AFTER DEATH — WHAT?

Also available in the Colin Wilson Library of the Paranormal:

AFTER DEATH — WHAT?

Researches into Hypnotic and Spiritualistic Phenomena

CESARE LOMBROSO

Rendered into English by
WILLIAM SLOANE KENNEDY

Introduction by Colin Wilson

Volume Four
in the Colin Wilson
Library of the Paranormal

THE AQUARIAN PRESS

After Death — What? first published in 1909
This Edition 1988

© The Aquarian Press 1988

British Library Cataloguing in Publication Data

Lombroso, Cesare
After death — what?: researches into
hypnotic and spiritualistic phenomena.—
(The Colin Wilson library of the paranormal)
1. Spiritualism
I. Title   II. Series
133.9'3   BF1286

ISBN 0-85030-706-6

*The Aquarian Press is part of the
Thorsons Publishing Group, Wellingborough,
Northamptonshire, NN8 2RQ, England.*

Printed in Great Britain by
Woolnough Bookbinding, Irthlingborough, Northants

1 3 5 7 9 10 8 6 4 2

INTRODUCTION

Although now virtually forgotten, Cesare Lombroso was undoubtedly one of the greatest scientific geniuses of the nineteenth century. And the story of his gradual conversion to a belief in the paranormal is surely one of the most interesting moral fables in the history of psychical research.

Cesare Lombroso was born in Verona in 1835, the son of Jewish parents. At that time, Verona was under the domination of the Austrians, so he was officially a subject of the Habsburg empire. As a member of a 'subject' people, he became — like most Italians — a man of revolutionary opinions. Moreover, the political turmoil caused his father — a gentle, cultured man — to lose most of his money, so the family existed in near-poverty.

Now the Austrians were, of course, Catholics, so they warmly supported the Church of Rome and its 'traditionalist' views. Just as naturally, the young Lombroso — an immensely intelligent young man — came to detest religion and everything to do with it. The simile is painfully hackneyed, yet it must be said nevertheless that he took to science like a duck to water. For Lombroso, as for the young H. G. Wells a few years later, it represented salvation. Even at school, Lombroso read the 'banned' works of the philosopher Vico, which tried to show that society is an organic growth, not some divine creation. Lombroso's schoolmasters were Jesuits, and he felt that they were trying to thrust him back into the Middle Ages. The Emperor Franz is said to have remarked 'I want obedient, not educated, subjects'. Then, in 1848, when Lombroso was thirteen, the first trumpets of freedom sounded, and the battle to liberate Italy began. And during the next twenty years, Lombroso watched

with deep satisfaction as the stranglehold of the
Austrians — and the Church of Rome — was broken.

Understandably, Lombroso became an enthusiastic
follower of the 'materialistic' philosopher Auguste Comte,
who believed that all religion is mere superstition, and
that the human race will one day emerge into a
triumphantly scientific stage of its evolution. And as a
disciple of Vico, he was also fascinated when the historian
Paolo Marzolo produced a book called *Historical
Monuments Revealed by the Analysis of Words,* trying to
unravel the early history of religion through philological
comparisons. Marzolo was greatly disappointed by the
uncomprehending — if favourable — reviews of this book,
until he saw one in a Verona newspaper by 'C. Lombroso',
which showed real understanding of what he was saying.
Assuming that the unknown reviewer was a lonely scholar
of advanced age, Marzolo invited him to call — and was
flabbergasted to meet a youth of sixteen. Lombroso
became a friend and disciple of the great man.

When he passed his medical examinations at the age
of 21, Lombroso was more materialist than ever. He even
scorned the philosophy known as vitalism, according to
which the difference between living matter and dead
matter lies in some vital spark or 'life force'. For Lombroso,
living creatures are machines, and should be studied as
such. In the account given by his biographer Hans
Kurella, Lombroso sounds rather like the young Freud,
determined to clear away all the 'metaphysical' rubbish
and establish the science of psychiatry on a solid
materialist foundation. He began studying cretinism, and
laid great emphasis on the measurement of skulls. In
1859, he served as an army surgeon in the war against
the Austrians, then became professor of psychiatry at
Pavia, and director of the lunatic asylum at Pesaro. There
he continued to study cretins and criminals, and to seek
for the tell-tale signs of 'degeneracy'. He also studied the
brains of dead madmen, carefully staining the nerve
fibres, hoping to pinpoint some purely physical source of

insanity. He was unsuccessful. But he was excited by
Darwin's theory of evolution — *The Origin of Species*
appeared in 1859 — and even more excited when, in 1870,
the German pathologist Rudolf Virchow announced that
he had discovered certain 'atavistic' features in the skulls
of criminals. This looked like the key that Lombroso had
been searching for, and he began to spend all his spare
time studying the corpses of criminals. In 1876 he was
appointed professor of forensic medicine at Turin, and
immediately began making a careful study of inmates of
the local prison. In the same year he announced to the
world his epoch-making conclusions in a book called
Criminal Man (L'Uomo Delinquente). According to
Lombroso, criminality is basically a throw back to our
caveman ancestors, and a large proportion of criminals
(about 40%) actually have some 'caveman' characteristics
— sloping foreheads, receding chins, and other 'atavisms'
that can only be seen under the magnifying glass or
microscope. Many decent citizens who happened to have
a somewhat Neanderthal appearance were understandably indignant; there was a furious controversy, and
Lombroso suddenly became famous. He had already
acquired a certain notoriety four years earlier when he
announced that the disease called pellagra is caused by
a poison contained in maize. (He was wrong — it is caused
by a deficiency of vitamin B_2 — but then, all the other
experts were wrong too — most of them blamed a tiny
parasite.) What outraged his wealthy contemporaries was
his analysis of agrarian poverty and his criticism of the
great landed gentry who never suffered from pellagra.
Lombroso's views led to social ostracism, and the loss of
large numbers of his patients, so that he lived for a long
time in comparative poverty. But this probably saved him
from the consequences of too much fashionable success
as a medical man, and enabled him to devote himself
whole-heartedly to his investigations.

Criminal Man caused widespread controversy; so did
his views on women, which would have enraged

supporters of women's lib. His study of criminal women led him to explain that 'woman displays to the same degree as the child the lineaments of moral idioc -- except that she is saved by maternal love and sympathy. Nevertheless, women are basically non-moral, and exhibit traits of character 'which prevent her from approaching to the same degree as man that balance between rights and duties, between egoism and altriusm, which is the ultimate goal of moral development'. In other words, woman is really a natural criminal, except that her biological make-up — maternal feelings, etc — prevent her from plunging into the pit. He also explains that strong erotic feelings do not occur in women — or at least, when they do, the women are 'an approximation to the masculine type'.

Lombroso did not, of course, claim that all criminals are caveman throw backs, and he came to strongly recognize the influence of environment on criminality. What irritated his contemporaries — all over the world — was that his views seemed to be based on a flat denial of free will. As a scientist, he did not even recognize its existence. He caused further outrage in 1888 in his book *The Man of Genius* when he propounded his view that genius is a form of neurosis or insanity. He was inclined to believe that inspiration is closely related to an epileptic attack. Large sections of *The Man of Genius* are devoted to case histories of madmen who nevertheless displayed remarkable abilities — abilities undoubtedly due to their lack of certain inhibitions that are natural to 'civilized man'. So his theory of genius is closely related to his theory of criminality, which proposes that criminals are a throw back to an age before law and civilization, when men behaved like wild animals — a state that has changed since we learned that we have to live together and observe 'the social contract'. For good measure, Lombroso also threw in studies of Wagner and Verlaine to illustrate that genius involves symptoms of degeneracy. (A contemporary named Max Nordau achieved fame by elaborating

Lombroso's theories in a book called *Degeneration* which argued that nearly all modern art and literature is a clear sign that modern society is plunging downhill.)

We can see, then, that Lombroso was an instructive example of a man who has been 'conditioned' to violent rebelliousness by his upbringing, and who ran true to form for most of his adult life — a kind of Karl Marx of psychology. Yet, as the readers of this book will discover, there came a point where he ceased to run true to form — or rather, where the ruthless logic of his rationalistic premises led him into strange regions of speculation.

At this point, it is necessary to go back a few decades to the time when Lombroso was enthusiastically reading Paolo Marzolo's *Historical Monuments* — the year 1850. In that year, the world was overtaken by another great revolution, which became known as Spiritualism. Everyone knows the story of the strange goings-on in the home of the Fox family of New York State in 1848 which convinced millions of Americans that man had at last achieved contact with the world of those who had 'passed on'. The first Spiritualist Meeting was held in the Corinthian Hall in Rochester in November, 1849, and by the following year, spiritualism was already spreading across Europe. Lombroso would undoubtedly have said 'like a plague'. Like all scientists, he regarded it with horror and suspicion, hardly able to believe that this revival of mediaeval witchcraft was really sweeping across the world in the middle of the nineteenth century. And during the next twenty years or so, Lombroso's researches into criminality and insanity prevented him from paying much attention to this form of 'collective insanity'.

But, as he explains in the opening chapter of this book, the world of the unknown forced itself on his attention in the year 1882, when he was asked to examine the 14-year-old daughter of a distinguished man. The girl had developed hysterical blindness at puberty, but had apparently developed compensatory powers — the ability to see through her ear and smell through her chin. The phenomenon was known as hyperaesthesia, and had been observed by many respectable physicians, as Lombroso remarks. With her eye blindfolded — as a precaution — she was able to read a letter held close to the top of her nose — too close for normal reading. (In the 1820s, a German doctor, Justinus Kerner, had studied a girl called Friederike Hauffe, 'the Seeress of Prevorst', who could read from a book laid flat on her stomach.) She also read it when it was held near her left ear. When her sense of smell transferred itself to the back of her foot, she winced and writhed when disagreeable smells — like smelling salts — were brought close to her heel, but not when they were held under her nose. What intrigued Lombroso even more is that she seemed to have rudimentary powers of prophecy, and was able to foretell things that would happen to other members of the family.

Lombroso was puzzled, but refused to abandon his scientific attitude. In the past few years, science had once again begun to take account of hypnotic phenomena. Hypnosis had been discovered at the end of the previous century by a disciple of Anton Mesmer; but the physicians of Paris and Vienna had risen up against Mesmer, declared him a charlatan, and insisted that hypnotized subjects were merely pretending. And for most of the nineteenth century, any doctor who expressed an interest in hypnosis was likely to be treated with disdain by his colleagues. But in the 1870s, the famous French physician Jean-Martin Charcot had become interested in a curious phenomenon first discovered by Mesmer: that patients could often be cured by magnets. As odd as it sounds to us, many doctors found that they could cure, say, paralysis in an arm by stroking the arm with a magnet, or sometimes just with a metal object (gold seemed to be particularly efficacious). One odd phenomenon was that if a patient had been cured of deafness in the right ear by 'magnetism' or metalotherapy, the deafness often transferred itself to the left ear. And when Charcot had himself witnessed such 'cures' again and again, he began — about 1878 — to experiment with hypnotism. It dawned on him that the patients he could cure with magnets or metals were suffering from *hysterical* symptoms — a woman suffering from hysterical pregnancy might show all the symptoms of real pregnancy — and that hysteria and hypnosis were very closely related indeed. The psychical researcher F.W.H. Myers concluded that a part of the mind he called 'the subliminal self' was responsible for these strage effects — Sigmund Freud later preferred to call it 'the unconscious'.

So when Lombroso began to investigate hypnosis (he called it somnambulism) — as described in the first chapter of this book — in the 1880s, he could look to the example of the great Charcot (ten years his senior). He soon became convinced that the phenomenon of thought transference (or telepathy) was genuine, that it could be explained in scientific terms. But what about the peculiar powers of the eminent Dr C. (mentioned on page 27), who was always having premonitions that turned out to be true? He was so sure that there would be a great fire at the Como Exposition of 1894 that he persuaded his family to sell their Fire Insurance shares. As an honest man, Lombroso had to acknowledge that such things really happened — and that in that case, his 'positivist' conception of the universe was not as sound as it looked.

In fact, what we witness in this remarkable book is the astonishing story of how a materialistic but rigidly honest scientist was forced to acknowledge the existence of phenomena that he would once have dismissed as superstition. In 1888 he published a paper about his experiments in hypnotism, much of which is repeated in this first chapter. Then, in 1891, he was persuaded to undertake some experiments with the medium Eusapia Paladino, an illiterate peasant woman who could produce the most amazing effects — she could float into the air and lie there as if on a couch, and cause tables and chairs to float around the room. She also occasionally cheated

— but her cheating was so clumsy that it was easily detected. Lombroso's biographer is deeply embarassed that Lombroso was taken in by her; he says irritably that Eusapia was 'indeed a miracle — a miracle of adroitness, false *bonhomie*, well-simulated candour, naïveté, and artistic command of all the symptoms of hystero-epilepsy'. Kurella was present at many of the seances but, unlike Lombroso, he simply declined to believe the evidence of his eyes. Kurella thinks that Lombroso was willing to be taken in by mediums like Eusapia because he himself had met so much scepticism from academics, and was therefore sympathetic. But as we read Lombroso's own account in this book, that explanation seems unnecessary. He wrote in a letter to a friend, Dr Ciolfi, 'I am ashamed and sorrowful that with so much obstinacy I contended the possibility of the so-called spiritualistic facts. I say the *facts*, for I am inclined to reject the spiritualistic *theory*; but the facts exist, and as regard facts I glory in saying that I am their slave.'

And, as we shall see, it was this obsession with facts that finally led Lombroso to 'swallow' the most difficult assumption of all: that in some way, people continue to exist after death. It took a long time. At an earlier stage, he wrote: 'Not one of these facts (which we must admit to be facts, since we cannot deny that which we have seen with our own eyes) is of a nature to render it necessary to suppose . . . the existence of a world different from that admitted by neuro-pathologists.' And he speculated that when a hypnotized subject is 'paralysed' by the effects of hypnosis, certain centres in the brain become more powerful, and can channel enough energy to raise a table. But little by little, he had to admit that these 'scientific' explanations failed to cover all the facts. When he studied tribal witch-doctors and shamans, he was repeatedly told by them that they produced their phenomena (so similar to those of mediums like Eusapia) with the aid of the dead, and he slowly found himself giving more and more weight to this explanation. One of his most remarkable cases involved the investigation of a 'poltergeist' in the Via Bava in Turin. He describes it in this book in the chapter on haunted houses, although he does not mention the amusing circumstance that when he first went to the wine shop, the proprietor, Signor Fumero, told him that they *had* had a ghost, but that it had gone away since Professor Lombroso had visited the house. 'You interest me extremely,' replied Lombroso. 'Allow me to introduce myself' — and he presented his card. The embarrassed proprietor had to admit that he was so tired of sensation-seekers knocking on his door that he had been using the story about Professor Lombroso to keep them at bay. They then went down to the wine cellar, which was in darkness. As they entered, there was a sound of smashing glass, and a bottle struck Lombroso's foot. And as they stood there, three empty bottles began to spin on the floor and shattered against the table leg.

One basic feature of poltergeist cases is that there is usually present some young person who seems to be — quite unconsciously — causing the trouble, often an adolescent who has just reached puberty. Such a person is known as the 'focus' of the disturbances. In this case, Lombroso identified a young waiter as the focus, and when he was dismissed, the disturbances ceased. It looked as if this particular ghost could be explained in terms of the 'subliminal mind' of the waiter — although in this case there was no question of hypnosis or hysteria. And the study of more haunted houses gradually convinced Lombroso that there are two types of haunting: one in which there is a 'medium' or focus, and the other, which may continue for centuries, in which the only explanation seems to be a haunting by a 'spirit' of some kind.

If I may be allowed to end this introduction on a personal note, I should like to remark that Lombroso's experience has been very similar to my own. When commissioned to write a book called *The Occult* in the late 1960s, I also began as a total sceptic, accepting only that 'supernatural' occurrences are due to some unexplained powers of the human mind. When, in 1980, I was asked to write a book called *Poltergeist*, I still took it as a self-evident truth that poltergeists are some strange manifestation in the unconscious minds of disturbed teenagers. Long before I had finished writing that book, I had recognized that the weight of evidence is against this view. And when I had finished it, I had no doubt whatever that a poltergeist is a 'spirit' — probably a spirit of the dead. Hans Kurella concluded that Lombroso's final conversion to 'life after death' was a painful aberration due to the decay of his faculties (although Lombroso was only 47 when he became interested in the subject). If so, then I must confess that I suffer from the same aberration, and that I take a certain pride in being able to point to the great Lombroso as one who shares my views.

COLIN WILSON

PREFACE

WHEN, at the close of a career — richer in fierce logomachy and struggle than in victory — in which I have figured as a champion of the new trend of human thought in psychiatry and criminal anthropology, I began investigations into the phenomena of spiritism and afterwards determined to publish a book on the subject, my nearest friends rose against me on every side, crying, " You will ruin an honorable reputation, — a career in which, after so many contests, you had finally reached the goal; and all for a theory which the whole world not only repudiates, but, worse still, thinks to be ridiculous."

But all this talk did not make me hesitate for a single moment. I thought it my predestined end and way and my duty to crown a life passed in the struggle for great ideas by entering the lists for this desperate cause, the most hotly contested and perhaps most persistently mocked at idea of the times. It seemed to me a duty that, up to the very last of the few days now remaining to me, I should unflinchingly stand my ground in the very thick of the fight, where rise the most menacing obstructions and where throng the most infuriated foes.

And one cannot in conscience blame these opponents, because spiritistic phenomena, as commonly conceived, seem designed to break down that grand idea of monism which is one of the most precious fruits of our culture, retrieved by so sore a conflict from the clutches of superstition and prejudice; and because, furthermore, when contrasted with the precision of experimental phenomena — always accurately tallying with each other in time and space — spiritistic observations and experiments, so frequently varying with different mediums, according to the time of day and according to the mental state of the participants in the séance, notwithstanding their frequent repetition and reinforcement by accurate mechanical instruments, and however carefully sifted out by the most severely scientific experimenters (one need only name such men as Crookes, Richet, Lodge, James, Hyslop), are always wrapped in a dim atmosphere of uncertainty and show a tinge of mediæval science. But note this well, that, however doubtful each separate case may appear, in the ensemble they form such a compact web of proof as wholly to baffle the scalpel of doubt.

In psychical matters we are very far from having attained scientific certainty. But the spiritistic hypothesis seems to me like a continent incompletely submerged by the ocean, in which are visible in the distance broad islands raised above the general level, and which only in the vision of the scientist are seen to coalesce in one immense and compact body of land, while the shallow mob laughs at the seemingly audacious hypothesis of the geographer.

CESARE LOMBROSO.

TURIN, October 29, 1908.

Cesare Lombroso

CONTENTS

ILLUSTRATIONS

AFTER DEATH—WHAT?

AFTER DEATH—WHAT?

CHAPTER I

Hypnotic Phenomena

IF ever there was an individual in the world
opposed to spiritism by virtue of scientific edu-
cation, and, I may say, by instinct, I was that
person. I had made it the indefatigable pursuit
of a lifetime to defend the thesis that every force
is a property of matter and the soul an emanation
of the brain, and for years and years had laughed
at the idea of centre-tables and chairs having
souls!

But if I have always had a passionate devotion
to my own special science, my own flag, I have
had a still more ardent love of the truth, the verification of the fact.

Now, although I had such an aversion to
Spiritualism that for years I refused even to
be present at a test séance, I was fated to be a
witness, in 1882, as a neuropathologist, of certain very singular psychic phenomena for which
no scientific explanation whatever has been found,
except that they occurred in hysteric or hypnotized individuals.

TRANSPOSITION OF THE SENSES

I refer to the case of a certain C. S., the fourteen-year-old daughter of one of the most active and intelligent men in all Italy. The girl suffered from no ailment except sciatica. Her mother was healthy, intelligent, and robust. Her two brothers at about the age of puberty had an extraordinary increase of stature, accompanied by a certain degree of pulmonary trouble. The girl also, — who was of pleasing aspect, height four feet four and one-half inches, the pupil of the eye somewhat "midriatic," sense of touch normal, and sensitiveness to pain and to colors normal, — when near the age of puberty, rapidly increased in stature to the amount of six inches, and, at the first hints of the menstrual function, experienced severe hysterical troubles connected with the stomach (vomitings, dyspepsia), so that during one month she could swallow only solid food, and in another only liquids; the third month hysterical convulsions were the symptoms, — a state of hyperæsthesia so marked that the patient believed a wire placed on her hand to be as heavy as a bar of iron. Another month blindness developed, with hysterogenic points on the little finger and on the rectum, which, when touched, exhibited not only convulsive movements, but motor paresis in the legs, with exaggerated spastic reflex movements, contractions, and muscular energy increased to such a degree that the pressure of the hand on the dynamometer caused a rise from 32 kilograms to 47.

At this point extraordinary phenomena manifested themselves; that is to say, somnambulism appeared, during which the girl showed singular activity in domestic labor and great affection for her parents and unusual aptitude for music. Later a change in her character appeared, — a virile audacity and immorality. But the most extraordinary circumstance was that while she had lost the power of vision with her eyes, as a compensation she saw with the same degree of acuteness (7 in the scale of Jaeger) at the point of the nose and the left lobe of the ear. In this way she read a letter which had just come to me from the post-office, although I had blindfolded her eyes, and was able to distinguish the figures on a dynamometer. Curious, also, was the new mimicry with which she reacted to the stimuli brought to bear on what we will call improvised and transposed eyes. For instance, when I approached a finger to her ear or to her nose, or made as if I were going to touch it, or, better still, when I caused a ray of light to flash upon it from a distance with a lens, were it only for the merest fraction of a second, she was keenly sensitive to this and irritated by it. "You want to blind me!" she cried, her face

making a sudden movement like one who is men-
aced. Then, with an instinctive simulation entirely new, as the phenomenon itself was new,
she lifted her forearm to protect the lobe of the
ear and the point of the nose, and remained thus
for ten or twelve minutes.

Her sense of smell was also transposed; for
ammonia or asafœtida, when thrust under her
nose, did not excite the slightest reaction, while,
on the other hand, a substance possessing the
merest trace of odor, if held under the chin, made
a vivid impression on it and excited a quite
special simulation (*mimica*). Thus, if the odor
was pleasing, she smiled, winked her eyes, and
breathed more rapidly; if it was distasteful, she
quickly put her hands up to that part of the chin
that had become the seat of the sensation and
rapidly shook her head.

Later the sense of smell became transferred to
the back of the foot; and then, when any odor
displeased her, she would thrust her legs to right
and to left, at the same time writhing her whole
body; when an odor pleased her, she would remain motionless, smiling and breathing quickly.

Next appeared phenomena of prediction and
clairvoyance, for she foresaw, with what I would
call mathematical exactness, and sometimes fifteen or sixteen days previously, the day of her
cataleptic fits, — the hour in which they were
to occur and the particular metal to be used in

checking them. Thus, on the 15th of June she predicted that on July 2 she would be delirious and would then have seven cataleptic fits that would be healed with gold; on the 25th of July pharyngismus and pains in her limbs; on July 6 cataleptic fits at the first drop of water that should be sprinkled on her, and a state of calm thereafter up to the 12th, when she would be taken with a fit at six o'clock in the morning, with a tendency to bite and tear things, which would not be quieted but by a half-teaspoonful of quinine and three drops of ether. All took place precisely as she had predicted. On the 14th she predicted that the four fits to come on the 15th would be cured with lead; and, to tell the truth, this was found useful, but gold helped still more. If there was any mistake made here, it was not in the selection of gold (which she had foretold the use of with precision) nor in the number of the fits. She later predicted things that were to happen to her father and brother, and two years afterward they were verified. She clairvoyantly saw from her sick-bed her brother in the *coulisses* of a theatre (as in fact he was), distant more than half a mile from the house.

Nor are such phenomena as these at all isolated. As early as 1808 Petetin cited the cases of eight cataleptic women in whom the external senses had been transferred to the epigastric region and into the fingers of the hand and the toes of the feet (*Électricité Animale,* Lyons, 1808).

In 1840 Carmagnola, in the *Giornale dell' Accademia di Medicina,* describes a case quite analogous to ours. It concerned a girl fourteen years old, in whom, as in the other case mentioned, the menstrual function had begun only a few months previous, and who was troubled with convulsive coughing fits, with headaches, swoonings, sobbings when she drank, fits of dyspnœa, mimetic convulsions during which she would sing, sleeping spells that lasted for three days, and true fits of somnambulism during which she saw distinctly with the hand, selected ribbons, identified colors, and read even in the dark.

Wishing to look at herself in the mirror, she put her hands before it, and, when she saw nothing there but these, lowered them in order to see her face. Not succeeding in this, she grew enraged, and, stamping on the floor, ran away. The first act (lowering the hands) was spontaneous, instinctive, and the exact counterpart of the action of the " C. S." mentioned above, who would cover up the lobe of the ear when it was irritated by the finger of the experimenter ,or by an unexpected ray of light, — a phenomenon in itself sufficient to exclude simulation. That my readers may no longer claim that these are matters of recent discovery, let them note that in this case, as in that of Petetin, the application of gold or of silver always calmed the frenzies of the girl and made her light-hearted again, — so much so that during her fits she would run eagerly about hunting for those metals. One day she touched bronze, believing it to be gold; but, although her delusion was complete, she got no comfort. Silks and furred things deprived her of all strength. Little by little she improved, although she relapsed on the occasion of every menstruation.

Despine tells us of a certain Estella of Neuchâtel, eleven years old, who was afflicted with paresis as the result of an accidental wound in the back (*trauma*), but had improved by the use of the baths of Aix, and after magnetic treatment was found to have suffered transposition of the sense of hearing to various parts of the body, — the hand, the elbow, the shoulder, and (during her lethargic crisis) the epigastrium, and at the same time acquired greater skill in swimming and horseback riding. The application of gold produced extraordinary energy.

Frank (*Praxeos Medicæ, Univ. Torino*, 1821) publishes an account of a person named Baerkmann in whom the sense of hearing was transposed to the epigastrium, the frontal bone, or the occiput.

Dr. Augonova studied at Carmagnola, in 1840, a certain G. L., a girl fourteen years old, who had become dyspeptic and amenorrhœic as the consequence of a fit of displeasure. During somnambulistic states, toward the middle of the night, she would identify pieces of money placed before the nape of the neck and distinguished odors by the back of her hands. Later, at the end of April, sight and hearing got themselves transposed to the epigastric region, so that with her eyes bandaged she could read from a book held a few steps away.

The same doctor records his observations of a woman (Piovano), aged twenty-two, afflicted with hysterical catalepsy and epileptic fits, who in the artificial somnambulistic condition could see now with the nape of the neck and now with the epigastrium, and who heard with the feet. She claimed that she saw in her own body thirty-three worms, which after the lapse of a certain time she actually voided!

And then the phenomenon is to be correlated and joined with what was well enough known at the time, but was not noticed, respecting ordinary somnambulists who see very well either with the eyes wide open, but insensible, or with the eyelids shut, or else the head thrown back and the eyes lifted up as in the case of persons asleep. Evidently they see with some other part of the body than the eye. Preyer and Berger, who in their time observed this class of facts, just as Hedenhain does to-day, believe they interpret them truly on the hypothesis of greater tactual sensitiveness and more acute visual power. It is true that these are frequently noted in such cases; but supposing that this may explain at the utmost the visual power in a darker room (a circumstance which does not apply in the cases just noted), still it cannot explain the transposition in the case just mentioned, in which the tactile sensitiveness is observed to be absolutely identical both before and after as well as during the attack, and vision shows the same degree of acuteness in the two states or stages. In the case just cited visual perception resides in two points of the skin. But the sense of touch is the lowest, and does not suffice, at any rate, to explain the reading of a manuscript.

If more modern authors did not bestow any attention on cases like these, and Hasse could call them "illusions," it is because, in obedience to a tendency which is praiseworthy even when excessive, they were willing to admit only those facts which could be scientifically explained. It was for this reason that scientists were so cautious in believing in the performances of the magnet, and many of the results that the magnetizers empirically obtained, — catalepsy, hypnosis, hyperæsthesia, — matters which are now, up to a certain point, accurately accounted for (Heidenhain). The truth is that it is absolutely impossible for us to give a scientific interpretation of these facts, — facts which bring us to the vestibule of that world which is properly spoken of as being still occult because unexplained.[1]

Still, the mysteries of clairvoyance may in part be explained by a kind of auto-suggestion, by that sharp instinct of one's own condition that enables the dying person to specify the last hour of his life. Yet there may be more in it than that: perhaps the regular unfolding of the phenomena of one's own nervous illness can be better observed, since, during the extraordinary excitement of the somnambulistic ecstasy, we acquire a deeper consciousness of our organism, in the living interlocked wheel-work of whose states, or conditions, there are registered potentially (in the germ) the varied succession of morbid phenomena.

Here belongs an act noted for the first time by our countryman Salvioli (in my *Archivio di Psichiatria e Scienze Penali*, vol. ii. p. 415), — namely, that in somnambulism the flow of blood to the brain is greater than in the waking hours, and greater consequently the activity of the psyche, in the same way that there is an increase in the muscular excitability. Indeed, the invalid girl I referred to some pages back, who acquired in the somnambulistic state an increase of energy of twelve kilograms registered on the dynamometer, yet affirmed to me that in that state she

---

[1] Further on, in Chapter X, I shall make some statements concerning the *double* which will serve as a provisional explanation.

was unable to possess her soul in quiet, but must be ever grinding out new ideas.

But the foregoing conclusion no longer serves when clairvoyance attains such a pitch of power as to predict what would happen to a father and brothers two years after the time of the prediction, nor can it explain to us scientifically the transposition of the senses.

The sole fact that emerges here in a marked manner is that the phenomena take place in hysterical subjects and during severe hysterical attacks.

TRANSMISSION OF THOUGHT (SUGGESTION)

A similar state of things has been noted in the cases (for the most part unstudied by science) of suggestion, or the transmission of thought from one mind to another. Such are the circumstances communicated to me by Grimaldi and Ardu, in the case of a certain E. B., of Nocera, a young man twenty years old, who became subject to hysteria in consequence of thwarted love at the age of fifteen. This lad had the cranium dolicocephalic (76), face extraordinarily asymmetric, with a feminine look; acuteness of vision; sense of touch normal, though keener on the left; sensitive to all the metals, and especially to copper and gold, which calm the palpitations of his heart and the pain of the muscles (myalgia). Being, as he is, a person

of exaggerated sympathies and antipathies, of
timidity so extreme as to fear the shadow in
a dark corner, highly changeable and capricious
in his disposition, influenced by suggestion to
such an extent as to obey the command not to

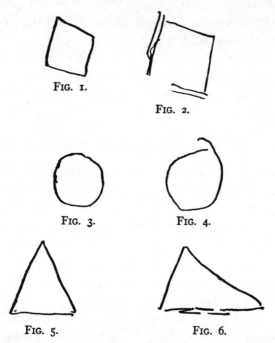

FIG. 1.

FIG. 2.

FIG. 3.

FIG. 4.

FIG. 5.

FIG. 6.

feel the keenest pains inflicted on him with a
needle and a red-hot iron, he also exhibits the
phenomena of transposed senses. He could divine
a word or a number in another's mind and reproduce figures drawn behind his back at a certain distance while his eyes were blindfolded by

a thick bandage passing around the head over the ears.

If a rhomb is drawn for him (Fig. 1), he reproduces it roughly (Fig. 2) and hesitatingly, but succeeds much better with the circle (Figs. 3, 4).

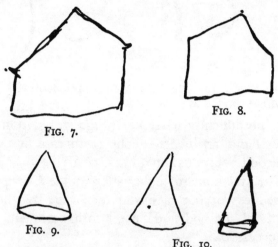

FIG. 7.

FIG. 8.

FIG. 9.

FIG. 10.

Considerable difficulty is encountered in the reproduction of a triangle (Figs. 5, 6). After a longer meditation or reflection than in the first case, he draws two sides. The third, that of the base, is drawn with visible uncertainty. Instead of being a right line, it is broken in zigzag fashion.

Scarcely is this experiment finished, when the subject, whose face is a little inflamed, complains of a severe pain in his head. We remove the bandage and allow him to rest for a little while. After ten minutes the experiments are resumed.

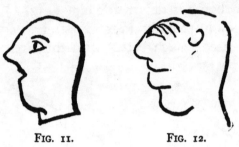

FIG. 11.   FIG. 12.

In executing the figure of a polygon (which might also be deemed the profile of a hut), he finds no difficulty whatever (Figs. 7, 8). On the other hand, an inverted cone requires a first and a second reproduction (Figs. 9, 10).

The symptoms of exhaustion suddenly appear, — redness of the face and torpor in the movements of the body. Hence two experiments are unsuccessful.

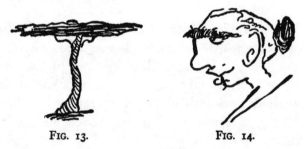

FIG. 13.   FIG. 14.

He next reproduces the head of a man (Figs. 11, 12), adding ears, however, and the figure of a bird (Figs. 15, 16), with the addition of feathers, but does not succeed in reproducing a small tree (Figs. 13, 14), although he gives a confused idea of it in his tracings of a woman's head.

We suggest in writing the word *Margherita,* and it is reproduced, as also the words *Andrea,*

FIG. 15.   FIG. 16.

etc. (Figs. 17, 18, 19, 20, and 21). His first attempt to reproduce *Margherita* resulted in *Maria.* But on the second attempt he gets it right (Margherita).

The suggestioner wrote *Andrea* (Fig. 17), re-

FIG. 17.   FIG. 18.

produced as in Fig. 18, in a style much like that of a boy copying an example.

The suggestioner next wrote the words *Amore* and *Maria,* erasing the first by a line drawn through it. This was reproduced as in the drawings shown in Figs. 20 and 21.

After the subject is tired, he reproduces nothing more. When mentally bid to open an ink-stand or a door, he succeeds almost without effort, although he is blindfolded; but the continuation of the trials puts him into somnambulistic and

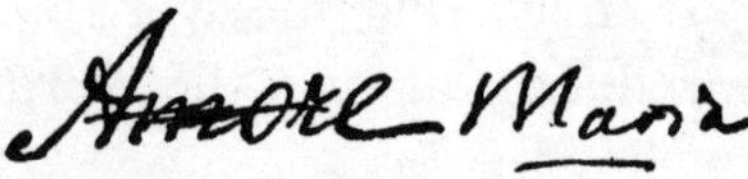

FIG. 19.

cataleptic states. Pressure on the temples causes him to pass into the somnambulistic state, from which he wakens when bidden.

In the series of elaborate movements inspired by mental suggestion we found errors which might have led us to believe we had met with so

FIG. 20.

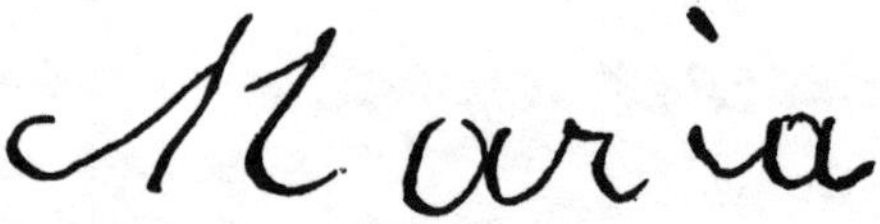

FIG. 21.

many failures. On the contrary, they fitted with admirable clearness into the list of graphic errors just described.

The idea was once conveyed to him by suggestion that he open the door of the room. He ran to open it, and up to this point the experiment was successful; but in place of stopping there he called in a loud voice for the servant. The phenomena must positively be classified as pertaining to the hysteric and hypnotic condition of the individual.

These evident proofs of the transmission of thought by neurotics stimulated us to undertake similar experiments [1] on a large scale. Out of twenty subjects studied in whom transmission of thought was successful (in that they were able to divine the name of a paper, a number, etc.), twelve were neuropathics and were the ones who guessed most rapidly and with the greater precision.

They succeeded better if they were able to put themselves into the condition of mono-ideism, bandaging their eyes and stopping their ears. In three cases immediate contact facilitated the reading; or, rather, it was the indispensable condition thereof. In three others it had no influence whatever. In one instance emotion was of assistance, the transmitter being a lady who was loved by the subject. Sometimes the human figure, as contrasted with lines and flowers, was better transmitted, with a difference in its favor of ten per cent. And this is comprehensible, because living figures are more energetically perceived; and when one does not feel deeply he cannot transmit thought.

[1] *Studies in Hypnotism*, 1882.

In some cases the transmission is facilitated by the use of alcoholic drinks or of coffee, which stimulate the nervous centres.

But these observations of mine were a very small affair compared with the hundreds and thousands of similar ones (controlled more minutely in details) which were made in England and France.

In England the celebrated Society for Psychical Research instituted very delicate experiments upon individuals in the sleeping state and the waking state, causing them to draw on a blackboard a figure which another person on another floor or in another and distant environment sketched on a sheet of paper, — such as bits of complicated three-angled things, buildings, strange names (for example, " chevalon "). Now, the results of these experiments were very happy.   Successful were one in every $5\frac{1}{4}$ among those hypnotized by suggestion, and one in every 43 among the non-hypnotized.

Other more recent experiments of this English commission (the report of which already fills a volume) were conducted in the presence of Dr. Guthrie and Professor Herdmann.

The subject, or medium, in this case is Miss Relph, who remains seated while the objects selected are hidden behind a curtain and behind her back.   The experiments take place without contact.

OBJECT THOUGHT	OBJECT DIVINED
Red paper cut in the shape of little egg-holders with a white egg inside.	Something red, longer than it is wide.
Blue paper in the form of a soup-plate.	Is it azure colored? Wider on top than in the middle; still wider like a soup-plate.
Red paper cut in the form of a vase.	Is it red? I see only the color.
A sword.	Something that shines; silver or steel; long and slender.
A red circle.	Is it red? It is round.
Silver paper cut in the shape of a tile-kiln.	It is of shining silver, like a coffee-pot; a tile-kiln.
A yellow rectangle.	Is it yellow? Longer than wide.
A louis d'or.	It is shining yellow, of gold; it is round.
Three of hearts (card).	It is a card with two red dots. A three of hearts or something similar.
Five of clubs.	It is another card with five black points.
Eight of diamonds.	It is a card with many red points; a ten.
A card with two red crosses.	It is something yellow. I do not see well. It is a card with red dots.

No one could believe that the laws of probability would permit even a distant approximation to results like these. For mark well that even the errors, or rather semi-errors, represent a state of imperfect transmission, though as-

suredly bearing but a small proportion to the bulk
of the case.

But more important results are obtained from
experiments made by the comparative method
with subjects in a state of waking or of hypnotism. Richet, after having assured himself that
the probability of drawing any particular given
card from the 52 playing-cards in a pack is 428
out of a total of 1833 trials, made the same experiments with cards held in the hand of a friend,
the selection of each card to be that which the
friend fixed on in his mind. He obtained the
figure 510, — a gain of 52 over the probable
figure. In this case the degree of probability did
not exceed $\frac{1}{16}$.

Experimenting with 218 photographs and like-
nesses, while the probable figure would have been
42, he obtained 67.

In a third series the number of the cards (to
be exact) was $\frac{17}{31}$. In this series, for eight times
in succession, the card turned up marked precisely the same, while the probability of obtain-
ing eight identical cards in succession is $\frac{18}{52}$, which
is equivalent to $\frac{1}{7,164,958,643,456}1$.

Taking up suggestion, the members of the
London Society for Psychical Research obtained
9 successes out of 14 experiments at the first trial,
and 5 successes out of 5 at the second. That is
to say, while in the first experiment the figure of
probability was 0.25, the true figure was 9.

In other similar experiments by Stewart $\frac{45}{118}$ was obtained.[1] If the case had been that of playing-cards, the number of the cards indicated would have had to be 22 and not 45. Operating upon individuals subject to hysteria, but not hypnotized, Ochorowitz obtained 13 successes out of 31, the task being in these cases to divine a letter, a number, a name (such as Maria), or a taste.

By the employment of suggestion with hypnotized persons he afterwards got 15 successes out of 20, whereas, according to the estimate of the probabilities, he would not have been able to get more than 1 success in 24.[2]

From all this Richet would make the following deductions:

First. The thought of an individual is transmitted, without the aid of outward tokens, to an individual near him.

Second. This mental transmission of the thought affects the second of the individuals with varying degrees of intensity.

These transmissions of thought become still more extraordinary when they are perceived to take place at a distance, and at distances sometimes enormous. Furthermore, cases of this kind would be seen to be still more frequent if our scepticism did not hinder us from collecting and recording them with scientific accuracy.

---

[1] *Thought Reading*, 1883.   [2] *La Suggestion*, 1890.

Thus a few years ago (in 1887) the report ran that a little Novarese girl had had a mental perception of the illness of her mother, who was at Settimo-Torinese. A few days later De Vesme, by direction of the Italian Psychological Society, verified the fact that at half-past twelve o'clock on the 17th of February, 1887, Anna Voretto, while busied about her affairs, was suddenly taken ill and died on the next day. At nine o'clock P. M. of the 17th the sister of the woman received a telegram telling her to come with the child (Stella), daughter of the dying woman. Now seven witnesses depose to the fact that the child had showed herself highly agitated ever since one o'clock of the 17th, asking to go to her mother *because she was ill.* The next day, on the train for Novara, the child cried out that mamma was dead.

Professor De Sanctis not long ago communicated to me the following narrative of a similar case of telepathy or presentiment:

" During the second half of last September I found myself in Rome without my family, who were in the country. Inasmuch as during the previous year thieves had visited my house, my brother was in the habit of coming to pass the night with me. One evening, — I am uncertain whether the 16th, 17th, or 18th of September, — it being a gala night at the Costanzi Theatre, in honor of the Spanish journalists then present in Rome, my brother told me he was going there. Hence on that evening I returned home alone. I began to read something, but soon perceived that I was filled with apprehension. I shook off the unpleasant thoughts and began to undress, but an inner uneasiness disturbed me. I went to bed trying vigorously to fight down the idea that the Costanzi Theatre was afire and that my brother might be in danger. I extinguished the candle, but the idea of the fire fairly possessed me and so tortured me that I was obliged (a thing contrary to all my habits) to light the candle again and await my brother's return with open eyes.

"I was actually in a state of terror, as a boy might be. About half-past twelve I heard the house-door open, and presently said to my brother, 'Well, did you have a good time?' as if to give the direct lie to my fears. What was my wonder to hear him reply, 'Good time indeed! A little more, and we should all have been burned to death!' Then he told me of the panic that had taken place when the fire first broke out at the Costanzi, the particulars of which were given next day by the journals.

"On comparing the exact time when the affair took place at the Costanzi with the time when I began to be obsessed with the idea of the fire, we found that the two were coincident."

Professor Mercandino obtained the following

account from a female client of his whose sons had undertaken the ascent of Mount Cibrario. She went to bed and slept tranquilly up to the middle of the night. At two she awoke with a start, seeming to see her son Gustave upon the precipitous rocks and to hear him groaning and refusing to follow his brother Cesare, who was giving him a stimulating liqueur to drink and kept vehemently urging him to rise, even calling him a coward. Next day, wh n they had returned, they affirmed that sure enough at two o'clock in the morning that had occurred which the mother at the same hour had clairvoyantly perceived, and that Cesare in his distress had thought, " If mamma could see us!   Oh, if we could only get home again! "

Tschurtschenthaler tells an incident of a boy subject to convulsions and having a hysterogenic point. This boy's two brothers were in America. One day, without having been in any way notified of it, he declared, first, that he saw them on the sea, and afterwards disembarking in Liguria, and he made these asseverations on the very day and at the very hour when the event actually occurred.

Dr. Pagliani writes me of having studied the case of a certain Caroline A., a woman of twenty-four years (two years married), a somnambulist and often cataleptic, who, by taking the hand of people and smelling it, would divine their thoughts, even when they did their thinking in a foreign tongue to her unknown. He noticed that the thought was transmitted to a distance by an iron wire, even as far as six metres.

I will add to these instances two, procured by me, of the truth of which I can have not the slightest doubt.

A lady whom I will designate as Madame V. was at the theatre in Florence at half-past ten on an evening in November, 1882, when suddenly she uttered a cry and refused to remain any longer at the theatre, saying that she felt that her father was seriously ill. Arrived home, she first found a telegram containing the news that her father was dying at Turin, and then a second telegraphic message to the effect that he had died at half-past ten. Madame V. was subject to hysteria.

Mrs. F. J. had in her house a maid whom a soldier (lover or husband, whichever he was) came almost every evening to see, with the permission of the mistress. One evening, at the usual hour, this man asked admittance. Mrs. J., seized with fear, caused the doors to be barred and refused him admission, justifying herself later to her husband by saying that the idea entered her head at the time that the man wanted to assassinate her and rob the house. That night a pane of glass was broken, the house entered, and certain sums of money taken, though

of small account.   No one was any longer thinking of the occurrence, when one day the servant-
maid unguardedly allowed the truth to leak out
among the neighbors, — how that night when the
mistress had repulsed her betrothed he had plotted
to kill her, seize the keys, open the strong-box, steal
a large sum, and flee with her to a foreign land.

Now, in these cases, it is in vain to assert, as
I used to do at first, that thought, being a phenomenon of movement, can be transmitted to
either a short or a long distance.   For it may
be justly opposed to this that the force of vibratory motion decreases as the square of the distances, and that therefore, even if transmissions
of thought to a short distance may still be explained thus, we cannot understand those between
two distant points, which dart through space to
affect the mind of the percipient without dis-
sipating themselves on the way, and beginning
their flight from an instrument like the brain
which is not fixed upon an immovable base.

But what it behooves us to note in these cases
is that the majority of the transmissions were
those of hysterics and epileptics.

THE PREMONITIONS OF HYSTERICS AND EPILEPTICS

And then how explain premonitions, — predictions made, not by eminent persons, geniuses,
individuals of sound mind in a sound body, but

by invalids, or even during our dreams, when ideation is so vague and wandering, and when our psychic personality loses its sense of individuality?

A certain Castagneri wrote to De Vesme in September, 1886, how on the 8th of that month a servant-girl named Bianchi-Capelli had dreamed that her mother, a fruit-vender at Cesena, had been cheated out of three hundred lire and that her brother was ill. She was profoundly disturbed, and nothing availed to give her peace. On the 11th she received letters setting forth that on the very day after the night of her dream the two identical events took place, as De Vesme was able to authenticate by testimony.

I had in my care, for treatment, the famous Dr. C., one of the most distinguished of our young savans, and at the same time one of the most neurotic, in whom since puberty hysteria had been present in its true form, with not a few marks of degeneracy and grave hereditary defects. For some years he had noticed that he possessed powers of premonition, and it was his consciousness of this that one day hindered him from taking a single step to meet a friend who had telegraphed that he was coming. The doctor had a sure feeling that he would not come. He frequently announced to his mother the arrival of a letter, or a person whom he had not seen and whom he minutely described.

But the most important fact for us, because the best authenticated, is that on the 4th of February, 1894, he predicted the burning of the Como Exposition (which actually took place on the 6th of July) with such firm assurance as to induce members of his family who had had other proofs of the accuracy of his predictions to sell all the shares of the Milan Fire Insurance Company for the sum of 149,000 lire ($29,800). It is important to note that, as the time of the fire drew near, he felt the certainty of it less, — in the conscious state, — although he automatically repeated the prediction, as those about him remember, especially on the morning of the day when the fire took place, thus verifying in this case (at least for the conscious state) what Dante records (*Inferno,* Canto X) of the prophetic powers of the shades, with special reference to Farinata, who predicted his exile, while other spirits in his circle of Hades showed themselves entirely ignorant of every present event.

" I made the prediction offhand, on the spur of the moment," he himself wrote me, " and cannot conceive how I could have attained so intense a conviction, no consideration of a technical kind having any influence on my prophecy. At that time I could not have seen anything more than the enclosing fence of the exposition, the building of the main edifice not having progressed very far.

" I am unable to say whether previous to that day there was any vague presentiment lurking in me. Certainly I did not have a clear and definite idea before I observed the sign of the fire insurance company.

" I remember very well that at that moment I had no hallucination, either visual, caloric, or the like. So far as I was concerned, the fatal necessity of that disaster had acquired the certainty of a thunderbolt: it was not a thing to be discussed, but seemed to be an intuition of the truth, so to speak.

" It was the surprise awakened in me by this inexplicable state of mind that persuaded me to act in conformity with the presentiment; and so much the more readily because, in spite of my scepticism about Spiritualism, I have had at other times to note the truth of my presentiments.

" I will add that the shares of the Milanese company formed an asset of the highest credit in the market, and that the sale of them was very easy, because such investment of money was then much more remunerative than that in funds or annuities.

" After the shares had been sold, I gave no more thought to the matter, and in the month before the fire the idea had apparently dropped out of my mind altogether.

" But the person who attended me asserts, and is ready to testify to it, that when I was distraught I would frequently repeat in the dialect of Como, ' All must burn,' and that on the very morning of the fire I uttered these words several times."

The doctor was born of parents who were first cousins and neurotics. He had an epileptic sister. His cranium very large, of 1161 centimetres capacity; face asymmetrical; hair grown white at twelve years, and later becoming black; ears mobile; field of vision narrowed for the red and the blue, with attacks of vertigo. He had the strange power of dilating at will the pupil of the eye. Since the age of nineteen he had had epileptic-hysterical fits, accompanied by hallucinations.

The *Proceedings of the Society for Psychical Research*, March, 1897, contain an account of a most extraordinary case of premonition. It concerns a lady who was summering with her ten-year-old daughter at Trinity. One day when the little girl was out of doors playing in a favorite spot by the sea and near the railway, the mother heard an internal voice which urged her to send and fetch the child or something frightful would happen to it. She hastily called the nurse and bade her run quickly and bring her. She soon had her again safe and sound. A half-hour afterwards a train was derailed and smashed to pieces right where the little girl had been accustomed to play and where she certainly would have been if she had not been sent for. Three of the four trainmen were killed.

These phenomena of premonition and prediction are of such frequent occurrence that many more might be selected out of contemporary narratives, — such, for instance, as De Witt's *Italian Brigandage*, from which the following narrative is cited:

On the morning of November 4 Lieutenant Perrino rose at five o'clock and said to the mistress of the house, who was preparing his breakfast, that he had no wish to eat on account of an ugly dream he had had in the night. Perrino was a man approaching thirty years, his complexion dusky-carnation, slow in his movements, rather fond of his ease and comforts, and habitually melancholy.

On the evening of the 3d of November he was in a cheerful frame of mind, and there was nothing about him to indicate the misfortune impending over him. On going to bed, his head had scarcely touched the pillow when he was fast asleep; but in his dream he seemed to himself to have been bound to a tree, with his orderly, and the two to have been shot by brigands.

His hosts and Captain Rota laughed heartily at his story. The next day, with half a company of men and two carabineers, he set out for the farm hamlet of Melanico, — a quarter where brigands were usually to be looked for, — to make the usual daily reconnoitre. These forty-two soldiers and their officers ought to have had with them a company of the national guard; but Captain De Matteis, with a hundred and fifty national guards, having learned that the environs of the forest of Bosco were swarming with ferocious ruffians, made a halt a mile from the village, and begged the captain of the other troop to do the same. Rota would pay no attention to him, and went with his scanty troop to confront a hostile force numerically ten times stronger than his own.

Arrived at a certain point, he spied on a promontory four horsemen who were the pickets of the united bands of brigands encamped in no trifling numbers behind the promontory. In order to reach the summit of this, the captain directed his platoon of soldiers to traverse a ploughed field, which on account of the rain of the day previous was muddy and ill adapted for walking. He and the nimblest men of his company had run over a good part of that field. Lieutenant Perrino, on the other hand, and the feeblest walkers had got stuck in the mud up to their knees and were much farther behind than the troop that had followed the horse of Captain Rota. Just then Perrino had halted on a little tract of solid ground in the middle of the field where three or four oak-trees spread their branches. All the ploughed ground was enclosed between hillocks and meadows held fallow for pasturage, and from these places, which were higher than the others, the eye could easily range over the broad bottom-land where was the troop of soldiers. All of a sudden, dashing out from the high ground on the sides, ten half-squadrons of mounted brigands, each composed of about forty men, almost simultaneously opened fire on the scattered troop, riding up to discharge their guns and then making off out of sight to have time to reload. After a long and useless resistance the troopers were one after another surrounded, shot by sharpshooters, captured, abused or tortured, and killed.

The first group to fall into the hands of the brigands was that of Lieutenant Perrino. He and his orderly, inasmuch as they were captured alive and unhurt, were tied together, bound to an oak-tree, and both shot at the same time. The dream had come true.[1]

The dream that led Dante's son Jacopo to find the thirteen lost cantos of the Paradiso is a matter of history.

Dante Alighieri died during the night of September 13–14, 1321. His sons Jacopo and Piero at once set about the task of collecting the different parts of the great poem, which were still scat-

[1] *The History of Brigandage*, by A. De Witt, Florence, 1884, p. 317.

tered here and there.   Jacopo especially interested himself in the work.

But the enterprise was difficult.   Boccaccio in his Life of Dante relates that the two sons repeatedly searched in vain every nook and cranny of the house and all of his manuscripts, the search extending over months.   They were quite mortified " that God had not lent the great poet to the world long enough at least for him to be able to compose the small remaining part of his work." And " they had been induced by the persuading powers of certain of their friends to endeavor, in so far as in them lay (they were both rhymers) to supply the missing portion in order that it should not remain imperfect."   But in the meantime Jacopo had a most wonderful vision.   He " saw his father come to him, clothed in the whitest garments and his face resplendent with an extraordinary light."   Jacopo seized the opportunity to ask the shade of his father several questions, and among others this, " Whether he had completed his work before passing into the true life, and, if he had done so, what had become of that part of it which was missing and which they none of them had been able to find.   To this it seemed to him that the second time he heard the reply, ' Yes, I finished it '; and then the spectral form took him by the hand and led him into that chamber where he (Dante) had been accustomed to sleep when he lived in this life, and, touching a certain place in one of the walls, said, ' What you have sought for so much is here.' At these words both Dante and sleep fled from Jacopo at once."

Jacopo Alighieri, agitated both by joy and by fear at the same time, rose, although it was mid-dark of the night, and, having traversed in haste the deserted streets of Ravenna, came to the house of Pier Giardini, a notary who had lived on terms of great intimacy with the elder Dante, and related to him what he had seen. They resolved to investigate at once. " For which purpose, although it was still far in the night, they set off together, and went to the designated place, and there they found a blind, or curtain, of matting affixed to the wall. Upon gently raising this, they saw a little window never before seen by any of them, nor did any one know it was there. In it they found several manuscripts, all mouldy from the dampness of the walls, so much so that if they had remained there much longer they would have been spoiled. Having tenderly brushed away the mould and read them, they saw they were the thirteen cantos so long sought by them."

To this instance we are able to add two recent dreams, one a clairvoyant vision and the other a dream of premonition, both of which were authenticated by the courts of justice and by the town treasurer.

The first concerns a Miss Loganson, a girl nineteen years old, living in Chicago, who saw in a dream the scene of the assassination of her brother Oscar, a farmer in the town of Marengo, about fifty miles northwest of Chicago. For many days she kept accusing a farmer, his neighbor. At first no one paid any attention to her; but at length she was permitted to send a telegram, the reply to which was, " Oscar has disappeared." Thereupon the girl started for Oscar's farm, accompanied by another brother and by the police. She led them directly to the house of a person named Bedford. It was locked, and the police had to force the door. Traces of blood were found in the kitchen. Miss Loganson, however, did not stop there, but went at once toward the hen-house, the yard of which was paved. " My brother is buried there," she said. The police called her attention to the fact that the pavement had not been disturbed since the hen-house had been built. But, owing to the insistence of the girl and her terrible agitation, consent was given to dig. Under the pavement they first found the brother's overcoat, and digging deeper came upon his corpse nearly five feet down. A description of Bedford was immediately telegraphed in every direction, and he was arrested at Ellis, Nebraska.

Miss Loganson could never give any explanation of her discovery of the crime. She simply said that for several days continuously the spirit of her brother had haunted her and agitated her.

The other dream I have mentioned has to do with Rosa Tirone, a servant girl, an hysteric thirty-five years old, who had formerly been in love with a young man of her village but had not been able to marry him owing to the precarious condition of his health. The young man died at the age of twenty-five.

One night in November, 1908, Rosa dreamed that her quondam lover and fellow-townsman said to her, "I don't want to see you working as a servant-girl any longer; play these four numbers: 4, 53, 25, 30"; and he repeated them, in order to impress them on her mind. Then he added, "I'm so thirsty; draw a bucket of water from the well and give me a drink." In fact there was a well close by, and she drew up water and quenched his thirst.

The next day Rosa Tirone ventured a considerable sum on the four numbers. They were all winning numbers in the drawing of the following Sunday.

The only distinctive feature of this woman, who had already received four sentences for swindlings and thefts, is that she exhibits a purely masculine type of character as well as the tendency to fantastic mendacity that is a trait of those afflicted with hysteria. She would brag of owning villas, lands, money, and also discussed

her investments as if she had a *bona fide* property. Before the fortunate dream came to her she
had had a premonition of her good fortune, for
the same identical lover had said to her in a dream
'that she would become rich.

There is enough in all these observations to
enable us to conclude that there exists an immense series of psychical phenomena that completely elude the laws of psycho-physiology, and
that have solely this feature in common and this
certainty, — that they take place more readily in
individuals subject to hysteria, or who are neuropathic, or who are in the hypnotic or dreaming
condition, just at the moment, in fact, when the
normal ideation is more or less completely inactive, and in its stead the action of the unconscious dominates, which is more difficult to subject to scientific examination of any kind.

In short, in the foregoing pages cases are cited
and verified in which there are manifestations
(even exaggerated) of a function whose organ
is as completely inactive as if it were lacking.

Fig. 22. Eusapia Paladino in 1907.

CHAPTER II

Experiments with Eusapia

AFTER having convinced myself of this, the chief objection had disappeared which I had to occupying myself with spiritistic phenomena, as phenomena that could not really exist because contrary to physiological laws; and, although the thing was still repugnant to me, I ended by accepting, in March, 1891, an invitation to be present at a spiritualistic experiment in full daylight in a Naples hotel and *tête-à-tête* with Eusapia Paladino. And when I then and there saw extremely heavy objects transferred through the air without contact, from that time on I consented to make the phenomena the subject of investigation.

Eusapia Paladino was a poor orphan girl, born at Murge in 1854, and abandoned by the roadside, so to speak. As a young girl she was received out of charity as nurse-maid in a family of the upper bourgeoisie.

From the time when she was a little girl she had manifestations, either mediumistic or hallucinatory, whichever they were, without being at all able to explain them to herself, — such as hearing raps on pieces of furniture on which she was leaning, having her clothes or the bed-covers stripped from her in the night, and seeing ghosts or apparitions. In 1863 Damiani, — who at a séance in London had already heard a mediumistic communication from " John " to the effect that there was a medium in Naples, John affirming her to be his daughter, — Damiani, I repeat, was present at a spiritualistic séance in the house of the family in which Eusapia was living. During this séance her participation in the proceedings was attended by the most extraordinary phenomena of raps, movement of objects, etc. From that time on Damiani and Chiaja got a true mediumistic eduction through her; and the poor nurse-girl, finding in this a means of gain and a method of introducing variety into her miserable occupation, went on from time to time attending séances, until the business of mediumship became her sole occupation.

The description of all the experiments made in Europe with Eusapia Paladino would fill a huge volume. We shall simply content ourselves with describing in full the seventeen séances held in Milan in 1892, with myself and with Aksakoff, Richet, Giorgio Finzi, Ermacora, Brofferio, Gerosa, Schiaparelli, and Du Prel, — séances in which the most marked precautions were taken, such as searching the medium, changing her garments, binding her and holding her hands and feet, and adjusting the electric light on the table so as to be able to turn it off and on at will.

EXPERIMENTS WITH EUSAPIA PALADINO

(MILAN, 1892)

PHENOMENA OBSERVED IN THE LIGHT

I. MECHANICAL MOTIONS NOT EXPLICABLE BY THE MERE DIRECT CONTACT OF HANDS

1. *Lateral Levitation of the Table under the Hands of the Medium seated at one of the Shorter Sides thereof.* We employed for this experiment a fir table made expressly for the purpose. Among the different movements of the table employed to indicate replies it was impossible not to note the raps frequently given by its two sides, which were lifted simultaneously under the hands of the medium without any preceding lateral oscillation. The blows were given with force and rapidity and generally in succession, as if the table were fastened to the hands of the medium. These movements were the more remarkable in that the medium was always seated at one end of the table, and because we never once let go of her hands and feet. Inasmuch as this phenomenon appears very frequently and is produced with the greatest ease, in order that we might observe it better we left the medium alone at the table with her two hands completely

above it and her sleeves turned up as far as the elbows.

We remained standing about the table, and the spaces above and below it were well lighted. Under such conditions the table rose at an angle of from 30 to 40 degrees and remained thus for some minutes, while the medium was holding her legs stretched out and striking her feet one against the other. When we then pressed with one hand upon the lifted side of the table, we experienced a marked elastic resistance.

2. *Measure of the Force applied to the Lateral Levitation of the Table.* For this experiment the table was suspended by one of its ends to a dynamometer attached to a cord. The cord was tied to a small beam resting on two wardrobes. Under such circumstances the end of the table was lifted 15 centimetres and the dynamometer indicated 33 kilograms. The medium sat at the same short end of the table with her hands completely above it to the right and left of the point where the dynamometer was attached. Our hands formed a chain upon the table, without pressure, and in any case they would not have been able to do more than increase the pressure applied to it. The desire was expressed that the pressure should diminish instead of increase, and soon the table began to rise on the side of the dynamometer. M. Gerosa, who was following these indications, announced the diminution as

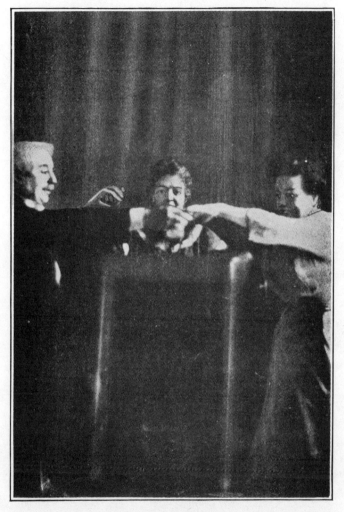

Fig. 23.   Motion of a Table not Due to the Direct Contact
of Hands.

expressed by the successive figures 3, 2, 1, 0 kilograms. In the end the levitation was so great that the dynamometer rested horizontally on the table. Then we changed the conditions, putting our hands under the table. The medium especially put hers, not under the edge where it might have touched the vertical cornice and exerted a push downward, but under the very cornice that joined the legs together, and touched this, not with the palm, but with the back of the hands. Thus all the hands could only have diminished the traction upon the dynamometer. When the wish was expressed that this traction might again increase, M. Gerosa presently announced that the figures had increased from 3.5 up to 5.6 kilograms.

During all these experiments each foot of the medium remained beneath the nearest foot of her neighbor to the right and the left.

3. *Complete Levitation of the Table.* It was natural to conclude that if the table, in apparent contradiction with the law of gravitation, was able to rise on one side, it would be able to rise completely. In fact, that is what happened, and these levitations are among those of most frequent occurrence in experiments with Eusapia. They were usually produced under the following conditions: The persons seated around the table place their hands on it and form the chain there. Each hand of the medium is held by the adjacent hand

of the neighbor on each side; each of her feet is under the foot of her neighbor; these furthermore press against her knees with theirs. As usual, she is seated at one of the short sides (end) of the table, — the position least favorable for mechanical levitation. After a few minutes the table makes a lateral movement, rises now to the right and now to the left, and finally is lifted wholly off its four feet into the air, horizontally, as if afloat in a liquid, and ordinarily to a height of from 10 to 20 centimetres (sometimes, exceptionally, as high as 60 or 70), then falls back on all four feet at once. Sometimes it stays in the air for several seconds, and even makes fluctuating motions there, during which the position of the feet under it can be thoroughly inspected. During the levitation the right hand of the medium frequently leaves the table with that of her neighbor and remains suspended above it. Throughout the experiment the face of the medium is convulsed, her hands contract, she groans and seems to be suffering.

In order better to observe the matter in hand we gradually retired the experimenters from the table, having noticed that the chain of several persons was not at all necessary, either in this or in other phenomena. In the end we left only a single person besides the medium, and placed on her left. This person rested her feet on the two feet of Eusapia, and one of her hands on

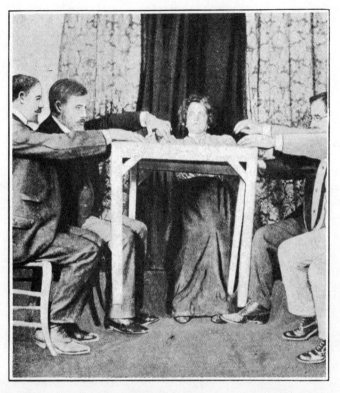

FIG. 24. FROM A PHOTOGRAPH OF COMPLETE LEVITATION OF THE
TABLE BY EUSAPIA.

the latter's knees.   With her other hand she held the left hand of the medium, whose right lay on the table in full view of all, or was even lifted into the air during the levitation.

Inasmuch as the table remained in the air for several seconds, it was possible to secure several photographs of the performance.

A little before the levitation it was observed that the folds of the skirt of Eusapia were blown out on the left side so far as to touch the neighboring leg of the table.   When one of us endeavored to hinder this contact, the table was unable to rise as before, and was only enabled so to do when the observer purposely allowed the contact to occur.   It will be noticed that the hand of the medium was at the same time placed on the upper surface of the table on the same side, so that the leg of the table there was under her influence, as much in the lower portion by means of the skirt as in the superior portion through the avenue of the hand.   No verification was made as to the degree of pressure exerted upon the table at that moment by the hand of the medium, nor were we able to find out, owing to the brevity of the levitation, what particular part was in contact with the garment, which seemed to move wholly in a lateral direction and to support the weight of the table.

In order to avoid this contact it was proposed to have the levitation take place while the me-

dium and her coadjutors stood on their feet, but
it did not succeed. It was also proposed to place
the medium at one of the longer sides of the
table. But she opposed this, saying that it was
impossible. So we are obliged to declare that
we did not succeed in obtaining a complete levitation of the table with all four of its legs absolutely free from any contact whatever, and there
is reason to fear that a similar difficulty would
have been met in the levitation of the two legs
that stood on the side next the medium.

4. *Variations of Pressure exerted by the Entire Body of the Medium seated upon a Balance.*
This experiment was very interesting, but very
difficult to perform; for it will readily be understood that every movement of the medium,
whether voluntary or not, on the platform of the
balance, could produce oscillations of the platform
and hence of the lever, or beam. In order that the
experiment might be conclusive, it was necessary
that the beam of the balance, once it had taken
a new position, should remain there for a few
seconds to permit the measurement of the weight
by means of the shifting of the weight on the
beam. In the hope that this would work all right
the attempt was made. The medium was seated
in a chair on the balance, and the total weight
was found to be 62 kilograms. After a few oscillations there was a marked descent of the beam,
lasting several seconds, and this permitted M.

Gerosa, who stood near the beam, to measure the weight immediately. It indicated a diminution of pressure equivalent to 10 kilograms.

A wish having been expressed that the opposite result might be obtained, the extremity of the beam quickly rose, indicating this time a rise of 10 kilograms.

This experiment was repeated several times, and in five different séances. Once it gave no results, but the last time a registering apparatus enabled us to get two curves of the phenomenon. We tried to produce similar deflections ourselves, and succeeded only when many of us stood on our feet on the platform of the balance and rested our weight now on one of its sides and now on another, near the edge, with very vigorous movements, which, however, we never observed in the medium, and which, indeed, were impossible in her position on the chair. Nevertheless, recognizing that the experiment could not be regarded as absolutely satisfactory, we rounded it out with one that will be described in Chapter III of this book.

In this experiment of the balance, also, it was noticed by some of us that success seemed to depend on contact of the garments of the medium with the floor upon which the balance was directly placed. The truth of this was established by a special experiment on the 9th of October. The medium having been seated on the balance, that

one of our number who had taken upon himself
to watch her feet soon saw the lower folds of her
dress swelling out and projecting in such a way
as to hang down from the platform of the balance.
As long as the attempt was made to hinder this
movement of the dress (which was certainly not
produced by the feet of the medium), the levitation did not take place. But as soon as the lower
extremity of the dress was allowed to touch the
floor, repeated and very evident levitations took
place, which were designated in very fine curves
on the disc that registered the variations of
weight.

5. *The Apparition of Hands on a Background
slightly Luminous.* We placed upon the table a
large cardboard smeared with phosphorescent
material (sulphide of calcium) and placed other
pieces of the same cardboard in other parts of
the room. In this way we very clearly saw the
dark silhouette of a hand projected on the cardboard of the table, and upon the background
formed by the other pieces we saw the black
outline of the hand pass and repass around
us.

On the evening of September 21 one of us several times saw the apparent shadow, not of one,
but of two hands, outlined against the feeble
light of a window closed merely by panes of glass
(outside it was night, but not completely dark).
These hands were seen to be in rapid motion,

but not so much so as to hinder our seeing their outlines. They were completely opaque. These apparitions (of hands) cannot be explained as cunning tricks of the medium, who could not possibly free more than one of her hands from control. The same conclusion must be drawn as to the clapping of two hands, the one against the other, which was heard several times during our experiments.

6. *The Levitation of the Medium to the Top of the Table.* Among the most important and significant of the occurrences we put this levitation. It took place twice, — that is to say, on the 28th of September and the 3d of October. The medium, who was seated near one end of the table, was lifted up in her chair bodily, amid groans and lamentations on her part, and placed (still seated) on the table, then returned to the same position as before, with her hands continually held, her movements being accompanied by the persons next her.

On the evening of the 28th of September, while her hands were being held by MM. Richet and Lombroso, she complained of hands which were grasping her under the arms; then, while in trance, with the changed voice characteristic of this state, she said, " Now I lift my medium up on the table." After two or three seconds the chair with Eusapia in it was not violently dashed, but lifted without hitting anything, on to the top

4

of the table, and M. Richet and I are sure that we did not even assist the levitation by our own force. After some talk in the trance state the medium announced her descent, and (M. Finzi having been substituted for me) was deposited on the floor with the same security and precision, while MM. Richet and Finzi followed the movements of her hands and body without at all assisting them, and kept asking each other questions about the position of the hands.

Moreover, during the descent both gentlemen repeatedly felt a hand touch them on the head.

On the evening of October 3 the thing was repeated in quite similar circumstances, MM. Du Prel and Finzi being one on each side of Eusapia.

7. *Touchings.* Some of these are worthy of being chronicled with some detail on account of certain circumstances capable of yielding interesting bits of information as to their probable origin; and first of all should be noticed those touchings felt by persons beyond the reach of the hands of the medium. Thus, on the evening of October 6, M. Gerosa, who was at a distance from the medium of three places (about four feet, the medium being at one short end of the table and M. Gerosa at one of the adjacent corners of the opposite end), having lifted his hand to be touched, several times felt a hand strike his to lower it; and he, persisting, was struck with

a trumpet, which a little before had been sounded here and there in the air.

In the second place should be noted touchings that constitute delicate operations impossible to be performed in the dark with that precision which was observed in them by us.

Twice (September 16 and 21) Signor Schiaparelli's spectacles were removed and placed on the table before another person. These spectacles are fastened to the ears by means of two elastic spiral springs, and it will be readily understood that a certain amount of attention is requisite in order to remove them, even in broad daylight. Yet they were removed in complete darkness with such delicacy and deftness that their owner had to touch his temples with his hand in order to assure himself that they were no longer in place.

In all of the extremely numerous manœuvres executed by mysterious hands there was never noted any blunder or collision such as is ordinarily inevitable when one is operating in the dark; and the darkness was in most of our experiments, with one or two exceptions already indicated, as complete as it could possibly be.

It may be added in this connection that bodies quite heavy and bulky, such as chairs and vessels full of clay, were placed upon the table without encountering any one of the numerous hands resting upon it, — a matter which was especially difficult in the case of chairs that would cover a large part of the table's surface owing to their size. A chair was once even turned down on the table and placed longitudinally without annoyance to any one, although it occupied nearly the whole top of the table.

8. *Contacts with a Human Face.* One of us, having expressed a desire to be kissed, felt the contact of two lips. This happened twice, September 21 and October 1. On three separate occasions it happened to one of those who were present to touch a human face with hair and beard, and the touch of the skin was undeniably that of a living man's face. The hair was much coarser and ranker in growth than the medium's, but the beard seemed very soft and fine.

9. *Sound of a Trumpet.* On the evening of October 3, a trumpet having been placed behind the medium and behind the curtain, all at once we heard it sound several notes. Those who were near Eusapia were in a situation to assure themselves with the greatest certainty that the sound did not come from her direction.

10. *Other Instances of "Apports."* One of us, at the beginning of the séance, had laid his overcoat on a chair beyond the reach of the medium. At the close it was seen that several different objects had been brought and laid on a phosphorescent cardboard that was on the table. The owner of these articles recognized them at once

as having been in an inside pocket of his over-coat. Hereupon the medium began to lament and make signs of displeasure, complaining of something that had been put about her neck and was binding her tight. We produced light and found that the overcoat was not in the place where it had been originally laid, and then, giving our attention to the medium, discovered that she had on the overcoat in question, her arms being slipped into it, one in each sleeve. During the sitting her hands and feet had been always controlled in the usual way by the two who sat next her.

II. Phenomena hitherto observed in the Dark now at length obtained in the Light, with the Medium in Sight

In order to attain complete conviction, it remained for us to attempt to secure important phenomena in the light. But, as darkness is very favorable to their production, we proceeded, in the sitting of October 6, as follows: In order that one part of the room might be left in darkness, it was separated from the rest by a curtain (divided in the middle), and a chair was placed for the medium before the aperture in the curtain. Her back was in the dark part, while her arms, hands, face, and feet were in the illuminated portion. Behind the curtain were placed a little chair and a small bell, about a foot and a half from Eusapia, and upon another more distant chair was placed a vessel full of moist clay.

In the illuminated part of the room we formed a circle around the table, which was placed before the medium. The room was lighted by a lantern with red glass sides.

Presently the phenomena began. We saw the inflated curtain blowing out toward us. Those who sat near the medium, on opposing their hands to the curtain, felt resistance. The chair of one of them was vigorously pulled, then five stout blows were struck on it, which signified "less light." We thereupon softened the light of the red lantern with a shade; but a little afterward we were able to remove the shade, and instead the lantern was set on our table in front of the medium. The edges (*lembi*) of the curtain where it was divided were fastened to the corners of the table, and, at the request of Eusapia, the upper parts were also folded back above her head and fastened with pins.

Then above the head of the medium something began to appear and disappear. M. Aksakoff rose, put his hand in the aperture of the curtain above the head of the medium, and announced that fingers had touched him several times; next, his hand was grasped through the curtain; finally, he felt something thrust into his hand. It was the little chair; he held it firmly; then the chair was snatched away from him and fell to the floor. All present put their hands through the curtain and felt the contact of hands. In the dark background of the aperture itself, above the head of the medium, the usual firefly-like bluish gleams appeared several times. M. Schiaparelli was forcibly struck through the curtain both on the back and side. His head was covered by the curtain and drawn into the dark part, while he with his left hand kept holding all the time the right of the medium, and with his right the left hand of M. Finzi. In this position he felt himself touched by the warm bare fingers of a hand, saw the light-gleams describing curves in the air and lighting up a little the hand and the body which was carrying them. Then he took his seat again; whereupon a hand began to appear in the aperture without being withdrawn so suddenly and in a more distinct way. M. Du Prel, without letting go of the hand of the medium, put his head into the aperture above her head and received some hard blows from several quarters and by more than one finger. The hand still showed itself between the two heads.

Du Prel resumed his place, and M. Aksakoff held a pencil up to the opening. It was grasped by the hand and did not fall to the floor. In a little while it was flung through the aperture onto the table. Once a closed fist appeared on the head of the medium. It opened slowly and showed the hand open, with the fingers spread apart.

It is impossible to state the number of times

that this hand appeared and was touched by us.
Suffice it to say that no doubt was any longer
possible. It was actually a living human hand
that we saw and touched, while at the same time
the entire bust and the arms of the medium remained in sight and her hands were continuously
held by her neighbors on each side.

When the sitting was over, Du Prel passed first
into the darkened part of the room and called
out to us that there was an imprint in the clay.
In fact, we ascertained that this had been dis-
figured by the deep print of five fingers, which
explains the fact that toward the end of the
séance a piece of clay had been thrown upon the
table through the aperture in the curtain. The
imprint of the hand was a permanent proof that
we had not been under an hallucination.

These things were repeated several times in
the same way or under a form a little different
on the evenings of the 9th, 13th, 15th, 17th, and
18th of October. Although the position of the
mysterious hand would not permit us to assume
that it belonged to the medium, nevertheless, for
greater security, on the evening of the 15th an
elastic rubber band was applied to her left hand
and wound around each finger separately, and
thus allowed one to distinguish at any moment
which of the two hands each neighboring sitter
had in custody. The apparitions took place just
the same, as they also did on the evening of the

17th, and finally on the 18th, although with less intensity, under the rigorous control (solemnly attested by them) of MM. Richet and Schiaparelli, each of whom gave special attention to this part of the investigation.

One evening, in full light, Schiaparelli brought a block of new writing-paper and asked Eusapia to write her name. She grasped his finger and moved it over the paper as if it were a pen. She then said, " I have written." But we could find no trace of writing, and she showed us that the writing was there, but in the inside of the tablet, or block of pages. In a second trial the signature was visible on the stick that held up the window curtain at a height of more than two metres at least, and nearly four from the table.

In a last trial the name was found to be badly written on the next to the last page of the tablet of paper, and yet the leaves had not been turned over nor the tablet lifted up.

And now let us glean the most interesting cases from the memoirs of the most eminent experimenters.

At Naples, in 1895, with my eminent associates Bianchi, Tamburini, Vizioli, and Ascensi, I again tried these experiments in a room in our inn chosen expressly for the purpose. And here, in full light, we saw a great curtain which separated our room from an alcove adjoining (and

which was more than three feet distant from
the medium) suddenly move out toward me, en-
velop me, and wrap me close. Nor was I able
to free myself from it except with great difficulty. A dish of flour had been put in the little
alcove room, at a distance of more than four and
a half feet from the medium, who, in her trance,
had thought, or at any rate spoken, of sprink-
ling some of the flour in our faces. When light
was made, it was found that the dish was bottom
side up with the flour under it. This was dry,
to be sure, but coagulated like gelatine. This
circumstance seems to me doubly irreconcilable,
— first, with the laws of chemistry, and, second,
with the power of movement of the medium, who
had not only been bound as to her feet, but had
her hands held tight by our hands. When the
lights had been turned on, and we were all ready
to go, a great wardrobe that stood in the alcove
room, about six and a half feet away from us,
was seen advancing slowly toward us. It seemed
like a huge pachyderm that was proceeding in
leisurely fashion to attack us, and looked as if
pushed forward by some one.

In other successive experiments made in full
light with Professor Vizioli and with De Amicis,
having asked Eusapia (whose feet and hands
were tightly bound and held by us) to have her
" John " move a little bell that had been placed
on the floor about a foot and a half from her, we

more than once saw her skirts extend themselves
to a point, as if forming a third foot or like a
swelled up arm. When I grasped this arm, it
presented a slight resistance to me, as if it were a
bladder filled with gas. And this immaterial arm
(shall we call it?) finally, in full light, under our
very eyes, all of a sudden seized the bell and
rang it!

I shall now present some of the experiments
tried at Milan and Genoa before the Society for
Psychical Studies by Morselli (1906–1907), Mar-
zovati, and myself, and described by Barzini in
his *Mondo dei Misteri* (1907).

The medium (Eusapia) frequently performed
experiments suggested by the caprice of those
present (see Barzini). One evening we asked
her to produce on our table a trumpet then on
a chair in the corner of the inner cabinet; and,
while we were looking at Eusapia sitting there
motionless, we heard the little trumpet fall to
the floor, and then for several minutes we heard
it moving lightly along, as if a hand were grazing it without being able to grasp it. One of
the experimenters held out the interrupters (or
cut-offs) of the electric light intrusted to him
toward the cabinet, about six feet from Eusapia,
and said, "Take them!" They were at once
taken out of his hand, and several metres of the
cord to which the cut-offs were attached slipped
through his fingers. He pulled the cord to him

forcibly and felt an elastic but strong resistance. After a brief and gentle pull he exclaimed, " Turn on the light! " and one of the lamps was lighted.

These events sometimes occur so rapidly as to take one by surprise and leave in one's mind a very legitimate doubt as to their nature; but very frequently they are slow and labored, and reveal an intense and concentrated energy.

During the séance Professor Morselli felt his right arm grasped by a huge hand, the position of the fingers of which he could accurately distinguish. At the same time Eusapia cried out, " See! " and the green lamp was lighted and again extinguished. Now, the cut-off of this green lamp, attached to a long cord that hung from the ceiling, was all the while in the pocket of Professor Morselli, who had not perceived the entrance of a hand there.

We all observed that the lamp was lighted and extinguished without the click of the cut-off being heard. While we were talking, as if to confirm our impression the lamp set to work lighting itself and extinguishing itself in the same silent manner as before.

We ought not to forget one thing: the lighting and extinguishing of the lamp corresponded to a slight movement of the index finger of Eusapia in the hollow of my hand. This synchrony between the phenomena and the movements of the medium occurred almost always in our experiments, and it is noteworthy that in these cases the active force of the medium proceeds from the side opposite to that on which the phenomenon is verified as having taken place. For instance, if the right fist of Eusapia is contracted, the person on her left will probably feel the touch of a hand, and is often able to recognize that it is a right hand. There is here a most singular crisscross, an inversion which it may be important to authenticate, in default of anything better.

A big table weighing about 24½ pounds, situated in the empty recess in front of the window, and upon which some one had laid boxes of photographic glass plates and a metronome belonging to Professor Morselli, moved forward to us, then retired. The metronome got into action and began its regular tic-tac. After a while the apparatus is closed, then resumes its action, then is closed again. Now, to set a metronome in operation and stop it is not a difficult nor a long piece of work, but it is minute, and, above all, is not an operation that metronomes are in the habit of doing of themselves.

Frequently the objects that arrive on the table of the medium are accompanied by the black curtain in such a way that it is exactly as if they were brought by persons hidden in the cabinet and who put the curtain between the objects and their hands. In another séance we saw the dynamometer, which was almost in contact with the edge of the curtain, come up on the table, move about, and disappear behind the curtain. We do not hear the light noise that would have been made in laying it up somewhere, and we remark among ourselves that one could think it were being held by some person. Whereupon, lo and behold! out of the cabinet, above the head of the medium, there steals forth a hand, holding the dynamometer as if it were showing it to us. Then the hand disappears, and after some minutes the dynamometer reappears on the table. The pointer marks a pressure of 110 kilograms. It is the pressure that would be exerted by a very robust man.

There can be no doubt but that the thought of the participants in a séance exercises a certain influence upon phenomena. It seems as if our discussions were listened to in order to get from them a suggestion for the execution of the various performances. We have only to speak of the levitation of the table, and the table rises. If we rap rhythmically on its upper surface, the raps are exactly reproduced, and often in the same spot apparently. We begin to speak of the luminous appearances which have sometimes been exhibited in Eusapia's sittings, and which we have not yet seen in this sitting, when, suddenly, behold! a light appears on the knees of the medium, disappears, and then again shows itself, this time on her head, descends along her left side, becomes more intense, and finally disappears when it reaches the hip.

In continuation, Professor Morselli gives notice that he has discovered some person behind the curtain, feels its body resting against him, and we see its arms enveloped in the curtain. Unexpectedly, Barzini pokes his head into the opening of the curtain in order to look into the cabinet. It is empty. The curtain is swelled out and its voluminous folds are empty. That which on one side seems to be the form of a human body in relief, on the other appears as a *carità* in the stuff, — a *moulage*, or mould. One recalls the " *homo invisibile* " of Wells.

Barzini touches with his right hand, which is free, the swelling of the curtain on the outside face, and positively encounters under the stuff the resistance of a living head. He identifies the forehead, feeling the cheeks and the nose with the palm of his hand; and, when he touches the lips, the mouth of the thing opens and seizes his hand under the thumb. He feels distinctly the pressure of a sound set of teeth.

The carillon (or music-box), intended to make a little diversion, comes upon the table as if it had fallen from above, and, resting there entirely isolated, plays for several seconds, while we look curiously on. In shape it is like a small coffee-grinder. Being so simple and so slightly musical, this instrument requires, in order to be played,

the co-operation of the two hands, — one to hold
it firm, and the other to turn the crank. Its *glu-
glu* has scarcely ceased when we hear the mandolin sliding along over the floor. M. Bozzano sees
it come out from the cabinet and stop behind Professor Morselli, where it strums two or three
times. Thence it climbs up on the table, turns
upside down, and ends by depositing itself in the
arms of Barzini like a baby! As we placed our
hands on the strings, we felt them vibrating under
the touch of the unknown force, and thus also
acquired the proof of touch as to the reality of
the phenomena.

We observe that the movement of the mandolin, as of all the objects transported, has a kind
of orientation. In other words, the objects never
move in a circle: they are subject to transference, but not to revolution. They move precisely
as if they were held by a hand, — advance and
retreat, move to the right or to the left, but keeping one and the same relative position.

The mandolin always has the handle turned
toward the medium. The chairs which take their
curious walks and climb up on the table always
look as if they were being dragged along by the
back. Professor Morselli brought with him a
little cord about sixteen inches long, and at a
given moment put it on the table. It disappeared
and then returned, wiggling and squirming like
a dog's tail. When he expressed the wish to

have knots tied in it, immediately it disappeared into the cabinet and soon after returned knotted in three places. These knots were equal, large, well made, symmetrical, and equidistant.

In a fifth sitting, in which Morselli had carefully tied Eusapia to a cot-bed, he was obliged to testify, after every instance of apparition, that she had been untied or tied in a different manner.

SPECTRAL APPEARANCES AND MATERIALIZATIONS

During the first five or six years of her public career as a medium Eusapia devoted herself more to phenomena of movement — to self-moving objects of furniture and to apports — than to spectral appearances. After the first years spectral hands began to be seen (sometimes joined to arms of various size), and, more rarely, feet. In the last few years these phantasms of arms and hands appear more frequently in the middle and at the end of the séance. Sometimes they accompanied translocation of chairs and mandolins, etc. Sometimes they appeared solely for the purpose of showing themselves — frequently being pale, diaphanous, of a pearly tint.

Bottazzi (*Nelle Regioni inesplorate della Biologia*, 1907) multiplied observations of this kind. For instance, he saw a black fist come clear out in front of the left-hand curtain and approach a lady, who felt herself touched on the back of

the neck and on the knees. On another occasion
a natural hand, the warmth and solid nature of
which were felt, was placed on his arm, and then
re-entered the body of Madame Paladino, as if
it were a case of phantasmal prolongation. Indeed, Galeotto once distinctly saw emerge from
the left side of Eusapia two identically similar
arms, — one (the true one) held by the controller, and another spectral (or " fluidic "), that
detached itself from her shoulder, touched the
hand of the controller, and then returned to
merge itself in the body of Eusapia.

These " fluidic " arms are the ones with which
the mediums move objects from eight to twelve
inches farther than the extremity of their own
proper limbs; furthermore, the thrusts given by
them frequently produce pain just as if they were
the true arms.

Sometimes, in good séances, these phantom
limbs are somewhat prolonged, but not farther
than four and a half feet from the table.

At the end of Eusapia's séances, especially the
more successful ones, true spectral appearances
occurred, though much more rarely. Among the
more important of these, inasmuch as it was seen
by many and was repeated, I note not only the
apparition of the deceased son of Vassallo,[1] but
also the one first confessed to me personally by
Morselli (however put in doubt afterwards) of

[1] See Vassallo, *Nel Mondo degli Invisibili*, 1902.

his mother, who kissed him, dried his eyes, said certain words to him, then again appeared to him, caressed him, and, to prove her personal identity, lifted his hand and placed it on the right eyebrow of the medium ("It is not there," said Morselli), and then placed it on her own forehead, on which, near the eyebrow, was a little blemish. Morselli was seated at the right of Eusapia, while on the other side was Porro (see the figure).

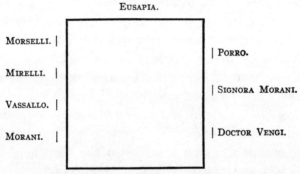

FIG. 25.   DIAGRAM OF TABLE AND SITTERS.

I myself had the opportunity of examining a similar apparition in Genoa in 1903. The medium (Eusapia) was in a state of semi-intoxication, so that I should have thought that nothing would be forthcoming for us. On being asked by me, before the séance opened, if she would cause a glass inkstand to move in full light, she replied, in that vulgar speech of hers, "And what makes you obstinately stuck on such trifles as that? I can do much more: I can cause you to

see your mother.   You ought to be thinking of
that."

Prompted by that promise, after half an hour
of the séance had passed by, I was seized with a
very lively desire to see her promise kept.   The
table at once assented to my thought by means
of its usual sign-movements up and down; and
soon after (we were then in the semi-obscurity of
a red light) I saw detach itself from the curtain
a rather short figure like that of my mother,[1]
veiled, which made the complete circuit of the table
until it came to me, and whispered to me words
heard by many, but not by me, who am somewhat hard of hearing.   I was almost beside myself with emotion and begged. her to repeat her
words.   She did so, saying, "*Cesar, fio mio!*"
(I admit at once that this was not her habitual
expression, which was, when she met me, "*mio
fiol*"; but the mistakes in expression made by
the apparitions of the deceased are well known,
and how they borrow from the language of the
psychic and of the experimenters), and, removing
the veil from her face for a moment, she gave
me a kiss.

After that day the shade of my mother (alas!
only too truly a shadow) reappeared at least
twenty times during Eusapia's séances while the

----

[1] At that moment Eusapia was certainly held by the hand by two persons, and her height is at least four inches greater than that of my poor
mother, of whose appearance she had not the faintest idea.

medium was in trance; but her form was enveloped in the curtain of the psychic's cabinet,
her head barely appearing while she would say,
" My son, my treasure," kissing my head and
my lips with her lips, which seemed to me dry
and ligneous like her tongue.

One of the most typical and strange instances [1]
is that which happened to Massaro, of Palermo,
in the séance of November 26, 1906, at Milan.
Some time previously, having evoked at a turn-
ing-table the spirit of the son recently deceased,
he had received from him the promise of a materialization at Milan. Having got a hint of the
séances of Eusapia, he decided to be present.

At the sitting of the 26th, Morselli having taken
a place in the chain, Madame Paladino remarked
quite suddenly that she perceived a young man
who came from a distance, and, after being
questioned, specified " from Palermo "; and
afterwards said, " Portrait made in the sun."
Whereupon Massaro remembered that he had
in his letter-case a photograph of his son taken
out of doors (in the country). At the same
time he was aware of being sharply tapped on
the breast at the very spot where he had that
picture of his son, and felt himself kissed twice
on the right cheek through the curtain that hung
near him; and the kisses were followed by very

1 From the volume entitled *I Fenomeni Medianici*, by Francesco
Facchini Luraghi, Milan, 1902.

arch caresses, though most delicate withal. Then
all of a sudden the significant touches were repeated, but this time by a hand that insinuated
itself with eager movements into the inside pocket
of the coat just where the letter-case was. This
it opened just at the compartment that held the
portrait. During this second appearance caresses
and kisses were held back at first; then he felt
himself seized around the body, drawn near the
curtain, and repeatedly kissed. Finally there was
projected on the curtain the apparition of a head
bound with a white bandage, — a head which he
recognized as that of his son.

A few months before he died, Chiaja presented
me with some bas-reliefs obtained (all of them)
from Eusapia when in a state of trance by placing clay wrapped in a thin fold of linen on a
piece of wood in a box, and this covered with
a board securely weighted down by a heavy stone.
Upon this the medium placed her hand, and
after she had entered into the trance state cried
out, "It is done!" The box was opened and
there was found the hollow print either of the
hand or the face of a being whose facial expression was mingled of life and death. I was
not present at these sittings. But the testimony
of Chiaja (a man of honorable memory) and that
of an illustrious Neapolitan sculptor who took the
reliefs from the moulds or imprints (Figs. 26 to
29) is my firm guaranty as to the transaction; as

FIG. 26.   MEDIUMISTIC SCULPTURES — THAT TO THE LEFT BY JOHN KING
(EUSAPIA), AND THAT TO THE RIGHT BY NICOLÒ R., 1905.

is also the opinion of Bistolfi, according to whom, in order to obtain in a few minutes those touches which, seen near at hand, are meaningless, but which from a distance assume a terrible and positively death-life expression, repeated trials would be necessary, and we should have to grant to the medium an extraordinary artistic ability, whereas she is without the very first elements of the art. Let us add that, since the clay is covered with a thin veil, the warp and woof of which can still be made out in the imprint, even a veteran artist could not succeed by mere pressure, and, as Bozzano notes, the hand would have to leave, not an imprint proper, but a vague channelling.

The *bona fide* nature of these occurrences is also proved to me from their having been repeated under the eyes of Bozzano at meetings of the Circolo Scientifico Minerva of Genoa, in 1901–1902, and in France under the control of Flammarion at Monfort l'Amaury, who repro duces a remarkable death-like mask, the very image of Eusapia.[1] The same phenomena have been produced under my own eyes in Milan and Turin.

[1] [See p. 76 of Flammarion's *Mysterious Psychic Forces* (Small, Maynard & Co., Boston, 1907).]

CHAPTER III

Experiments with Accurate Scientific Instruments

BUT the great mediumistic problem cannot be solved without the assistance of those accurate instruments by the use of which we are saved from every possible error of judgment. Crookes long ago noted, in the case of Florence Cook, that with appearance of the phantasm she lost almost the half of her weight. The same thing is true of Miss Fairland, who by the formation of a phantasm diminished her weight by sixty pounds, — the full half of her normal weight. Morselli noted a diminution of weight in Eusapia, after the trance state, amounting to 2200 grams. Arsonval at Torigio remarked that at the moment of the levitation of the table Eusapia's weight was augmented by the weight of the table. Eusapia, like Home, can vary the weight of her body both downward and upward (*i. e.* in less and in greater degree), first from 62 to 52 kilograms and then rising to 72 kilograms. She can effect the same result in the case of an object placed upon the balance, although at least the hem of

FIG. 27. PLASTER CAST OF IMPRESSION IN CLAY OF MEDIUM'S FOOT.

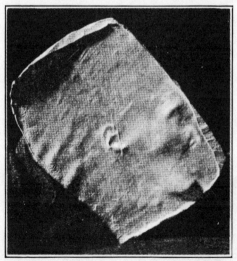

FIG. 28. BAS-RELIEF OF HER FACE EXECUTED BY EUSAPIA (CHIAJA).

FIG. 30. EXPERIMENT WITH CARDIOGRAPH AND RECORDING CYLINDER.

her draperies or her dress must touch the foot of the weighing-machine (*bascule*).

In our experiments with Eusapia we obtained similar results. Having placed two Regnier dynamometers on the table at a distance of three feet from the medium, — asking her to exert the greatest pressure she could, — we saw the indicator go to 42 kilograms, and this of itself, in full light and during one and the same manipulation. But when she is out of the trance state Eusapia has never before been able to reach more than 36. During the performance she asserted that she saw her " John " pressing in his two hands the instrument which she in her ignorance called " the thermometer." And she kept writhing her hands, held tight by us, and trying to turn them toward the dynamometer. While this was going on, I observed that the pupil of her eye contracted and her breathing grew deeper even to the point of dyspnœa.

In February, 1907, we placed in the mediumistic cabinet a Marey cardiograph (see Fig. 30) at a distance of three feet from the psychic, who had her back turned to it and her hands controlled by two of the experimenters. The cardiograph was connected with a pen running upon a cylinder smoked with lampblack. The connection was made by a tube traversing the walls of the cabinet. The writing pen was located 51 centimetres from the left lateral wall of the cabinet and about a mètre and a half from the medium. Everything being ready, we begged " John " to press the button of the cardiograph.

After a few minutes we hear the noise of the pen running over the cylinder, which being re-

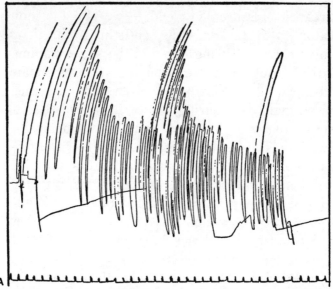

FIG. 31. CARDIOGRAPHIC TRACINGS BY "JOHN" (A IS THE TIME IN SECONDS ON THE DESPREZ REGISTER).

volved gives us two groups of curves that rapidly decrease (see Fig. 31). One part of the second group is intertwined with the first because we were not able in the darkness to remove the cylinder in time. The first group corresponds to about 23 seconds and the other to about 18 seconds. These tracings indicate either a prone-

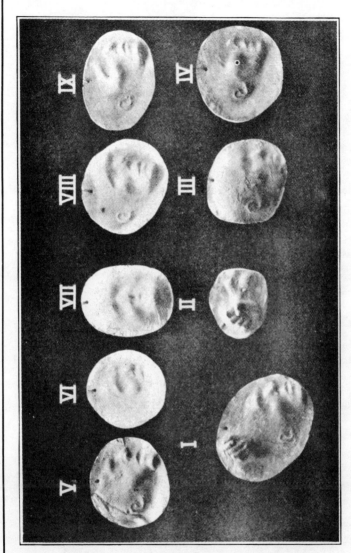

FIG. 29. TRANSCENDENTAL SCULPTURE: BAS-RELIEFS OF EUSAPIA'S FACE AND HAND.

ness to exhaustion or else weak volitional energy. To comprehend this, see the tracings (Fig. 32) made by one of us for one second pressing uniformly and rhythmically on the button of the cylindrical cardiograph.

The psychic, who in the normal state does not exercise any influence at a distance on the electroscope, one evening when she had just been awakened from a profound trance was placed by

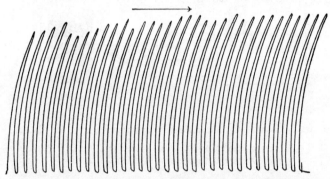

FIG. 32. CARDIOGRAPHIC TRACING BY EXPERIMENTER.

Dr. Imoda with her hands suspended ten centimetres above the electroscope. For two minutes nothing happened. Then of a sudden began the drooping of the pieces of gold leaf, which after four minutes fell rapidly. This is something that, correlated with the impression made by the medium on photographic plates wrapped up in dark paper, confirms the fact of her radio-activity in the trance state, and harmonizes with the frequent appearance of white fluctuating clouds

similar to the luminous vapor on the upper surface of the table during the séances, — it being
a property of the cathode rays to determine the
formation of vapor when they pass through air
saturated with humidity.

And now we come to the experiments of Foà

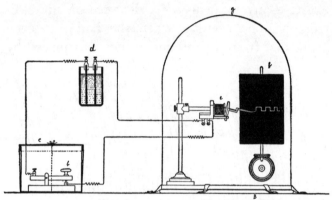

FIG. 33.   APPARATUS FOR REGISTERING MOVEMENTS OF THE MEDIUM. —
ROTATING CYLINDER UNDER BELL-GLASS.

and Herlitzka and Bottazzi (*Rivista d' Italia,*
1907).

Drs. Foà and Herlitzka thus write:

In order to register objectively the movements
that the medium has the power of producing,
we have constructed (see Fig. 33) a rotating
cylinder (*f*) around a vertical axis. The cylinder completes one entire revolution in six hours.
Around the cylinder is wrapped a sheet of white
paper covered with a layer of lampblack. Upon
this black surface a fixed point moves, removing

the lampblack, and through the movement of the cylinder marking on the paper a white horizontal line. If the pointer moves from above downward, it designs on the paper a delicate vertical line. The pointer could be put in motion by a small electro-magnet (e), the Desprez register united to an accumulator and a telegraphic key. The rotating cylinder and the Desprez register are placed under a bell-glass, which is set on a stout plank (B). The bell-glass, the lower rim of which is stout and thick, was fixed upon the plank by means of a narrow band passing through three eye-holes formed of little ribbons sealed with sealing-wax to the board. The rim of the bell-glass served as a hold, or stop, for the band.

Through three holes made in the thickness of the wooden plank, the conducting wires proceeding from the registering apparatus issued from beneath the bell-glass only to be immediately encased in glass tubes which hindered the wilful or casual contact of the wires with each other and the consequent breaking of the electric circuit. Of the wires, one went to the accumulator (d), the other directly to the telegraphic key, from which next in order a third wire, insulated in a glass tube, went to the other pole of the accumulator. All parts of the wire that could not be insulated by glass, at the binding-wires of the accumulator, were wrapped with

insulating ribbon and covered with a ribbon band
(*fettucia*) sealed with our seal. Finally, the telegraphic key itself was enclosed in a cardboard
box (*c*) nailed to the plank, and shut by means
of two bands placed crosswise and sealed. Two
little holes in the box gave passage to two glass
tubes containing the conducting wires.

Accumulator and key were fixed upon the same
plank as the cylinder. Thus it was impossible
to make a mark upon the cylinder except when
the key was pressed down.

Besides this registering mechanism, we prepared some sheets of lampblacked paper in order
later to secure imprints; some photographic
plates carefully folded in black paper for the
purpose of putting in evidence eventual radiations that should penetrate through the opaque
media; and, lastly, a dynamometer.

We were able to prepare experiments with
assured objective results.

The medium told us that she could have moved
the key of our apparatus without breaking the
protecting structure if this had been of cloth instead of cardboard. So, for the second sitting,
we modified our apparatus, and in order not only
to register the movements taking place, but also
to measure their intensity, we abandoned electric registration, substituting for it the manometric method.

For this purpose (see Fig. 34) we connected,

by means of a glass rod, a vessel (*a*) full of water (and furnished with a tube aperture (*b*) near the bottom) to a U-shaped manometer (*c*) containing mercury. The top opening of the vessel was covered by a strong india-rubber cloth (*d*) tightly bound to the receptacle itself.

In this way we had an enclosed space full of liquid, at the farther extremity of which was inserted the manometer. And since upon the mer-

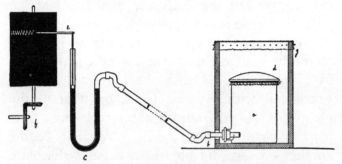

FIG. 34. EXPERIMENT WITH THE MANOMETER (TO MEASURE MOVEMENTS AND THEIR INTENSITY).

cury floated a little rod furnished with a point (*e*) which made tracings on the rotating cylinder (*f*), every pressure was registered and measured in an objective document.

Experience had taught us the uselessness of sealing the bell-glass, so we gave that up. But instead we took the cylinder and the manometer out of the medium's cabinet and placed them in a visible and controllable position throughout the séance. In the cabinet we placed only the glass receptacle for water, upon the rubber cloth of which the power of the medium was to be tested. This water vessel stood in a wooden box (*g*) over the top of which a cloth was stretched and nailed. The rubber cloth itself was covered with a layer of lampblack.

But even our precaution of covering the apparatus with cloth was to be shown up only too well as being of no service whatever, for at a certain moment the cloth was heard to tear.

In the presence of a phantom form one of us (F.) held a photographic plate, wrapped in paper, above the head of Eusapia and felt the plate seized by a hand covered with the curtain. M. Foà grasped it with his own hand, but that of the phantasm slipped from his and struck him. The plate is changed, and the invisible hand begins another contest, during which it holds the plate fast for several seconds. At last an unexpected blow given to the plate makes it fall on the little séance table, though without breaking it.

In continuation of the game, Dr. Arullani goes up to the little table No. 1. But it advances briskly against him and pushes him back. The doctor grabs it, and a contest ensues. During the contest the table is heard to crack. The table in question is strong and made of whitewood; height, 80 centimetres; length, 90; width, 55; weight, 7.80 kilograms.

Dr. Arullani calls for a pressure of the hand

from the curtain, and the medium replies with the voice, " I will first break in pieces the table and then shake hands." Hereupon three new complete levitations of the table take place, and each time it falls back heavily on the floor, and later goes into the cabinet, all the time smashing itself up, then comes out with violent movement, thrashing around before everybody, and, its joints all apart, is finally broken to pieces, even the separate boards being broken up. Two of the legs, still united by a small strip of wood, hang poised in the air for a moment above us and then descend upon the little séance table.

The co-experimenters of Professor Mosso thus sum up the objective phenomena established and authenticated by them:

1. The registration of our apparatus took place while the rotating cylinder was outside of the séance cabinet in such a way that no one could approach it without being seen, while at the same time the transmitting apparatus was in a wooden box higher than the elastic cloth, or membrane, and entirely visible. One of us felt, simultane-ously with the taps on the membrane, the pres-sure of the right hand of the medium in his left, during which time also the other hand of Madame Paladino was in that of Professor Foà.

The apparatus stood on the left of Dr. Her-litzka, whose left hand held the right hand of the medium, while her right was held by the one who sat next.

2. The stout table went all to pieces before the eyes of all of us, untouched by any one; the nails were pulled out and the joints and separate boards smashed. The breaking up took place, as has been said, on one side of the medium and also in front, to the left, in the midst of many of the company, and in a good state of the light.

3. The photographic plate, nailed under the table, passed with swift motion to its upper surface, while all present were on their feet and forming the chain, and in the best light possible, — all of us, including the medium, being at a distance from the table, which was in open space and distinctly visible on all sides.

The objective records of the phenomenon were these: When the séance was over, the photographic plate was found to be on the table instead of under it, and two of the nails that had held it up were missing. Before the event occurred, Eusapia made the one of us who had nailed the glass plate under the table give her his hand to hold, while her right was at the same time held by two others of us.

4. The photographic plate (wrapped up in black paper) which one of us had held on the head of the medium and which for several seconds had been struggled for by what we called a hand, showed after development the dark negative im-

print of four large fingers (Fig. 35). This is evidently a case of radio-activity and not of luminosity, because the impression was made through an opaque medium. Two of the plates gave uncertain results.

Our manometer had made on the smoked paper varied markings, the highest of which correspond to a pressure of 56 millimetres of mercury. The proportions of the elastic cloth being known, that indicates that upon this cloth there had been exerted a pressure equal to about 10 kilograms. Upon the gutta-percha cloth covered with lampblack there was found the imprint of the cloth; only it was partly torn.

Bottazzi (*Nelle Regioni Inesplorate della Biologia Umana*, 1904), and Galeotti at Naples, undertook on a grand scale, in experiments with Eusapia, the application of graphic registration to mediumistic phenomena. From Bottazzi I have gleaned the following accounts: —

Conceive a metallic cylinder covered with a sheet of white paper that has been smoked, — a cylinder that turns continuously on its axis with a uniform motion more or less rapid. Just touching the cylinder is the point of a pen, or stylus, which at one end is fixed to a support. The style may rest in a vertical plane in the centre of which is a horizontal axis. When the style moves over that plane, the point describes on the cylinder a

curved line, the arc of a circle that has for its
centre the axis around which the style moves.
The style should be held by means of a counter-
weight in a fixed horizontal position. Upon the
surface of the séance-table let there be a telegraphic key, and let the button of the key be
connected with the style by means of a cotton
or silk thread. Then say to the medium, " Press
down the button without touching it with your
visible hand, but solely by means of your mediumistic force." The medium presses it down. The
click of the key is heard, that is to say, the rap
of the metallic point of the key upon the metal
block underneath. But at the same time, through
the operation of the thread, the lowering of the
button has drawn down the style, the point of
which has traced a line on the smoked paper.

The telegraphic key was set in motion several
times. It was screwed down on a piece of board,
and hence was not misplaced or overturned.

We all heard the rapid lively taps of characteristic timbre. And as a proof that we were
not the victims of collective illusion or hallucination, the tracing revealed to us three groups of
registrations and two isolated strokes interca-
lated among them. Fortunately, the electro-magnetic signal operates in a mode quite different
from that of our sense organs and is never deceived nor can be deceived. Those little vertical
lines, that are almost indistinguishable one from

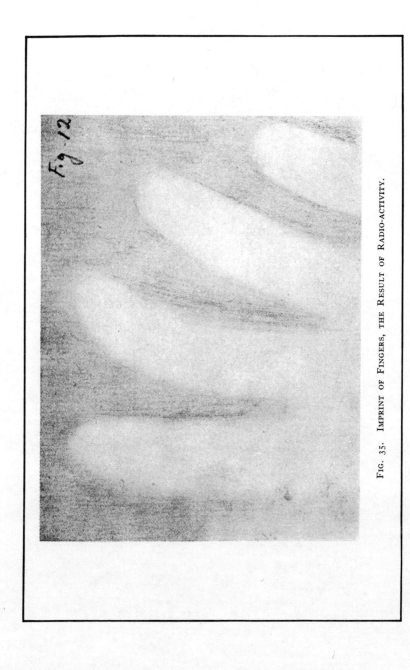

Fig. 12

FIG. 35. IMPRINT OF FINGERS, THE RESULT OF RADIO-ACTIVITY.

the other (because, owing to the low velocity of the cylinder, they succeed each other at too short intervals, less than the fifth of a second), correspond to an up and down movement of the key. Looking sharply at the original tracings with a magnifying lens, one discovers that the marks when they are thick are registered with a frequency of about $2\frac{1}{2}$ for every $\frac{1}{5}$ of a second, that is to say, about 13 to a second.

Here is another method of manometric registration:

You are to suppose fastened upon the top of a stool a Marey receiving tympanum, upon the central button of which, glued to the middle of the sheet of caoutchouc (more resistant than the sheets ordinarily used in physiological researches), had been fastened with strong glue a disk of wood for the purpose of increasing the superficies upon which the pressure of the invisible hand of the medium was to be exerted. The tympanum was connected by means of a tube with a François Frank mercury manometer, which, in a branch of the U-shaped tube, has a float furnished with a style that writes on the usual lampblacked cylinder. Every pressure exerted on the little wooden disk glued on to the elastic membrane is transformed (by transference of force) into a lifting of the float and of the style of the manometer, and every depression into a lowering thereof.

Now, if the tracing be observed, groups of ascending and descending white lines will be found, some higher, some lower. Naturally, to the higher lines correspond strong pressures, to the medium ones pressures of medium intensity, and to the lowest ones weak touches of the disk. The pressures given, especially the strongest, cannot produce the highest lines except when they are exerted on the membrane of the tympanum, which, as has been said, is fastened upon the stool.

As respects displacements of this stool, or as respects the taps rapped on it, or the movements imparted to the caoutchouc tube connecting the tympanum and the manometer, or even as regards the bruises or batterings of it, the former do not have any effect at all, and the latter are translated into little vertical lines on the manometric tracing. An invisible hand or foot would have to strike or step on the little disk, would have to press on the membrane of the receiving tympanum and that with force, since to obtain the highest lines it is necessary to depress the disk to the utmost limit.

In other séances Bottazzi (see his *Nelle Regioni Inesplorate,* etc.) places on the table of the medium a letter weigher (balance scales) and the lampblacked cylinder, and adjusts the style against the paper. Madame Paladino is asked to lower the little tray of the balance without touching it. The cylinder is put in motion, and the point traces on it a horizontal line during several successive turns. Some seconds pass, when, lo! the left-hand curtain is seen to advance resolutely toward the table (as if pushed by a hand hidden behind it, whose fingers are plainly seen in relief), take hold of the tray

FIG. 36. LINE TRACED BY A SUPERNUMERARY PHANTASMAL HAND.

of the balance, forcibly depress it, then draw back and disappear.

We stop the cylinder (says Bottazzi), and all testify to the fact that the point has traced (badly, to be sure, because the invisible hand made the balance oscillate) a vertical line upon the smoked paper. Eusapia's hands were in our custody (see Fig. 36).

The next day (continues Bottazzi) I wanted to see how much the index of the letter balance registered when the little tray was depressed as far as in the experiment of the day before, and found that the pressure exerted on the tray must have been equivalent to 370 grams.

On the table of the medium, in these Bottazzi experiments, were the following objects: a cage of iron wire with a key (*tasto*) inside of it; two Erlenmayer goblets containing the two known solutions of ferrocyanide of potassium and chloride of iron; one or two spring-keys; and a little Gaiffe electro-magnetic mechanism suitable for use as an electric cut-off, or interrupter. The other spring-key (the mate of that just spoken of) was outside of the cabinet on a chair.

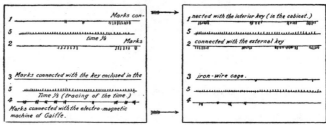

FIG. 37. — SYNCHRONOUS REGISTRATIONS OR MARKS (NAPLES PHYSIO-LOGICAL LABORATORY, MAY 15, 1907).

In the séance we are about to describe, the two keys operate marvellously well. Eusapia had at length learned to follow synchronous movements to perfection.

Scarcely had the invisible hand begun to cause taps on the interior key to be heard when Bottazzi put the other key on the table and invited Eusapia to strike them both at the same time.

The result of the experiment is visible in the two figures herewith presented, in which there are reproduced not only those which will be presently mentioned, but also the marks traced by the points of the two Desprez registers (the two upper lines), not counting the curve of time (*tempo*) connected with the two spring-keys.

The tracings show different groupings of synchronous taps. The number of the taps is not always the same in the two corresponding groups. But that comes from the circumstance that in each group the taps begin first on the interior key or first on the exterior one, and then the taps of the other key take place. But the synchronism is always perfect. The taps present a different record on the tracing and different from that perceived by our ears. As to this, the first thing to be considered is that the mediumistic raps are rapid and shorter, while those made by the visible hand of Eusapia are more gentle and hence more prolonged. The second point respects the force with which they were made, the criterion being the intensity of the sensations they provoke in us. Now the ones exterior to the curtain were quite weak, hardly audible; the interior ones were very strong, and appeared, not simply taps, but blows of a fist bestowed on the button of the key, delivered leisurely, not forcibly driven into the two surfaces of the table.

The results obtained may be summed up thus: The heavy table in the cabinet was shaken violently many times, with visible effort on the part of the medium, who made use of her arms and legs in such efforts. It was also from time to time drawn forth by bounds and leaps from the cabinet by the anterior left-hand corner, corresponding to the right side of Madame Paladino, and lifted up in such a way that after the sitting it was found twisted around, from front to rear and from left to right, about ten degrees measured on the level of the floor. Very naturally all the objects on it were, for this reason, either displaced or overturned (some one way, some another).

Only the cylinder and the balance had preserved their original position. From the tracings we found on the smoked paper it follows that the cylinder had rotated from right to left, that is, in the direction opposite to the hands of a watch, and that the pointer of the letter weigher had traced very irregular marks, corresponding to the raps of the metallic clock upon the support of the letter balance, — sounds that we heard during the movements of the table.

RÉSUMÉ OF THE EUSAPIA PHENOMENA

CLASS I

The Eusapia experiments have been well summed up by Professor Morselli. The first class includes mechanical phenomena, with the production of movements in the case of objects still in contact with the psychic. These Eusapia readily effects, in the dark or in the light indif-

ferently, — always, be it understood, under full
" control."

1. Meaningless oscillations and movements of
the table.

2. Movements and rappings of the table that
have meaning. These also are very frequent, and
those that tally the conventional language employed by Eusapia — two taps " no," three taps
" yes," etc. — regulate for the most part the
method of procedure of the séances. In truth,
the typtology of Eusapia, considered as a whole,
is a little different from the marvellous communications of a personal nature or of a philosoph-
ico-social order given by other mediums.

By way of compensation the Eusapian table
has a very rich diction that may be called
" mimic " and which resembles that of a child.

3. Complete levitation of the table to a height
sometimes of 78 inches.

4. Movements of different objects very lightly
touched by the hands or body of the medium,
which cannot be reconciled with the extremely
weak pressure exerted by her.

5. Movements, undulations, inflations of the
curtains of the séance cabinet, without the possibility of their taking place by means of the
severely controlled hands or feet of Eusapia.

6. Movements and inflations of the garments
of the medium.

CLASS II

The second class is only the rounding out and finishing of the first class; that is to say, the mechanical effects are produced without contact with the person of the medium, at a distance which may vary from a few centimetres to several metres. They are the most disputed of all, because they can with difficulty be comprehended by the ordinary laws of physics, which teach that a mechanical force ought to act directly upon the resistance opposed to it by material bodies. And yet this mediumistic telekinesis [movement at a distance] is the most frequent thing to be seen at the séances of Eusapia Paladino. Let us cite in a summary way the chief phenomena of this class.

7. Oscillations and movements of the mediumistic table without contact.

8. Independent levitations of the table. We have been present at dances of the table *a solo* [without a partner] in full gas light when the medium was shut into the cabinet and tied there.

9. Undulations, inflations, and flinging of the curtains of the cabinet. These take place even when the medium is distant; for example, when she is lying down and firmly tied within the cabinet. It seems as if invisible personages must be lifting the hangings with their hands, —

drawing them back to open them, forcibly pulling them to close them, etc.

10. Movements impressed on material bodies by hands voluntarily turned toward them, but at a distance. This phenomenon takes place ordinarily in full light and at the end of sittings. It is the true externalization of motivity explained by De Rochas.

11. Spontaneous movements and the displacement of different objects at various distances, even at a distance of two and three metres from the medium.

12. Transference of distant objects to the top of the table. Very frequently, however, such objects preserve certain relations to the dark curtains, which, in the phenomenology of Eusapia, have a most important function to perform, — as if they served as a defence for invisible limbs.

13. Displacement of the chairs of the observers. Frequently we feel our chairs taken from under us, etc.

14. Functional movements of mechanical instruments at a distance. For example, the starting into operation of musical instruments (mandolin, guitar, pianoforte, trumpet) or of other small mechanisms (music-boxes, metronome, dynamometer, etc.), all at a distance from Eusapia.

CLASS III

The third class of mechanical phenomena concerns the alteration of the gravity of bodies, which are the least sure cases, although illustrious observers guarantee us that they are authentic.

15. Spontaneous changes of weight in a balance. We have witnessed oscillations of the arm of a steelyard when it could not be seen that Eusapia pressed it. But the phenomenon appeared dubious.

16. Changes in the weight of the body of the medium of from five to ten kilograms.

17. Levitation in air of the person of the medium.

Professor Morselli had the impression that any of these levitations was genuine at its beginning, but was unconsciously assisted by the two controllers at the finish.

A curious class of cases, up to this time little studied, is that of the thermo-radiant results of mediumistic phenomena. It consists of few, but interesting, phenomena.

18. Wind out of the dark cabinet is a very frequent thing and is felt at almost every séance. It is a true spouting fountain of air, coming from within the cabinet and behind the medium.

19. Intense cold. It is observed, for the most

part, by the two controllers, and is the prelude to many manifestations.

20. Radiations from the head and the body of the medium.

When the hand is placed near the head of Eusapia, particularly that part of it where there is an osseous opening, or sunken place, due to a fall in early life, there is felt a very perceptible " puff " or draft, now tepid and now chilly. It is impossible to say just how great significance such phenomena have had in the hypotheses made to account for the new nervous forces.

The class of acoustic phenomena is in part comprised in the three preceding, since very frequently movements at a distance are rendered possible by means of noise, — the sound, etc., of musical instruments in operation.

But there are some other special cases of this class, as, for example, —

21. Raps, blows, and other noises on the table.

22. Raps and blows at a distance from the medium.

23. Sounds of musical instruments. These are not really musical sounds, nor harmonious chords, and much less melodious airs. At the most, they are rhythmic time-beats.

24. Noises of hands, of feet.

25. Vocal human sounds.

Professor Morselli next passes to a class of

manifestations not less impressive; namely, to that which, according to the Spiritualists, must reveal the action of occult " intelligences," with lasting results upon inert material. Eusapia, through her lack of culture, is rather weak in this kind of phenomena.

26. Mysterious marks made at a distance. These consist of spots and tracings found on the table and the cuffs of the experimenters, and seem to be made by a pencil.

27. Direct writing. This would seem to be writing made directly by the " spirits," without any evident operation of a hand, — sometimes, however, with visible graphic materials (pencil, graphite) and sometimes without.

28. Imprints on plastic material. (See photographs, *ante.*)

29. Apports.

CLASS IV

This deals with materializations, that is, with *ex novo* creations, more or less organized, and possessing our human physical characteristics embodied in a material substance; which means beings opposing resistance to touch and to the muscular sense (tangible beings) and beings sometimes endowed with self-light (luminous existences), but more frequently capable solely of arresting the exterior rays of light (rendering themselves visible).

The first sub-class is that of solid materializations, which Professor Morselli calls " stereosts " and " plasmasts " (*stereosi* and *plasmazioni*).

30. Touchings, handlings, and pressures of invisible hands. These are very common phenomena in the séances, occurring either in the darkness or in weak light or by red light. And they are genuine human hands that touch, press, grasp, draw, lightly strike, knock against us, pull one's beard or hair, remove eyeglasses, and bestow cuffs or slaps.

31. Organizations having a solid form and the characteristics of limbs of the human body. They are ordinarily hands, arms, and even heads, that are felt through the dark curtain and that seem pieces or fragments of a creature that is being formed. Sometimes they give the impression (tangible) of being an entire person. Pressures or grasps of a hand through the curtain are usually but momentary, the hand and arm drawing back in haste; but sometimes they remain a good while and allow of handling, especially the faces. The unseen mouth also gives kisses, bites, and the like, — hindered, however, almost always by the stuff of the curtain.

31 (*a*). Organs identical with human hands, distinguishable to the touch as nude. On certain occasions the touches of true hands of flesh and bone are felt, having the characteristics of the limbs of a living creature. The skin of the

7

hands, their warmth, the superficies of the palm, the mobile fingers, are all perceived. If they are grasped, you get the impression of hands that are dissolving under your touch, that slip away as if they were composed of a semi-fluid substance.

32. Complicated actions of materialized forms (tangible-invisible). Those hands, those arms, those heads or half-persons, albeit remaining imperceptible to the sight even of those who look within the cabinet (behind the curtains by which they are covered), yet advance towards the observers, touch them, and handle them, draw them close and grasp them, or push them away, caress them, attract and kiss them, with all the motions of real and living creatures. Further, they perform actions still more complex, whether in the penumbral light of the cabinet or in front of it (through the intermediary of the dark curtains, which are swelled out and projected at need over the surface of the sitters' table, or in the direction of those near it, even of persons outside of the chain), or whether in full freedom of movement, and fairly in the midst of the company, to such an extent that certain members of said company feel themselves approached, embraced, and kissed.

CLASS V

This consists of luminous phenomena, — elementary, self-illuminating (the telephany of the psychicists), or visible by the electric light, but always inorganic essences.

33. Appearance of luminous points. These are the celebrated " little flames " of the Spiritualists. Eusapia produces them now and then, but not with the intensity of other mediums. They are undefinable gleams, for the most part with contours vague and blurred, sometimes like very bright globules, — after the style of the so-called " Batavian drops," but upside down. Again, they resemble true " tongues of fire," as they are seen figured upon the heads of the Apostles. They are evidently sometimes multiple and seem to chase one another. It is impossible for one who has seen them even for a single time to compare them (I will not say assimilate them) to artificial phosphorescences.

34. Appearance of clouds or dim white mists. These do not seem to be endowed with their own proper light, since they can be observed only by the weak illumination this side of the curtains or within the cabinet. Sometimes they surround Eusapia's head or rise above her body when she is lying stretched out within her cabinet, and do not depend on action at a distance.

35. Radio-active action on photographic plates folded up in dark papers, and on electroscopes which are discharged from a distance.

36. Formation of obscure prolongations of the body of the medium. They are the supernumerary limbs which all those who have experimented with Eusapia have caught glimpses of and described. Only half visible or seen in weakest light and when Eusapia's anatomical or true hands are in sight and well controlled, these neoplastic appendages of the body perform many of the phenomena more fully described elsewhere in this volume, — touches, handlings of individuals, shakings of chairs, etc.

37. The issuing forth from the dark cabinet of shapes having a resemblance to arms and hands.

38. Apparitions of hands. They are among the most common and the oldest of spiritistic manifestations. The hands that appear have outlines for the most part indecisive or evanescent, of a whitish color, nearly diaphanous, and with elongated fingers.

39. Apparition of forms obscure and of character indeterminate or not very evident. They are the incomplete materializations. Now, in the vague clare-obscure of the room, dark globes are seen emerging and disappearing (heads?) and indefinable penumbral appendages (arms, fists?). Now appear shadowy shapes with curved profile (*profilo adunco*) which are

conjectured to be bearded ("John King"). And, again, on the luminous background appear dim black spectral silhouettes which seem as if transparent, and got up in a most strange manner, and making fantastic gesticulations.

40. Apparition of forms having the human appearance, or character.

These are the " complete materializations," and form the apex of achievement so far attained by Eusapia. (Other mediums, among which are Cook and Madame D'Espérance, give much more marvellous instances.) With Eusapia they are faces accurately delineated, heads and figures and half-busts of personages who are identified and named, the medium availing herself of notions obtained from the traditional history of Spiritualism. In this case one must admit that Eusapia acts upon certain invisible defunct beings in such a way as to make them conduct themselves as living beings, — a fact demonstrated not merely by the playing of certain instruments and the sounds of voices, but by graphic registrations and reproductions of movements much more complex, and with instruments which she cannot influence with her individual will. Furthermore, Eusapia can bring before our eyes the images of deceased persons of whom she had no knowledge before the séance.

TRICKS

Many are the crafty tricks she plays, both in
the state of trance (unconsciously) and out of
it, — for example, freeing one of her two hands,
held by the controllers, for the sake of moving
objects near her; making touches; slowly lifting the legs of the table by means of one of her
knees and one of her feet; and feigning to adjust her hair and then slyly pulling out one hair
and putting it over the little balance tray of a
letter weigher in order to lower it. She was
seen by Faifofer, before her séances, furtively
gathering flowers in a garden, that she might
feign them to be " apports " by availing herself
of the shrouding dark of the room. It would
seem, also, that she had learned from certain
prestidigitateurs some special tricks; for example,
that of simulating human faces by movements
of the two hands wrapped with a handkerchief so as to look like a turban. And yet
her deepest grief is when she is accused of
trickery during the séances, — accused unjustly,
too, sometimes, it must be confessed, because we
are now sure that phantasmal limbs are superimposed (or added to) her own and act as their
substitute, while all the time they were believed
to be her own limbs detected in the act of cozen-
ing for their owner's behoof.

CHAPTER IV

The Power and Action of Mediums

(EUSAPIA PALADINO CLINICALLY STUDIED)

LET us see now if the explanation of all these marvellous phenomena can be found in the organism of the psychics, studying one of them (Eusapia) clinically and physiologically.

In external characteristics nothing abnormal appears, at first sight, except a lock of white hair surrounding a depression of the left parietal wall, — a depression caused, as was told me once, by a blow given her with a stewpan by her stepmother, or, according to another version, by a fall from a window at the age of two years.

Her weight is 60 kilograms, and the weight does not vary after the séances. She has stenocrotaphia (that is to say, the forehead is narrow across the bizygomatic diameter, being greater than the frontal, 127 to 113); is dolicocephalic, 73, which is, however, an ethnic feature; circumference of the head small, 530; asymmetry not only of the cranium, but of the face, on account of the greater development of the right portion. The left eye presents the phenomenon of Claude Bernard Hörner, as in epileptics; the

TABLE OF MEDIUMSHIP.

PSYCHO-NEUROTIC CONDITION INDUCED AND MODIFIED THROUGH MENTAL SUGGESTION BY EXTRA-HUMAN INTELLIGENCES IN THE MEDIUM.

The Waking State.
{ Intuitive mediumship.
{ Mediumship with physical effects of motion: displacement of objects.

Pre-hypnosis.
{ Intuitive mediumship.
{ Speaking "
{ Writing "
{ Typtological "
{ Mediumship with physical effects of motion: displacement of objects.
{ " " " " noises.

Speaking mediumship.
Writing "
Typtological "
Mediumship with physical effects of motion: displacement of objects.
" " " " levitation.
" " " " transferences.
" " " " noises.
" " " " lights.

Somnambulism.
Mediumship with doubtful materializations partially tangible.
" " " visible by opaque light.
" " " " " their own proper light.
" " " " " photographic action in the dark.
" " " " " pneumatographic action.

Catalepsy.

Typtological mediumship with physical effects of motion: displacement of objects.
" " levitation.
" " transferences.
" " levitation of the medium?
" " noises.
" " lights.
doubtful materializations. semi-integral, tangible.
" " visible by opaque light.
" " their own proper light.
" " photographic light in the dark.
" " photographic action in reflex light.
" " pneumatographic action.
dematerialization: apports?

Lethargy.

Typtological mediumship with physical effects of motion: displacement of objects.
" " levitation.
" " transferences.
" " levitation of the medium.
" " noises.
" " lights.
doubtful materializations, integral, tangible.
" " visible by opaque light.
" " their own proper light.
" " photographic action in the dark.
" " " " with reflex light.
" " pneumatographic action.
" " speaking.
permanent partial materializations.
dematerialization: apports.

pupils corectopic above and below; interiorly, they react poorly to the light, but, on the other hand, react well to adjustment. The arterial pressure, measured by the sphygmomanometer of Riva-Rocci, has given the following results: first trial, on the right 200, on the left 230; second trial, on the right 200, on the left 239. That is to say, she shows an asymmetry in arterial pressure that is common in epileptics, and, like these, exhibits marked tactual left-handedness, the esthesiometer revealing great obtusity in the ends of the right fingers (5 millimetres) and less in those of the left (2.5). Her general sensitiveness, studied with the sledge of Rhumkorff, presents, on the other hand, right-handedness, registering her electric sensitiveness as 73 millimetres on the right and 35 on the left, and the pain-causing sensitiveness (*la dolorifica*) as 60 on the right and 30 on the left, revealing itself as being in every way more delicate than in normal cases, in which the general sensibility, tested in the same way, marked 45 millimetres, and the dolorific 20. The barometric sensitiveness is unequal, thereby making confession that the same weight, when tested by the left, is heavier than when tested by the right; it shows differences of weight of 5 grams. The osseous sensibility is, at the diapason, 5 on the right, 8 on the left; is lacking in the forehead; with the little dynamometer of Regnier-Mathieu it marks 11 kilograms on the right and 12 on the left; when she was approaching the trance state, it marked 15 on both hands. With her right hand and arm extended she supports a weight of 500 grams for a minute and two seconds; with the left for two minutes. She has the hyperæsthesic zone, especially in the ovary. She has the bole in the œsophagus that women with hysteria have, and general weakness, or paresis, in the limbs of the left side.[1]

Her field of vision, studied by Dr. Sgobbo, seems ample and normal. The reflex actions of the tendons are duller on the right, or, rather, they are not excited there except when accompanied by the Jendrassik phenomenon. On the left they are *nil*. Nothing is observed with the apparatus of Arsonval and the Röntgen rays.

Once during full light, while she was in the normal state, she had her right hand held for her for four minutes over a photographic plate wrapped up in three folds of dark paper. This sufficed to cause her to enter into the trance state and to impart to the hand a feeling of electric tremor. When the plate was developed, at the place where her index finger had lain was found a formless stripe of the length of the finger. This fact, which is to be correlated with her mediumistic radio-activity, may be classified with another anomaly of hers observed by Flamma-

---

[1] Arullani, *On the Mediumship of Eusapia Paladino*, etc., 1907.

rion,[1] and which consists in a diaphaneity on the periphery or contours of the fingers, forming as it were a second vague contour. " When I have this sign, I can do wonderful things," she asserts.

Urine yellow (examined at Turin, 1901), in quantity of 2000 grams, with a specific gravity of 10.23, shows sugar 40 per cent, phosphates 1.20 per cent, chloride 3.598; light traces of albumen. After a séance the albumen was much augmented (0.5 per cent), and the sugar diminished (20 per cent). From analyses made later by Bottazzi it appears that the density of the urine after a séance is augmented, — 1023 instead of 1022; increase of albumen, 2 per cent in place of 1.25; azote, 11.28 per cent in place of 9.53; the electric conductibility increased to 177.10 instead of 150.10; the congelation point increased to 1.560 instead of 1.260.

Hypnotic phenomena, which are so closely connected with spiritistic phenomena as even to be confounded with them, are frequently exhibited by Eusapia, although she pays no attention to metals or magnets. Arullani (*op. cit.*), by merely grazing her forehead with his hand [" making passes "], can hypnotize her and cause her presently to fall into the cataleptic state.

Morselli, on the other hand, notes that it is

---

[1] See his *Mysterious Psychic Forces*, p. 198. Boston: Small, Maynard & Co., 1907.

easier for her to be magnetized than hypnotized, so that by methodical passes of his hand over her head he can free her from headache (*cephalæa*), and quiet her agitations of mind, and by upward magnetic passes provoke in her a state of semi-catalepsy, just as by passes in the reverse direction he can remove distortions of her muscles and paresis.

Twice only, however, did she have premonitions, and they were not at all clear, and she explains them with that fantastic pseudology of hers in such a varied way that they can with difficulty be discriminated. The first time was apropos of the theft of jewels of which she was the victim. She was notified of it, she says, in two successive dreams in the nights immediately preceding the deed. But it appears from her own account that the theft took place in a way entirely different from her dreams, so that, in order to get light on them and discover the criminal, she was obliged to abase herself before a rival of hers, — a certain somnambulist named Del Piano, who pointed out the guilty one as being her concierge, — an opinion which seems to have been the true one, since it was shared by the police.[1]

Another time — the night preceding her disqualification, or exposure, at Cambridge (and this was the most serious misfortune of her life)

[1] Ing. Grauss, *Annales des Sciences Psychiques*, 1907.

— " John " appeared to her and sadly shook his head. It seems that this phantom intervened again in Paris, when Eusapia was ill and had been intrusted to a nurse who neglected her and went to sleep instead of watching with her, and had administered to her sounding cuffs and pinches, so that Eusapia grew terrified and fled.

The same gentleman, M. Grauss (civil engineer), relates that, having been reproved by the commissary of police because, owing to her reproaching her doorkeeper with the theft, she had rendered useless all search in his house, she was so taken aback that she swooned away. The table thereupon began to be agitated and to express typtologically the thought of John: " Save my daughter, for she is going mad! Save her by suggestion! " And the engineer having replied that John was stronger than he, lo! an old man, meagre, with a long beard, appeared in broad daylight, and without saying a word placed his palm on M. Grauss's head and then on that of Eusapia, leaving him in a profound state of exhaustion. Eusapia woke up and soon forgot all her griefs.

As respects the lottery, — something in which nearly all the village population of the province of Naples are sinners, — she had no success whatever in premonitions, but in compensation possessed a singular telepathic power. Twice, when persons were presented to her as her admirers, while in reality they were her secret enemies, she repulsed them with brutal insolence without even looking in their faces. Her culture is that of a villager of the lower order. She frequently fails in good sense and in common sense, but has a subtlety and intuition of the intellect in sharp contrast with her lack of cultivation, and which make her, in spite of that, judge and appreciate at their true worth the men of genius whom she meets, without being influenced in her judgments by prestige or the false stamp that wealth and authority set upon people.

She is ingenuous to the extent of allowing herself to be imposed on and mystified by an intriguer, and, on the other hand, sometimes exhibits, both before and during her trance states, a slyness that in some cases goes as far as deception. I have noted some instances of this trickery at the close of Chapter III, under the sub-head " Tricks."

She possesses a most keen visual memory, to the extent of remembering five to ten mental texts presented to her during three seconds. She has the ability to recall very vividly, especially with her eyes shut, the outlines of persons, and with a power of vision so precise as to be able to delineate their characteristic traits.

But she is not without morbid characteristics, which sometimes extend to hysterical insanity. She passes rapidly from joy to grief, has strange phobias (for example, the fear of staining her hands), is extremely impressionable and subject to dreams in spite of her mature age. Not rarely she has hallucinations, frequently sees her own ghost. As a child she believed two eyes glared at her from behind trees and hedges. When she is in anger, especially when her reputation as a medium is insulted, she is so violent and impulsive as actually to fly at her adversaries and beat them.

These tendencies are offset in her by a singular kindness of heart which leads her to lavish her gains upon the poor and upon infants in order to relieve their misfortunes, and which impels her to feel boundless pity for the old and the weak and to lie awake nights thinking of them. The same goodness of heart drives her to protect animals that are being maltreated, by sharply rebuking their cruel oppressors.

Before the séance, and sometimes when it has begun, she can give notification of what she will accomplish, although afterwards she cannot remember whether she has done what she promised or not, and frequently does not succeed in doing what she boasted she would do.

At the beginning of the trance her voice is hoarse, and all the secretions — sweat, tears, even the menstrual secretions — are increased. Hyperæsthesia, especially sinistral hyperæsthesia, is succeeded by anæsthesia. Reflex movements of

FIG. 38.   EUSAPIA IN TRANCE (SPASMODIC LAUGHTER, ETC.).

the pupils and tendons are lacking. Tremors and myostenia occur, followed by amyostenia and paresis (especially dextral). When she is about to enter into the trance state, she lessens the frequency of the respiratory movements, just as do the fakirs, passing from 18 inspirations to 15 and 12 a minute; while, on the other hand, the heart beats increase from 70 to 90, and even to 120. The hands are seized with jerkings and tremors. The joints of the feet and the hands take on movements of flexure or extension, and every little while become rigid. The passing from this stage to that of active somnambulism is marked by yawns, sobs, perspiration on the forehead, passing of insensible perspiration through the skin of the hands, and strange physiognomical expressions. Now she seems a prey to a kind of anger, expressed by imperious commands and sarcastic and critical phrases, and now to a state of voluptuous-erotic ecstasy.

In the state of trance she first becomes pale, turning her eyes upward and her sight inward and nodding her head to right and left; then she passes into a state of ecstasy (see Fig. 38), exhibiting many of the gestures that are frequent in hysterical fits, such as yawnings, spasmodic laughter, frequent chewing, together with clairvoyance and a word often extremely select and even scientific, and not seldom in a foreign tongue, with very rapid ideation, so that she

8

comprehends the thought of those present even when they do not express it aloud or utter it in a mysterious manner. Morselli observed in her trance state all the characteristics of hysteria, namely, (1) loss of memory; (2) her personifications as John King, in whose name she speaks; (3) passional acts, now erotic, now sarcastic; (4) obsession, especially in the shape of fear that she may not succeed in the séances; (5) hallucinations; and so forth. Toward the end of the trance, when the more important phenomena occur, she falls into true convulsions and cries out like a woman who is lying-in, or else falls into a profound sleep, while from the aperture in the parietal bone of her head there exhales a warm fluid, or vapor, sensible to the touch.

And, as the medium produces spontaneous movements without the aid of the usual anatomical means, so she experiences visual and tactile sensations without the intervention of the usual organs of sense, since she informs us of things happening about us in positions inaccessible to her sight or to the sight of any one else, occurrences which afterwards are shown to be true.

Apropos of this, it is inaccurate to affirm that she exhibits knowledge which out of the trance state she would not have. During the entire séance the medium remains in full rapport

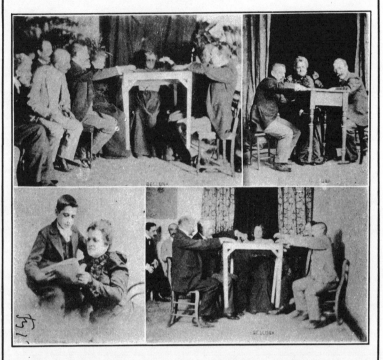

FIG. 39. (1. UPPER LEFT) MAGNESIUM LIGHT PHOTOGRAPH. PRESENT, PROFESSOR MORSELLI ON EXTREME LEFT. (2. UPPER RIGHT) LEVITATION OF THE TABLE AT 2 P.M. PRESENT, PROFESSORS PORRO AND MOTTZA. (3. LOWER LEFT) EUSAPIA WITH THE LAD PEPPINO, WHOM SHE WISHED TO ADOPT. (4. LOWER RIGHT) MAGNESIUM LIGHT PHOTOGRAPH (SÉANCES 1901–1902).

with all present, expresses her own opinions and her own will, whether *viva voce* (frequently pronouncing the words badly, like a progressive paralytic) or else with taps, which are now heard to proceed from the table and now from other objects, — the thought conveyed either in Italian or in a foreign tongue.

After the séance Eusapia is overcome by morbid sensitiveness, hyperæsthesia, photophobia, and often by hallucinations and delirium (during which she asks to be watched from harm), and by serious disturbances of the digestion, followed by vomiting if she has eaten before the séance, and finally by true paresis of the legs, on account of which it is necessary for her to be carried and to be undressed by others.

These disturbances are much aggravated if through the imprudence of any member of the company she is exposed to unexpected light, either before or after the sitting. This fact calls to mind the pythoness of Delphi, whose prophetic oracles shortened her life; also the sad case of Madame D'Espérance, who, through being exposed to brilliant light during a séance, suffered paralysis for many years.

I ought to add here a fact discovered by Dr. Imoda; namely, that when Eusapia is in the normal state she has no influence whatever on the electroscope. One evening when she had just awakened from the trance state, by holding her hands in the air above the electrode she was able after three or four minutes to produce a lowering of the gold leaf. Taken in connection with the impression of her fingers on photographic plates wrapped up in dark paper, this confirms the fact of her radio-activity in the trance state. It agrees, furthermore, with the frequent appearance of white fluctuating clouds, like luminous vapor, upon the surface of the table or upon her head during the séances, it being a property of the cathode rays to incite the formation of vapor, or mist, when they traverse a stratum of air saturated with humidity.

Nor are these morbid phenomena peculiar to Eusapia: they may be observed and verified in all the mediums.

The grandmother, mother, and one of the brothers of the famous medium Elena Smith [1] were subject to hypnotic and mediumistic phenomena. She herself had obsessions, hallucinations, from childhood up, and, later in life, fits of somnambulism, dysmenorrhœa, and, in the mediumistic trance, complete anæsthesia of one hand and *allochiria* [confusion of sensations], so that if pricked in the right hand she feels the pain in the left, and also believes she sees on the left objects which are really on her right.

[1] See Flournoy, *Des Indes à la Planète Mars*. Paris, Genève, 1900.

FIG. 40. EUSAPIA AFTER THE SÉANCE.

Mrs. Piper, when entering into a trance, begins with a slight convulsion, with peculiar shocks or starts, upon which follow stupor, stertorous breathings, a cry, after which she incarnates herself and the spirits communicate with her on the left side (the usual spiritistic left-handedness).[1] Her best communications are obtained at the beginning of the sitting. It must be observed that Mrs. Piper became a medium after her fright at a thunderbolt and after she had had two operations for the removal of tumors.

"When I am in a trance," writes D'Espérance, "I have a feeling of vacuity and lose the sense of space. I cannot tell where my finger moves; it is as if I were moving in water. . . . The transformation of vapor into a living being is so rapid that I cannot tell which is first formed, the body or its clothing. When the phantasm appears, I feel it so difficult to recover my thoughts and gather up my powers that I can hardly reply. I seem as in a dream and am unable to move. When Yolanda moves, she makes me perspire and exhausts me more than if I myself moved. When she materializes herself outwardly, I feel a stronger accession of power. When she touches some object, I feel my muscles contract, as if it were my hands that touched it. When she put her hands into melted

[1] Sage, *Madame Piper*. Paris, 1902.

paraffine, I felt my hands burn. When a thorn penetrated her finger, I experienced great pain. I saw her playing the organ; I saw her six times outside the cabinet. In the first moment of the semi-trance, when the phantasms have not yet appeared, I have a greater sensitiveness than the normal. I feel a person moving about in the house; I have a perception of the movements of the church clock and of the hissings of steam such as I do not have when in the normal state, and I am conscious of what persons present are thinking. When I touch the hands of Yolanda, I believe I am feeling my own, but perceive my error afterwards when I see four hands. When I stretch out my hands to touch her, I feel only the empty air. I have no sensation when a weight is placed on my feet. Nevertheless, one Sabbath I felt the entire weight of her body " (Aksakoff, *Un Cas de Dématérialisation*).

Politi, when out of the trance, does not exhibit any anomaly: in the trance this medium has convulsions, anæsthesias, terrific zoömorphic hallucinations, delirious ideas of persecutions.

All this is affined to hysteria, — just as (says Morselli very truly) tabes and general paralysis, without being due to syphilitic processes, develop more in those who have been syphilitic, just as those afflicted with gravel and asthma, while they may not be by nature gouty or rheumatic persons, have an affinity for those troubled with these diseases, although they have never had suffering in the joints.

The foregoing diagnosis suffices very well for the conclusion that the whole thing is a true hysteric equivalent, a new form of hysterical attack, just as, in my opinion, the creative frenzy (or *œstrus*) of genius is an equivalent of the psycho-epileptic paroxysm on a neurotic and morbid background.

Hence, when Professor Lucatello at Padua finds in Zuccarini complete cutaneous insensibility to pain, and somnambulism carried to the point of catalepsy, in consequence of a simple cutting of the skin (and Patrizi had already noted other hysterical anomalies, such as dissymmetry of the face with inferior development of the left half; the phenomenon of Claude Bernard Hörner, so frequent among epileptics; disparity of the visual function in the two eyes; ambidexterity; disproportion between the great opening of the arms (1.71) and the stature (1.60); habitual talking in her sleep, and deficient power of attention), that argues nothing against her mediumistic powers, but in part suggests and explains them, just as, in my opinion, the miracles of genius are explained by the neurotic concomitants.

And we are so much the more led at the very outset to believe that all the spiritistic phenomena take their rise in the abnormal state of the medium, since many of these phenomena always take place in her immediate vicinity, especially on the left side, and since the phantasmal arms and hands issue with more facility from her body and her garments, and the spectral forms appear for the most part above her head or that of her control standing by. Further, the rarer and more important are the phenomena (for instance, the apparition of phantasms), so much the heavier is the trance of the medium. Indeed, when movement of objects occurs, even at some distance away from said medium, synchronous movements are noticed in him or her. And, as soon as a phantasm appears, there is frequently noticed (for instance, in the medium Fairland, who was sewed into a hammock to allow the registration of variations in her weight) a gradual diminution of this, till it reached 66 pounds, — half her weight; and the moment the phantasm disappeared her weight began to increase (*Psychic Studies*, 1887).

This fact proves that the body of the spectral appearance is formed at the expense of the body of the psychic, and the matter is confirmed by the circumstance that in the first materializations of mediums many of the phantasms they evoke bear a certain resemblance to the face or the limbs of the medium, or even to the whole of his or her person, — something that must have fostered still further the suspicions as to trickery and deceit.

FIG. 41. FLOWERS DRAWN WITH COLORED CRAYONS BY A GERMAN
PEASANT WOMAN WHILE IN THE SOMNAMBULISTIC STATE.

I may add here the fact discovered by Rochas of the exteriorization of the sensitivity and motive power of the medium to the extent of several centimetres beyond his proper body. Now, the ability to extend this exteriorization to the psychic activity and prolong the motive power of that activity to a greater distance would suffice to explain a large part of the most mysterious phenomena of spiritism, especially since the phantasms, or spectres (the most important spiritistic phenomenon), often issue from the belly or the head of the medium (D'Espérance) and assume the medium's gestures and general appearance.

Moreover, the medium has some special characteristics. Not to speak of the strange epileptic-like look, even when out of the trance state he shows, according to Maxwell, zoömorphic spots in the iris of the eye; and, if he is not specially wicked, he becomes so in the trance. The medium may vary in intelligence from the ultra mediocrity of Politi up to the positive genius of D'Espérance and Moses. But in the trance state even the most stolid may develop an extraordinary intelligence, and Wallace tells of an ignorant, coarse-witted salesman who could discourse, when in trance, upon fate and prescience, whereas afterwards he could scarcely speak on common things.

The matter is worse still as respects the morality of mediums, many of them being ready deceivers and lascivious, while others, like the woman Smith and like Moses, are perfect saints. I have personally known some of them during intoxication, or when experiencing deep and joyful emotion, double their mediumistic powers. I have known of others who were not indubitably affected by albuminuria or diabetes, and yet during a séance these things appeared in them and grew worse.

For the most part, in order to develop their mediumistic powers, they require darkness, excitement, voices, cries, songs,[1] and (with the exception of the famous D'Espérance and Home) have no remembrance or consciousness of what they do in the trance, just as in the case of epileptics.

The proofs of the transmission of thought, whatever others affirm, are frequent and evident during Eusapia's trances.

I was thinking hard of being able to see my mother again: the table energetically assented to my thought unexpressed in words, and immediately afterwards appeared the image of my mother. Signor Becker mentally asks that his cravat be untied and removed, and his desire is immediately satisfied. Dr. Surada mentally wills that John pour water into a goblet in the medium's cabinet, and the thing is at once done: the glass full of water is transported to the table

---

[1] Maxwell recalls the incantations of witches and magicians.

FIG. 42 a. MEDIUMISTIC DESIGNS BY MACHNER.

and then placed to the lips of one of the controllers. The Countess of A. (at Venice, Professor Faifofer) sews under a fold of her dress a little bag containing a piece of money, and comes to the séance with the idea unexpressed in words that it be unsewed and abstracted; and, behold! no sooner does she concentrate her mind on the thought again at the séance than it is done. On another occasion she comes wearing a jewel on her head and in thought desires that it be transferred to the head of Eusapia, to whom she wishes to present it; and as soon as she thinks the thought anew the transfer takes place.

During trance, as we shall see, mediums acquire muscular and intellectual energy which they have not before had, and which can only rarely be explained by the transfer of thought from the minds of spectators (*i.e.*, by telepathy), and which therefore demand a special explanation, — that of aid from the spirits of the departed. They transfer during trance some of their most singular powers, such as left-handedness (Eusapia) and incombustibility (Home, who not only could touch a glowing coal without feeling pain, but could transfer this power to another).

Many of them manifest their activity in only one direction. The most common and least important, and often most liable to error, are the typtological mediums, who communicate by taps emanating from the table, and by the movements of a pointer placed over an alphabet spread out on the table. The most common and mediocre are the motor mediums, who cause tables, chairs, etc., to move.

There are healers among them, often most ignorant of medicine, and who can still obtain results. I have seen one of the most stupid of them (a woman), whom the Hindu fakirs would have recognized as a sister, benefit for fifteen or twenty days, by means of ridiculous muscular exercises, the health of a woman in the last stage of tabes.

And there are painter mediums, such as Sardou, Ugo di Alexis, Desmoulin, who without any ideas whatever sometimes depict and color objects. They seem to copy them by a transparent medium from a model. See, for example, the flowers painted during somnambulism by the peasant woman " R." who was absolutely ignorant of design. Note also the flowers and landscapes of Machner, a German sailor, who before he did this work had never taken a pencil in hand. And there are some who, like Desmoulin, execute in the dark oil paintings that would ordinarily require whole months of work, and which when awake these mediumistic somnambulists are unable to complete.

Then there are speaking mediums; also rhabdomancists, who locate metals in the earth; pneumatographers, who call forth direct writing

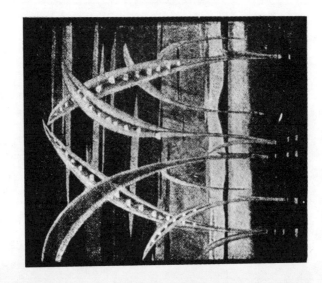

FIG. 42 b. MEDIUMISTIC DESIGNS BY MACHNER.

without making use of a pen; the dematerial-
izers, who bring in apports from without in spite
of windows and doors closed and intact; evokers
of phantasms; photofors, who bring out gleams
of light of a more or less circumscribed nature;
photographers, who print the forms of invisible
spirits upon photographic plates, even in the dark;
glottologues, who speak unknown tongues; fore-
seers, who prophesy; intuitive writers, who hear
in the brain a voice dictating to them what they
shall write, while acoustic mediums hear with
their ears the voice of spirits. Then we have the
musician mediums, who before the séance do not
know a note, and yet play on various instruments. Others handle glowing coals without
burning themselves. Others are the incarnaters,
who rapidly impersonate by word and look, etc.,
one or more deceased persons, one after the
other. Such a one is Randone, of Rome, who
impersonated for us the face and gestures suc-
cessively of an idiot, a church orator, a professor affected with general paralysis, etc.

There are some (such as Zaccardini, of Bo-
logna) who make a specialty of levitation and
nothing more. Eusapia and Home unite in themselves many of these features, such as materialization, direct writing, apports, levitation. But
the majority are mediums who produce physical
results of a motor nature. The minority (and
the most elect) deal with intellectual and mixed

phenomena. I noticed also in the life of Eusapia that her first manifestations were motorial; the last, phantasmal. Even in the trance only motorial phenomena are identified and studied at first. The spectral forms appear with her only in the last stages of the trance, when the lethargic condition has reached its most acute stage.

ACTION OF THE MEDIUMS

There is also another singular attribute of mediums which we must admit in order to explain certain spiritistic phenomena; namely, the fact that in the psychological atmosphere (*milieu ambiant*) of the medium in a trance, and by the medium's own action, the conditions of matter are modified, just as if the space in which the phenomena takes place belonged not to three, but to four dimensions, in which (according to the theory of the mathematicians) the law of gravity and the law of the impenetrability of matter would suddenly fail, and the laws that rule time and space would suddenly cease, so that a body from a far-off point may all at once find itself near by, and you may find a bunch of freshest flowers in your coat-pocket without their showing any trace of being spoiled; or a stone or a key or a garment may enter a room closed tight as wax; or one ring may pass within another; or knots may be formed or untied in a

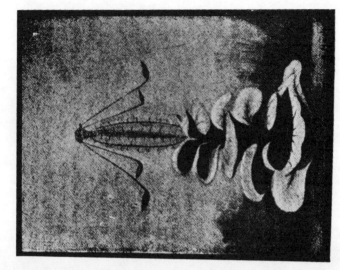

FIG. 42 c. MEDIUMISTIC DESIGNS BY MACHNER.

string tied and sealed at a certain point,[1] or the levitation not merely of inorganic, but of living bodies may take place. And we should have to

FIG. 44. EXPERIMENT WITH KNOTS FORMED IN A SEALED STRING, BY ZÖLLNER.

give this explanation, too, when Eusapia, merely by touching a sheet of paper with the finger of Schiapparelli, produces writing either on the last

---

[1] Zöllner, after having tied in a knot the two ends of a long slender cord and sealed the knot, unexpectedly placed it under the eyes of Slade expressing the desire that knots should be formed thereon; whereupon these suddenly appeared on it while Slade's hands were three quarters of an inch from the seal, which remained intact. In another trial Zöllner tied two thick rings to a string, which he knotted and suspended from the edge of a table upon which Slade was holding his hands. All of a sudden the rings disappeared from the string and were found at the foot of another table near by.

pages of a ream of paper or on the curtain-pole above the window; or when she makes roses drop out of my sleeves and Richet's while we are holding her hands; or when she levitates the table or slowly raises herself in the air above the table itself.

Perhaps, also, by inverting the laws of time, like those of space, we should be able to explain how mediums can at times succeed as prophets, — a fact authenticated with precision by Hodgson and by Hyslop in five or six instances in which the American medium, Mrs. Piper, figured. This medium predicted for persons perfectly well the malady each should be afflicted by, and who would cure them, and what complications would ensue.

Now, in order that an object may by apparent automatic movement pass out of a closed room without any opening of door or windows, it must needs be made to pass through wood or glass or bricks. But in order that this may take place (says Brofferio, *op cit.*, p. 195) one of three things must happen: either it must pass through the panes of glass without coming apart or breaking up, — that is to say, its atoms must pass through the interatomic spaces of the panes; or else it must be decomposed into imponderable material (an operation which we not very happily call " dematericalization ") before passing the walls, and afterwards be recomposed; or else,

FIG. 43. EXPERIMENT WITH RING AND KNOTTED STRING, BY ZÖLLNER.

in order to appear and disappear without passing through the walls at all, it would be necessary for it to pass into a fourth dimension of space and then, returning, emerge from that again. Before the eyes of beings living in a space of only two dimensions (just as the photographic figures in the electrotachiscope seem to move, maintaining themselves always in one plane) we could cause a flower painted within a circle to disappear, and then make it reappear outside of said circle, because we could lift it into the air and make it disappear in a third dimension, in height or depth (a thing of which those photographic beings could not have the slightest idea).

CHAPTER V

Mediums and Magicians in Savage Tribes

THAT mediums have so preponderating a power in spiritistic matters is a fact strengthened and buttressed by what is observed [1] among almost all primitive peoples and savage tribes, who believe in the powers of certain individuals, — magicians, wizards, prophets. These are all true mediums having an influence in the political and religious constitution of the community, individuals who act in our realm of space as if they were living in a space of the fourth dimension, upsetting our laws of time, space, and gravity: prophets and saints who predict the future and transport themselves through the air; witches who pass with their entire bodies through a keyhole and transport themselves in a flash to a distance of thousands of miles.

It is in vain to disparage the opinions of the vulgar; for if it is true that they do not possess the means of the learned scientist for the attainment of truth, nor his culture and talent, they supplement this by manifold illiterate and empirical observations, the result of which in the

[1] C. di Vesme, *Storia dello Spiritismo.* 3 vols. Torino.

end is superior in many cases to that attained by
the highest scientific genius. And so the influence of the moon and of meteors on the human
mind, the inheritance of disease, and the conta-
giousness of consumption were recognized by the
plain people before they were by the learned scientist. The latter received the assertion of these
facts with loud bursts of laughter, and perhaps
still does so (the learned academies do not exist
for nothing!).

It is to be noted that among the Hebrews an
insane man or a neurotic passed for a prophet;
and Saul, when he prophesied, stripped himself
naked, as madmen did (1 Sam. xix. 24. Richard
Mead, *Medic. Sacra*, III.). In 1 Samuel, also,
we see bands of false prophets running naked
through the fields and elsewhere, and we behold
them committing crazy and indecent acts in public, — cutting their hands, eating dung, going to
brothels and boasting of it, and the like deeds.

In the huge work on the *Scientific Exploration
of Algiers, Rel. di El Ajach,* we read: " The
people of Tripoli are famous for their sincerity
and for the great number of *medjdub* among
them " (p. 100). Further on, speaking of one of
them, he says: " He was the best of the medjdub;
his *djedjeb* (convulsion) was powerful" (p. 130).
" The word *medjdubim* stands in Tripoli for
those individuals who under special circumstances
fall into a condition that recalls exactly that of

the convulsionaries of Saint-Médard.   They are numerous in Algiers, and are better known under the name of *aicaovi* or *ammarim*."

Among the Kosa Kaffirs the doctor, or magician, receives his diploma or credentials (so to speak) after a mental malady, during which he believes he sees the powers of water, earth, and sky, and horses, and is mentally disturbed thereby. The facts are set before the chief, who according to their importance either approves of them or refuses to nominate him for the office.

The *yogis* of India are regarded as possessing the most perfect holiness, thanks to *yoga*, or union with God, a something attained by fixing the gaze on the point of the nose or on the navel. The *yogis* have the power of so governing the senses as not to perceive external sensations, or else of falling into a hypnotic trance.

Amongst the Batachi, when they find a man possessed of an evil spirit, they respect him most profoundly and look on him as an oracle. " They pointed out to me," says a traveller, " a girl whom they called ' the daughter of the demon,' because her father was mad.   She was continually visited by evil spirits and hence all her wishes were executed."

Modigliani observes that the Nias select for their magicians or doctors those afflicted with some special deformity, notwithstanding the fact that they have a supreme contempt for deformity. Above all, they choose those whom the genii (*bela*) strike with madness suddenly, thus showing that they (the genii) pick them out for their intermediaries. Then the Nias drive them out of the village to take up their habitation in the trees. And, when their compatriots find them perched up there, they pull them down, consign them to the chief magician, who instructs them for fourteen days, during which they are obliged to feast the whole village as well as their instructors. But they have their retaliation, for in their turn they are sumptuously feasted and cared for during life, so that many feign madness that they may obtain so rich an honor.

In Peru, besides the priests, the sacred virgins, etc., there were magicians or prophets of a secondary order who improvised prophecies (called *hecheloc*) while in the midst of convulsions and terrible contortions. They were venerated by the people, but despised by the more cultivated class.

The Patagonians have female magicians and doctors who prophesy while affected with convulsive fits. Men may also be elected to the priesthood; but they must dress like women and must always have exhibited from youth up special dispositions. Epileptics receive lawful election because they possess the divine spirit.

Among the Carajas of Brazil he who is born or becomes epileptic or neurotic, and so is disposed by nature to nervous ailments, becomes a doctor.

Kiernan says that among the nomadic peoples of Mongolia the symptoms exhibited by the fetichistic magicians (*shaman*) are so similar to epilepsy, in furious ragings and visions, that the two states were long confounded under the single name of "the sacred malady." It was always believed that this was due to some supernatural power, benign or malign; and they accordingly were in the habit of either placating it or driving it out.

Amongst the Zulus, the Bechuanas, and the Walla-Wallas the profession of medicine is hereditary, therefore the fathers choose certain sons, to whom they give counsel, even (it is claimed) after death. The same is true with the Siberian shamans. In certain Siberian tribes the medical gift or power (the shamanic force) comes upon one suddenly, like a nervous disease. It manifests itself in weakness and tension of the limbs, in tremors and inarticulate cries, fevers and convulsions and epileptic attacks, until the victims fall insensible. Afterwards they touch and swallow with impunity needles and glowing-hot pieces of iron. They also become delirious, until, all of a sudden, they take the magic drum and set up as shaman, or fetich doctor.

Among the Diujeric of South Australia those become doctors who from childhood up have had visions of the Devil. They have frightful dreams, with visions of incubi and the like.

The Kaffirs are an extremely superstitious folk. Superstition plays a great part in the relations of their life, and forms a part of their laws, customs, religion. Their religion consists in veneration of the spirit of the departed (*amadhlosi*).

They call their predicters, or diviners, *isanusi*, or *isangoma*. They may be regarded as the priests of the Kaffirs and are the intermediaries between the living and the dead. Their power over good and evil, like their power over the hearts of the Kaffirs, is unbounded. The art of divination may be exercised both by women and men, and all those who engage in this profession form a very distinct class among the South African stocks. Europeans confound diviners and magicians. On the contrary, diviners, or prophets, among the Kaffirs are defined as a religious sect who act for the benefit of the people. If one were to give to an *isangoma* (diviner) the title *untakati* (sorcerer), it would give him very serious offence. It would be like calling a policeman a thief in Europe. Among the Kaffirs the diviner is thought of as the protector of the people. To him it belongs to unmask the kings and wizards and bring them to judgment and punishment.

While the magician exercises his art for his own proper behoof, the diviner must work for

the common good by legitimate means, in the
character of a servant of the state. For this
reason he has the entire confidence and respect
of the Kaffirs. Before electing a diviner, it behooves to test his skill in the discovery of male-
factors, finding lost articles, and recognizing a
disease and its cause. Mastery in such things as
these is indispensable to a diviner. In addition,
he may also become an *inganga* (doctor) in other
departments of knowledge. There are specialists
for rain, hail, thunder, the grass, and what not.
Usually the diviner is also an expert in the medical art. However, all these specialties are not
necessary; they are merely attributes of the diviner, who ought to be able to communicate with
the spirits of the departed in order to disclose
their thoughts and secure their protection. In
the fulfilling of their task, imagination and deception co-operate.

He who possesses sensitive nerves and has un-
easy dreams is considered to be skilful in holding
communication with the spirits of those who have
passed beyond, and it is for this reason that
women have greater aptitude for divination. No
one can of his own volition and alone declare
himself a diviner. The candidates must for some
time be instructed by a wise diviner, chosen from
among the oldest of the tribe, and be nominated
with the consent of the chiefs. In the spring,
with the budding of the leaves, appear the first

symptoms of the future diviners. If at this season a young man has agitated dreams, he presently imagines that the spirits are in communication with him. He seems to hear their voices. He goes wandering about aimlessly in solitary places, dives into deep waters to receive communications from the spirits, and, when at night he returns to his home, he is dark of mood, refuses food (whereas formerly he ate like a wolf), and then falls into a state of ecstasy (see Fig. 45).

In continuation of these phenomena his parents conclude to have him examined by a diviner. If this man finds his vocation genuine, he orders him a medicine to strengthen his mysterious symptoms, puts a bunch of feathers on his head, and initiates him into the secrets of the science. The candidate continues his cure by means of medicine and rubbings. Seized with frenzy, he dashes himself against the rocky walls of the house or throws himself into the water, exposing his life to danger so seriously that his friends are compelled to watch him and keep him from succumbing. He charms serpents and winds them about his body and neck. During the different tests he grows visibly thinner, — which increases his worth, for the natives have little faith in fat diviners. Other diviners come into l..s hut; and not unfrequently it happens that they quarrel concerning their art, charging each other with being deceivers.

After a time the novice calms down, his appetite returns, his dreams are tranquil, and he begins practice as a finder of lost objects. Before being publicly received, he must prove himself before the people. Various objects are hidden in secret places, and, if he alone is unable to find them, other diviners come to his aid. If the trial gives good results, he is declared to be a true diviner.

Among the Kaffirs consecrations never take place without plenty of meat and beer, and the instructors of the new man, after having revealed to their colleague the secrets of the science, for fear that he should forsake them and return to his former life, kill in his honor the animal that suffices for a public banquet. His friends make him presents to supply his first necessities. In the sequel, with a good stock of cunning and self-possession, he can lead his clients about by the nose and procure wealth. That will not be difficult for him if he puts on a bold front and assumes a firm deportment. During his novitiate he has already had experience of that kind. If his predictions come true, he takes the fancy of the Kaffirs, becomes celebrated, and soon acquires a rich clientèle. If he makes an error, he needs only to say, as do the Spiritualists, that the spirits have deceived him to-day, or else that they were in a bad humor and would not reveal anything to him.

FIG. 45. THE PRIESTESS UYITSHIGITSHI DURING A PREDICTION.

The confession that a certain old Kaffir woman (magician) makes is very interesting. Her name is Paula, of Marianhill. For twelve years now she has been a Christian, but for forty years before this she was a celebrated diviner. She gives this curious account of herself and of her divining powers:

"When I was a young woman, after I had had my third child, I continued ill; I was attacked by convulsions and had visions; my appetite left me, I became as thin as a stake. My parents came to the determination to consult a diviner. But my father, who was famous in this craft, said, ' Bring her to me, I will make a clairvoyante of her.' My husband was at first opposed, fearing he should have to spend too much money, but finally I was approved by a diviner. His verdict was this: ' She is one of us.' I was taken to the house of a woman-diviner, who, with my father, taught me how to see clearly into mysteries. They brought me the three excellent medicines, Kindness, Gentleness, and Conformity with the Spirits of the Departed. I drank them for thirty days, then was thoroughly washed and rubbed with them. They placed goatskins on my shoulders as a sign of my merit. The spirits kept communicating more and more with me. In my dreams I saw the living and the dead. The spirits of my ancestors appeared to me under the form of gray lizards, sat on my shoulders, and encircled me.   I began to make predictions of future events.   People brought me money and other things.

"After passing all the proofs, I was declared capable and conducted to my own native town, where a great feast was held in my honor.   Oxen were killed and *utschwala* (the beer of the Kaffirs) was drunk.   My instructors each received two oxen as a gift.   I took a young cock and rubbed and drenched it with the medicines.   I then put it on the roof of my hut, and there it remained night and day, giving me notice by its crowing of the approach of my clients.   When the convulsions were about to attack me, I would cry, 'Help!   Quick!   come and help me!   The spirits are attacking me!'   The people would run up and sing and dance, stamping their feet.   About seventeen years ago the magistrate of Maritzburg had me called before him, for he had lost two horses.   I said, 'Go to the waterfall of Umgeni; you will find the two horses there tied, but the robbers have cut off their tails and their manes.'   A posse of policemen was sent to the place indicated by me and found the horses just as I said.   The thief, who was waiting near by to run them off, was put into prison."

For his investigations the diviner makes use of the bones of animals or of sticks which he throws on the ground, drawing his conclusions from the way the sticks fall.   When thrown high

Fig. 46. Kaffir Priestess.

up into the air, if they fall back horizontally, the question gets a negative answer. If they make as if they would strike the client, the answer is " Yes." And, if it is a case of a sick stomach, the sticks ought to fall on the man's belly. If, on the contrary, they hit another part of the body, it means that the evil lies there.

THE ARTIFICIAL CREATION OF MEDIUMS AND SORCERERS

Mediums, prophets, magicians, who are masters in a greater or less degree of nature, of time and space, have become rare in our day, because accurate scientific instruments (especially in meteorology) and the wisdom of scientific authorities supply them with greater certainty. But in ancient times and among barbarous peoples they were very common. And it is a curious thing that when they became scarce people created them artificially, by stimulating neuropathic symptoms in certain ones predisposed to these, instilling fears into them during infancy or even during conception, and compelling them to long fasts.

One of their chief methods in this creation of artificial magicians is the moulding and modifying of the whole character and life of the novice from birth up.

" The Aleouts," says Réclus, " when they beget

handsome boys, dress them and bring them up
as women, and sell them at the age of fifteen to
some rich man, although at the same time consecrating them to the priesthood. The first fresh-
ness of youth is scarcely over when they pass
with the greatest facility into sacred orders. In
Borneo the Dyaks who become priests assume
female names and dress, marry a man and a
woman, — the former to accompany them and
protect them in public. Further, the Aleout
priest receives as pupils the fittest girls, perfects
them in the art of dancing, of pleasures, and
of love, and they become women magicians and
priestesses " (Réclus, *Les Primitifs*, p. 83).

To make priests and prophets, they subject the
neophytes to special treatment, the priests select-
ing them from the two sexes indifferently. They
also apply to picked married couples to manufacture them by special treatment, — as fasting long
and often, and eating certain foods and avoiding
others. Scarcely is the expected child born than
they gather around it and bathe it with urine
and dung. When grown up, the novice must be
left whole days silent, alone. He then passes
through a series of initiations. To communicate
with the spirits, he must at intervals absent himself for a long time from the settlement, and
should go hunting and fishing now and then
alone. The farther they go in such a régime,
the more do they become alienated. They do

not know whether they are asleep or awake, take abstractions for realities, and create strong sympathies and violent antipathies around them. As among the yogis and fakirs of India and the shamans of Siberia, their supreme aspiration is to attain the rapt, trance-like state of ecstasy. They exhibit symptoms which may be classed with epilepsy. They possess strange lucidity of mind and hyperæsthesia, and believe in the persecution of demons who come to torment them. During their prophetic fury they abandon themselves to strange convulsive contortions, to unearthly howlings, foaming at the mouth, with face and eyes so congested that for the time they lose their sight. If they get hold of knives, they now and then wound themselves or others.

When all these initiations are passed, the selected individual becomes the magician (either "grand hangacoc" or "ancient hangacoc"). He assembles the members of the council, the justices of the peace, the arbitrators in public and private affairs, the comic poet, the doctor.

In the case of the Bilculas the initiation into medicine is accomplished with fastings and prayers; among the red Pollis, with fastings, dreams, and withdrawal into the forest and into solitude; among the black aborigines of Australia, by solitary search for the spirit of a dead doctor. It is the custom of the Indians of Gamina to have their candidate for the doctor's degree eat leaves of a special kind and live alone in the forest until the spirit appears.

The future "medicine-men" of the Wascos, the Caiusos, and the Walla-Wallas begin their careers as early as the eighth or tenth year. They must sleep in a wigwam on the bare ground, where they receive the spirit under the strange form of a buffalo-like dog, who makes important revelations to them. When the spirit fails to appear, they must fast until it does appear. They then impart to the head medicine-man what they have heard.

Among the Xosa Kaffirs the candidate remains in solitude in his hut until there appear to him in his dream the images of leopards, serpents, lightning-birds. These assist him in his task. Lastly appears to him the ghost of the deceased chief, which makes him dance and become restless.

In Sumatra the candidate must stay all day in a basket dangling aloft from the balcony of a house, and is furnished with a minimum of food. During the day he prays to the gods to make him invulnerable. If the basket sways to and fro, that means that the spirit has entered the candidate. Then they prick him and make holes in him with lance and sword, and the wounds cease to bleed and close up when he touches them with his hand.

A special diet is prescribed to the *thay-phap*

(prophet-doctor) of the Annamese. He is not allowed to eat the flesh of the ass or the buffalo, but must always eat of a plant that has heart-shaped leaves.

The *gangas* of Loango can drink only in certain places and at certain hours of the day. They have their meat diet much restricted, the flesh of certain quadrupeds being prohibited. In compensation they may enjoy a good many vegetables.

Another method is to incite convulsions and delirium by rapid motions of the head and by intoxicating substances.

The sect of the Aissaui among the Arabs of Algiers owes its origin to Mohammed Ben Hissa in the ninth century. This man, chief of a caravan, girt about by all the dangers that spring from the desert, — isolation, the simoom, robbers, and hunger, — resorted to extraordinary expedients of religious fanaticism where human power was of no avail. When famine stared the caravan in the face, he ordered the eating of scorpions and serpents in the name of Allah; and when these failed he taught them the *djedjeb*, the prayers that make hunger dumb. The *djedjeb* is a violent movement imparted to the head from left to right; the arms hang supine the while, and the bystanders keep time to the movements of the head and body. After an hour of such exercise there ensues a kind of fury and intoxication, which afterwards changes into a singular insensibility.

But let us consider particulars of more importance. The members of the sect are gathered in an appropriate room brilliantly lighted; the musicians begin beating on two enormous drums two slow taps and one very rapid. Then the brethren (or Aissaui) accompany them in a barbarous chant:

" Allah, Allah, Allah our Lord, Allah our Allah,
   Ben Hissah commanded to love Allah; the serpent
      obeys Allah;
   Ben Hissah makes me drink his remedy," etc.

This chant, although foolish and inconclusive as are all the songs of the idolatrous ascetics, yet, from the point of view of a European, excites a strange tremor, a boiling enthusiasm even in the veins of the most sceptical spectator.

Next, those of the faithful who were most smitten, so to speak, swept along by the singing, fall into the *djedjeb*, or sacred convulsion. The chorus now ceases, but the drums continue to accompany the contortions of the madmen, who sing:

" The head is exalted. Ben Hissah exalts it," etc.

In proportion as the Aissaui circle about in their furious dance the blood is seen mounting to their faces and the veins of the neck visibly swell. The breathing is now only a kind of hiss through the tightly compressed windpipe. Every trace of singing disappears to give place to an inarticulate sound which is the last effort of an obstructed respiration.

At this point in the proceedings the Aissaui seizes a bar of red-hot iron and strikes his brow and head with it, licks it with his tongue, bites it with his teeth. Says a distinguished traveller, " I have smelled the nauseous odor of the roasted live flesh of these fellows, and heard the crackling of their skin." So it was no illusion. Now Djedjeb becomes master of ceremonies. All are howling and running about, ferociously striking each other on the arms or shoulders. Some, on all fours, imitate the roaring of the lion and the cry of the camel. They ask from the chief something to eat, and receive from him cactus leaves and live scorpions, which they devour with delight.

An attaché of the French consulate at Algiers, not believing his own eyes, promised gold to one of the sectaries if he would devour in his presence a viper that had previously killed a cock and a hen. The Aissaui took the steps needed to get himself into *djedjeb*, and, having reached the point of supreme exaltation, ate the viper.

There are four other sects in Algiers similar to this. The tenth or fifth part of the population of a city, and often the whole city, is admitted to their ranks.

A society as widely extended as it is fantastic and cruel exists at the present time among the negroes of San Domingo. It is the Voudou Society. The origin of this word is unknown. Perhaps it is from *vou*, a serpent, and *dou*, a country. It is the name applied to the divinity, the institution, and its devotees. At San Domingo the god is the ordinary snake; at New Orleans, the rattlesnake. But the deity is of purely African origin, and especially of the Congo and Juidala regions. The priest of the god, Papa Voudou, exercises extraordinary authority over all the adherents of the sect, the same in Haiti as in their native Congo region. At the end of the room where the Voudouists are assembled is the chest in which lies the serpent. At one side are "papa," and "mamma" the priestess, the latter wearing a great ragged red cloak (red being the pure symbol of the deity). Papa, placing his foot and hand on the box, intones a barbarous chant:

> "Eh, eh, Bomba hen hen,
> Canga basio te,
> Canga mouni de li."

He communicates his excitement to "mamma," she to the whole circle of bystanders, who are agitated by lateral dancing movements in which head and shoulders seem to be dislocated. All the faithful are seized with a feverish exaltation. The whirling dance goes on in blind fury; the negroes become frenzied, sob, immerse their arms in boiling water, cut and slash their flesh with knife and finger-nails, have mortars placed on their backs and support strong men on them.

Similar things have been observed among the Ottoman dervishes. Every convent of dervishes has its own special kind of sacred dance, or, better stated, of epileptic convulsions. Some pray, making lateral movements with the head; others bow the body from left to right and from in front backward. But in the case of most of the members of convents, such as the Kufai, Cadris, Beyrami, they hold themselves tight by the hand in a circle. They put the right foot forward, throwing new life and energy into every step. The Kufai begin with chanting " Allah," wag their heads from side to side, and, each putting his arms on the shoulders of his neighbor, they turn ever more rapidly, so that they soon fall down in the *'haloth*, or ecstasy. While in this stage they submit to the test of red-hot iron, slash themselves with sabres, etc.

Similar marvels are told in the Bible of the priests of Baal, and by Lucian, and the monuments of Nineveh attest their truth. In India the priests of Siva and of Durga repeat the same kind of convulsive movements, followed by similar self-inflicted sufferings and (I would add) lascivious acts.

The same things are noted still among the

santons of Egypt. One of the most curious ceremonies is that practised by the howling dervishes in Egypt, and called the *zikr*. It is performed by uttering the word " Allah," at the same time continually wagging the head. Shaken and weakened by such motions, their bodies fall to the floor, their faces congested, mouths foaming like epileptics; and during these frenzies, like the convulsionaries of Saint-Médard, they mutilate and burn their flesh.

The coexistence of so extraordinary a custom among race-stocks so diverse and distant as the Semitic, Caucasian, and Hamitic, points to a source more profound and physiological than religion, which, springing from the sentiment of the people, is modelled upon them rather than modelled by them, and hence is not uniform.

On the contrary, we must place among the most characteristic tendencies of the human race the need of those artificial stimuli of the brain which we call intoxicants, and which increase in number and refinement with the growth of evolution. The strangest substances, as we shall see, have been employed by man for this purpose, — wine, alcohol, manioc, the kola nut, soma, ghee, *bitra,* opium, and even acetic lactic acid (tartar), and injection through the nostrils of the *niope* of Kamtchatka.

Peoples whose special life-conditions and training (for instance, negroes and the Aissaui), or

whose laws (the Mohammedans) do not permit
the use of alcoholic drinks or similar substances,
find substitutes in the lateral movement of the
head, — the most primitive method of intoxication that is known or possible. It is an actual
fact that the lateral movement of the body and
the head produces cerebral congestion. Any one
who will make the experiment for a few minutes
will be more than sure of it. The *Annals of
Medicine* (1858), for example, contain registered
cases of apoplexy and cerebral vertigo due to
movements of this character.

Once it was discovered that intoxication and
convulsions could be brought on by these methods
(conditions so anomalous that primitive folk were
unable to explain them as other than avatars of
the gods, as a new and sacred secondary personality), they thereupon proceeded to make use
of said methods to get into communication with
the divinities in the same way that they made
use of true epileptics and of madmen, and, later,
of intoxicated persons.

More frequently, indeed, they resorted to in-
ebriating substances. The priests of ancient
times, who were the first to note the action of
fermented beverages on the mind, at first re-
served them for themselves, declaring them
sacred, just as, for the same reason, they declared epilepsy sacred.

The legend runs that life arose from a drop

of divine blood that fell to the earth, — the meth, or mead, drink of the Norse Sagas; from the blood of Quasio, the wisest of the gods. Osiris and Lyæus, or Dionysus, were gods, discoverers of the vine and originators of civilization. Bacchus is the savior deity, the magician god, the physician god, a trace of whose great power still exists in the Italian oaths, " Blood of Bacchus! " " Body of Bacchus! " The Egyptians (see Rode) allowed wine only to their priests. Wine appears as a sacred liquor in their liturgies, libations, ablutions.

The Hindu priest is called a drinker of soma. To the fermented juice of the asclepias plant (*i.e.*, the soma) he attributed poetic inspiration, the courage of heroes, and the power of man to immortalize his life (namely, by drinking also the *amrita*, which is the same word as the *ambrosia* of the gods, — Greek *am-brotos,* Latin *immortalis;* or, as was later said, *aquavitæ,* alcohol).

The Rig Veda, viii. 48, says: " We have drunk the soma; we became immortal; we entered into the light."

In one of the *yasnas* of Zoroaster's writings the juice of *haoma* (the same as *soma*) " defers death."

The soma itself becomes a god, to be comforted or placated with fire. " Soma, thou who createst the Rishis, who bestowest blessings, who dost immortalize men and gods " (Rig Veda).

The soma drink was permitted only to the Brahmins, just as in Peru the coca was allowed only to the descendants of the Incas, and, among the Chibchas, to the priests, who made use of it as a means of authenticating their power. Let it be noted that the soma is called in Sanskrit *madhu*, which in Zendic signifies " wine," a fact which links the Norse *meth*, the Lithuanian *madus*, and the Sanskrit *mad* to the Italian *matto* (insane). Note, too, that the Bacchic delirium is a prophetic power, the peculiar possession of the god, and that Æsculapius, the god of healing, is the son of Bacchus.

It would seem as if those who first noticed the beneficent and maleficent effects of wine created the legend of the tree of the knowledge of good and evil. We may suppose this tree was the apple-tree, from the fruit of which the first fermented liquors were made.

The Assyrians had a sacred tree, the tree or plant of life. This was at first the asclepias, then the palm, from which latter a fermented liquor is made to-day.

Among the Egyptians it was the *ficus religiosus*, the fermented juice of which rendered the soul immortal.

Others, to bring on the divine madness, resorted to hypnosis, to ecstasy, to the fumes of poisonous gases.

The oracles of Delphi, Delos, Abae, Tegyra,

etc., in Greece, were in the hands of the priests. It was their device to have one, two, or even three women, under the influence of hysteria, deliver the prophetic oracles, after they had been intoxicated by the fumes of the laurel or emanations of other gases. The Pythian priestess essentially prepared herself by ablutions, by fumigations of laurel, and by burnt barley. She sat on a basin placed on a tripod, which itself stood directly over a crevice in the rock. From out this crevice rose the fumes of intoxicating and poisonous gases (hydroerburic and hydrosulphuric, Giacosa writes me) which enveloped the entire lower part of her body (Strabo, ix. 419) until she fell into the state of ecstasy or trance, sometimes eventuating in death.

She often spoke in verse or raved in disconnected nonsensical sentences, to which the priests gave appropriate meaning and even a rhythmic form, attaching to themselves for that purpose special poets. "In a dark and narrow recess of a cliff at Delphi," writes Justinian, "there was a little open glade, and in this a hole, or cleft, in the earth, out of which blew a strong draft of air, straight up and out as if impelled by a wind, and which filled the minds of poets with madness," — "*mentes vatum in vecordiam vertit*" (*Id.* xxiv. 6; Cicero, *De Divin.*, i. 3). At first the property of the gas was unknown. But certain shepherds were in the habit of feeding their flocks there, and one day a she-goat fell into the cleft and was immediately taken with convulsions. Now, undoubtedly, the superstition which (as in the case of *djedjeb* also) saw an intimate relation between convulsions and the divine inspiration, thereby consecrating epileptics as sacred beings, gave rise to the idea of employing these intoxicating vapors at Delphi for producing prophecy. In fact, they were at first associated with Bacchic intoxication. Some Pythian priestesses were Thuiadi, or Bacchantes, devotees of Dionysus (or Bacchus), and Dionysus, according to legend, dwelt a long time at Delphi.

Wherever gas escaped from the earth there were these oracles inspired by the intoxicating fumes, — for instance, at Lake Avernus, Heraclea, and Phigaleia, places which, believing themselves on this account in communication with Hades, claimed to be places for the evocation of the dead, and (what is more simple) for the inebriation, or intoxication, of the living, who thus became interpreters of the dead, or necromancers.

Thus the pathological, epilepsoid origin of the medium is attested by the universal consensus of all ancient and barbarous peoples, — a consensus carried to the point of adoration of epilepsy and to the artificial creation of epileptics in order thereby to secure a prophet, who is the genius of primitive peoples.

CHAPTER VI

Limitations of the Power of the Medium

THE foregoing facts prove the great influence of
the medium in spiritistic phenomena, — an influence which would seem to be the result of the
projection and transformation of his energy.
But it would be an enormous exaggeration to
believe that this explains all such phenomena,
although at first blush such a statement may
make us smile, when we take note of the medium's profound exhaustion after the séance, his
loss of force and of weight, and the perpetual
occurrence of the phenomena in the immediate
vicinity of his own person. Thus it is entirely
too easy a solution to suppose that, when the
transmission of thought at a distance occurs, the
cortical movement constituting thought is transmitted afar by the ether to a certain brain predisposed to another; that (as Ochorowicz puts
it) the molecular motion of the brain (which is
thought) is propagated around the thinker in the
shape of ethereal vibrations, and, meeting a second brain, is again transformed into the original
molecular movements and inscribes upon this
brain the thought of brain Number One; and

that, as this force is transmittable, it is also transformable, and, from being psychic force, becomes motor force, and *vice versa*, especially since we have in the brain certain centres the special function of which is the presiding over movement and thought, and which, when they are irritated, as in the case of epileptics, provoke now violent movements of the joints and now the great inspirations of genius.

Ermacora rightly calls my attention to the circumstance that the energy of vibratory motion is in inverse ratio to the square of the distance. Hence, if it be granted that transmissions of thought to short distances can be explained, yet it is hard to understand those cases of telepathy from one hemisphere of the earth to the other which some spiritistic manifestations afford. And it is difficult to understand how this vibratory motion [this " sightless courier of the air "] can pass to the organ of the percipient without waste, maintaining its long geographical parallelism of thousands of miles, starting as it does from an instrument not mounted on an immovable base.

If the exteriorization of motivity and of sense, which Rochas attributes to the medium, explains many mediumistic phenomena (as, for example, how the medium in the trance state can see things at a distance while he is in the dark and has his eyes closed, how he can feel the pricks or pinchings given to the phantasm, transport himself mentally and sometimes bodily to a distant point, cause a body at a certain distance to act and move about by means of the fluidic appendages of his double (see Chapter X), and even, perchance, give bodily shape to a phantasm, or, better, to an exact reproduction of his own body), — while, I say, exteriorization may account for these things, it still cannot explain the development in the medium of force and energy much greater than is natural to him, and which we must suppose he acquires by his relation to the phantasm he evokes, nor can it explain the formation of phantasms absolutely different from his own body.

As to the explication that has been proposed especially to fit the case of writing mediums, — namely, that only one hemisphere of their brain acts, preferably the right, while the left remains inert, thus explaining the unconsciousness of the right lobe, — an explication based on the extemporized left-handedness of many of the mediums (Smith), — if it be granted that it helps to explain automatism (see below), it yet does not serve in the case of those who write at one and the same time two communications, or even three. My readers will recall, as making against this hypothesis, the simultaneity and contemporaneity of certain phenomena in mediumistic séances.

For instance, in a séance at Milan, while Eu-

sapia was at the climax of her trance there appeared on the right — both to me and others
near by — the image of a woman who spoke a
word to me; in the centre of the room was
Eusapia asleep; near me and above me the
puffed-out curtain was blowing and swaying; at
the same time, on the left, a small table in the
cabinet was moving about, while out of the same
a small object was by invisible means brought
over the table in the centre of the main room.

Again, at Genoa, Barzini suddenly feels an
unknown hand moving in Eusapia's hair; at the
same time the left side of the portière, or curtain, is bulged stiffly out by a fist, which moves
forward, shaking the stuff of the curtain above
the heads of the controllers who are standing
around the medium; and simultaneously Bozzano, three feet away, feels himself touched several times on the shoulder.

"While some one behind me is touching me
and leaning against me," writes Visani Scozzi
(*La Medianità*, p. 287), "I see in the window the
profile of a person, and also another being touching Mainardi."

Dr. Imoda observed that, while a spectral form
was taking a plume from the hand of Mr. Becker,
another one was leaning his forehead on his
(Imoda's) shoulder.

On another occasion, while I was being caressed by a phantasm, Princess Ruspoli felt her

head touched by a hand, and Imoda had his own hand forcibly pressed by another hand.

I have said that some mediums write with both hands at once, at the same time carrying on a conversation with a third person (see Aksakoff). Mansfield wrote simultaneously with both hands in two different languages, while speaking of other subjects with persons present; among other things he announced the death of Jacobs, which was taking place at that moment (Moses). Moses also once noted three instruments of sound operating at once in a séance, — trumpet, table, and drum.

How can we explain the fact that the psychic force of a medium can not only be transformed into motor and sensory force, but simultaneously acts in three different directions and with three different purposes? And if it is impossible for a sane man, with senses undimmed, to turn his attention so fixedly in three different directions at once as to obtain objective phenomena, how is this possible for a medium in a state of evident insensibility?

Furthermore, there are things that take place against the will of the medium, and even of the so-called operating spirit. Having heard it asserted that during a séance at the residence of the Duke of Abruzzi the table set about beating time, with all four of its feet, to the tune of the royal march, I said jestingly that at Turin

even the tables and John King were monarch-
ists.   But I had hardly finished the sentence
when the table began to protest the contrary,
and with such resounding raps and blows that
they could be understood even by profane out-
siders inexpert in the typtological code.   And
when I said, " Oh, John, are n't you a monarchist,
then? " he denied it vigorously with the usual
two raps, — did so in several séances.   It then
occurred to me that possibly the idea might have
emanated from Eusapia, especially since the Neapolitan populace is warmly attached to the mon-
archy.   Being quite intimate with her, I led the
conversation up to the subject, and the poor little
woman, who in her adventurous life has too often,
and not always joyously, come into touch with
princes and kings, reaffirmed that she had no
opinions in politics, that she was not interested
in kings, and that the government that she would
prefer would be one that took thought for the
poor, nor did she ever in her subsequent talks
contradict herself.   And not even to the Duke of
Abruzzi, who remunerated her magnificently for
the séance, was she grateful for anything, griev-
ing that his Highness had not presented her his
visiting-card and did not show her those cordial
manners that others always exhibit.   Hence we
see that the monarchical manifestation did not
emanate from Eusapia, nor from John, but was, on
the contrary, in opposition to their predilections.

11

"Sometimes," observes Aksakoff, "the medium does not wish a certain name to be known, and yet the table reveals it. You are running over the alphabet and you get figures and words inverted or transposed with such rapidity that you cannot follow them or comprehend them.

"At times the spirits oppose their wills to that of the medium. For instance, a son who was a medium wanted to put himself in communication with his mother; but she refused, communicating to him typtologically, 'I don't want you to occupy yourself with Spiritualism'" (*Animisme et Spiritisme*, Paris, 1906).

Bozzano relates how that once, when he had proposed a second séance for the following day, Eusapia sharply opposed it, letting it be known that the too close succession of sittings exhausted her. But John not only protested that he wanted the sitting, but even went so far as to cuff her!

Aksakoff writes of a widower who founded a séance circle for the purpose of communicating with his wife, — a circle of relatives who all desired it; but they were not able to communicate with her, although they succeeded in communicating with others.

Stainton Moses, a very religious medium, a theologian, very often found in his automatic writings atheistic and satanic sentiments. "Almost all my automatic writings," he confesses, "were contrary to my convictions."

Pious mediums have involuntarily written blasphemies, obscenities, and a certain girl once confessed shameful things which she would rather have died than reveal.

One day Eusapia said to Mr. R., " This phantasm is going to be for you," and immediately after fell into a deep lethargy. Sure enough, a beautiful lady appeared, whose arms and shoulders were covered with the margins of the portières, in such a way, however, as to allow their outlines to be divined. Her head was covered with a veil of finest material; she breathed warm against the back of R.'s hand, ran her hand through his hair, and gently bit his fingers. In the mean while Eusapia was uttering prolonged groans, revealing painful effort on her part; but the groans ceased when the phantasm disappeared. This lovely apparition was seen by two others present and returned several times. The attempt was then made to photograph it, with the permission of Eusapia and John. But the phantasm signified with head and hand that she was opposed to this, and twice broke the photographic plates. She was then asked if she would allow the imprint of her hands to be taken; but this time also the ghostly visitor made repeated signs of denial both with head and hand, and, although Eusapia and John promised to make her yield to our wish, they did not succeed. At the last séance, however, Eusapia's promise as to this was very emphatic; the usual three taps several times signalled assent, and, sure enough, a hand was heard dipping itself in the liquid in the cabinet. After a few seconds R. had in his hand a block of paraffine with the imprint complete. But a fluidic hand reached out from the curtain and broke it into small pieces.

It was a case, we afterwards learned, of a woman, a former mistress of R., living, but now indifferent, who had a great interest in not leaving proof of her identity.

It is clear also from this case that, in spiritistic phenomena, a third will may intervene, which is not that of the medium nor of the sitters, but is opposed to the will of all these.

The spirits also sometimes compel a medium to take a certain course when he himself is opposed to it. Thus a certain extremely gluttonous medium was forbidden by his attendant daimon to make use of flesh-food, tea, coffee, or tobacco. When he disobeyed orders, raps were heard in the table; and, if he continued, the table opposed him. The result was that his health got to be completely re-established. But one day, when at sea he was about to smoke, the spirits threw him violently on the floor and drove a piece of the cigar into his mouth.

A widow believed to be mad by her physician brother, who thought of having her taken to a convalescent home, was in the habit of abusing her mediumistic faculty. The spirits several times ordered her to be moderate. But she would not obey, and one day they commanded her to get into a barrel. Her brother, seeing her in that position, was confirmed in his opinion, and had her shut up in an asylum for the insane. When she complained of it to the spirits, they said: "We did it on purpose. In this way you will tranquillize your mind."

These occurrences could be explained by admitting that they were in part willed by the victims because they redounded to their advantage. But cases are not rare of persons ferociously persecuted by the spirits to make them become mediums against their will. This was the very case with Dr. Dexter, a sceptic as to Spiritualism, and feeling a repugnance to occupying himself with it, but compelled to do so by a series of persecutions. One night when he was studying, he felt two hands seize him by the arms and give a violent shock to his hand. He heard two very loud raps in the wall, followed by a typtological communication to the effect that the spirits were going to exert power over him. He absented himself from every spiritistic reunion; but the phenomena increased to such a degree as to subject him to forcible levitation while he was in bed, nor did they cease until he agreed to become a medium.

In the home of Harry Phelps, the young son

of a Protestant bishop, chairs, tables, and large glowing firebrands began to move about; clothes were cut to pieces, or inflated to the semblance of human bodies. Every day the lad went to school the noises and movements followed him there, so that he was obliged to stay at home. During a few weeks seventy-one different objects were broken beside little Harry. When he went out driving, stones fell in the carriage, thrown by invisible hands, and the occurrences did not cease until he entered into typtological communication with the spirits.

So far the persecutions described would seem to have some cause, though disproportionate. But cases are recounted of persecutions inflicted without any reason, — any apparent reason, at any rate. The Russian factor Schtehaporw relates (in *Rebus*, 1886) the persecutions to which he and his wife were subjected. In November, 1870, there issued from the bed a red globe, which increased in size until it assumed the aspect of a huge balloon. Furniture was broken right and left. The unhappy married couple removed to the neighboring city to escape from the spirits; but hardly were they settled when the furniture began to dance a merry-go-round in the air. Knives, scissors, razors, were stuck in the doors and the walls. Garments and carpets would get into a state of spontaneous combustion; the clothes were burned on the woman's very back, though without pain to her; and finally the whole house burned down (Aksakoff).

We cannot be absolutely certain of the unconsciousness of the medium who provokes all these disasters; but it must certainly be a case of force extraneous to his will, because it is inadmissible to believe that any person whatever would wish to provoke occurrences injurious to himself. Under this head must be classed the original founders of Spiritualism, the Fox family in America, whose first revelations were in the nature of violent persecutions which they sought to escape by flight.

It is noteworthy that motorial and intellectual powers are manifested in the psychic trance which are very different from and much greater than the powers of the medium, and wholly incommensurate with these, and lead to the supposition of the intervention of another intelligence, another energy.

Thus, in respect to muscular energy, we have seen that several years ago the dynamometric force of Eusapia, corresponding to 36 kilograms, increased in full light, by the aid of a fluidic arm which she said was that of " John," to 42 kilograms; that is to say, there was an increase of 6 kilograms. In these latter days, when she is afflicted with diabetes and albuminuria, and suffers exhaustion on account of too frequent séances, her dynamometric energy has fallen to 12

and 15 kilograms.   Now in a séance with Morselli at Genoa the medium's force registered on
the dynamometer reached 110 kilograms, and in
a sitting in Turin John developed force sufficient
to break a table, — a force which we estimate
as being at least 100 kilograms.   And we may
with certainty estimate at 80 the energy necessary to lift a table with the publisher Bocca
seated on it, and at a much larger figure the
dragging along for several seconds of Bottazzi
and his chair, weighing both together 93
kilograms.

But if it is difficult to explain these phenomena
as being solely the projection and transformation of the psychic powers of the medium, what
shall we say of those cases in which she is slowly
lifted, with her chair, from the floor without making any effort with her feet, not merely without
any support, but against the will of the controllers, who rather seek to hinder her from rising?

And how explain the levitation of Zuccarini
(see Fig. 47); and of Home, who moves horizontally through the air around all the windows
of a palace and is levitated while he lies in bed;
or that of the Bari brothers, who traverse 45
kilometres in 15 minutes?

Here is the proper place to record the fact
that the centre of gravity of a body cannot be
changed spatially unless an external force acts
upon said body.   Displacements of separate parts

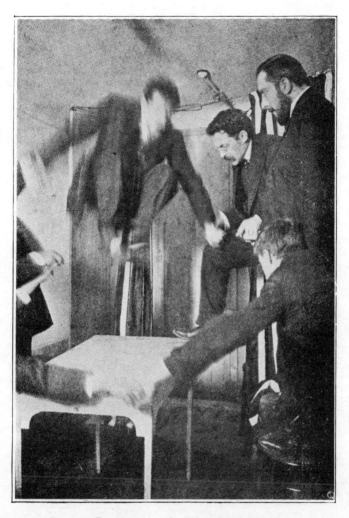

FIG. 47.   EXPERIMENT IN LEVITATION WITH ZUCCARINI.

of the body may, to be sure, take place by the action of internal forces alone, but the displacements of these parts are such as to maintain unaltered the position of their centre of gravity.

It is therefore evident that, the chair and the medium constituting a single system in which every force emanating from the medium himself is an internal force, the phenomenon of levitation cannot be considered as a phenomenon produced by energy proceeding from the medium, but ought to be deemed the result of some external force.

One more observation must be added to this proposition, an observation already made by Barzini at Genoa, — namely, that the movements of objects do not take place at haphazard, but have a kind of orientation. Mandolins, drinking-glasses, water-bottles, chairs, move as if held by a hand; the mandolin has its handle turned toward the medium, the chairs seem to be dragged along by the top or shoulder. Nay, sometimes the fluidic hand has been visible in full light, and seen holding objects, picking the strings of the mandolin, beating the tambourine, lifting things from boxes, putting the metronome in movement without a key. And it was a hand much larger than Eusapia's, resembling that from which the imprints were obtained.

It is true that the greater number of the motor

phenomena, as well as the most intellectual and
the most intense, emanate always from the immediate physical environment of the medium,
especially from his left side, where, being left-
handed in the trance, he is most powerful.   It
is true that these movements are preceded by
synchronous movements on the part of the medium; it is true that we see at times, emerging
in full light from the skirts or from the shoulders of such a medium as Eusapia, a fluidic limb
that performs the function of an arm, and that
acts, for instance, on the dynamometer.   But the
fact that the medium is a great aid to these forces
does not compel us to believe that they are his
or her exclusive creation.   As to the synchronous
movements, they repeat only what naturally takes
place at the initial step of every exertion of energy, of every movement, even of those to which
another gives the inciting cause; as when, for
example, the mother entices her babe, by the gestures of her arms as well as by the voice, to come
to her.   And yet it would not occur to any one
to affirm that by these gestures she effects the
movements of the child.

As to the matter of intelligence, how can we
explain the medium's seeing in trance, in a dark
room, with closed eyes, everything that takes
place before, behind, and around her, whereas
awake and in the light she can see only what
takes place before her and on each side?

Again, how explain, for example, the following occurrences? Eusapia is almost illiterate, spells out a printed page with difficulty, and does not understand handwriting unless it is read and explained to her. Now in a séance at Turin there entered the circle a young man with a bracelet in his pocket, and she not only divined that it was for her, not only succeeded by the aid of a fluidic hand at a distance of three feet from his hand in groping about his coat and extracting the bracelet from his pocket and clasping it on her own arm (her hands being all the while firmly held by controllers), but, on being asked what else the young man had in his pocket, replied, "A letter, and that letter contains a request." Now the young student knew that he had on his person papers containing chemical formulæ, but he did not remember at all a letter he had received from a person to whom he was indifferent, and much less did he know its contents, for he had not yet opened it. In full light the pocket of the student was turned inside out, and there indeed was the letter, in which some one asked him if he might come to see Eusapia. Now how could she, an illiterate person, not merely read the letter, but make a rapid summary of its contents? In this case none of the living company present assisted her. And how could Miss Edmunds, of New York, declare to Evangelides in trance that his son was dying in

Greece, — which was a fact, though so far as he knew the son was in perfect health?

Once, at Venice, at the rooms of Professor Faifofer, a medium who did not know Latin all of a sudden dictated *Sordidi sunt hic; pellenda sunt sordida* ("There are nasty-minded people here; away with obscenity!"). No one knew at whom she had shot this arrow until the table in its usual typtological language gave notice that "such a one has a book." In fact, the person in question, on polite request, owned up to having in his pocket *The Temple of Venus*. Now I can understand that the Latin may have been suggested telepathically by some one of the learned gentlemen present; but who could have apprised the medium of the presence of that book? Is it logical to admit that it was the owner of it who not merely suggested to her the idea, but brought on himself the mortification of the public confession of what might seem a serious fault? None of those present suffered scruples of that kind. The reproof therefore must have come from some one outside of the circle who felt and thought in a manner different from them.

Then, again, it seems to me a noteworthy circumstance that at Milan, as well as Naples and Turin, John would always respond at once, — and preferably in English, which was understood by only one of those present and was an unknown tongue to the medium. In the experiments of Bottazzi, Arabic words were included; and, in New York, Greek, Hindu, etc., were spoken by Miss Laura. It is true that one of the company at a séance may serve as transmitter of new cognitions; but is it not logical to infer that the medium who employs this language for the first time should feel great repugnance and make very slow headway in comprehending, speaking, and making use of it?

It has been observed that Eusapia has a great antipathy toward technical instruments of experimentation and is completely ignorant of how they are manipulated. Now it is curious to note that in experiments in Genoa, Naples, and Turin John could close and open interrupters, press Marey's drums, adjust a stethoscope, and put a metronome in movement.

And how explain the impromptu and very beautiful sculptures of Eusapia, who is entirely ignorant of the art of Pheidias?

And in what way solve the mystery of the spirit of Spencer Stafford revealing the principle of the telephone to D'Espérance (who was ignorant of physics) thirty years before its discovery?

The novel of *Edwin Drood*, left incomplete by Dickens, was finished by the fourteen-year-old medium James, a mechanic, and almost unable to read. He did not believe in Spiritualism, but

was besought by Dickens to continue the novel
under his dictation. It is interesting to note that
the orthography is English and not American,
and to observe the frequent passing from the
past tense to the present,— a special peculiarity
of Dickens's style. James entered into a trance
and saw Dickens fix him with his glance. He
did not know what he was writing, but, when he
awoke, found the floor littered with unnumbered
manuscript slips, and on every page the writing
was larger than on the one that preceded it
(Aksakoff).

The American Spiritualists are quite proud
of the philosophical book called *Arcana of Nature*, which Büchner himself highly appreciated.
When he sent his compliments regarding it to
the author, Hudson Tuttle, the latter repulsed
him, saying that he was only the medium to
whom the book was dictated by a spirit.

"For my part," writes Brofferio (*op. cit.*, pp.
141 *et seq.*), "I knew a writing medium to whom
Boccaccio, Bruno, and Galileo dictated replies
that for elevation of thought were assuredly more
worthy of the greatness of that trio than on the
level of the medium, and I could cite competent
testimony to the fact." So the responses that
Kant and Schopenhauer gave mediumistically to
Hellenbach were not unworthy of Schopenhauer
and Kant. Dante — or one who stood for him —
dictated to Scaramuzza three cantos in *terza*

rima. I read only a few strophes of these, but, so far as I can judge, they were very beautiful. Certainly the mere unaided medium, although strong in his own art, was not so in the poetic art. I will cite one more short example. An occult intelligence who had taken the name, or pseudonym, "Manzoni" was invoked with some insistence by four experimenters whom I know, whose motives I have no reason to doubt, and whose names I can furnish in private. The response to the insistent request was, as I am told, this sextain:

> " Perchè si spesso il fremito
> Della tua mano audace
> Suole dal sonno togliere
> Di desiata pace
> Gli spiriti incorruttibili
> Di quei che furo un dì? "

("Why does your bold but trembling hand so often arouse from the sleep of longed-for peace the incorruptible spirits of those who one day lived?")

Barcas gave keen replies to D'Espérance on musical acoustics, and there was no technical proficient present.

Although it is true that mediums for the most part put themselves in tune with their sitters and participate in their thoughts in such a way that, while it may seem they are inventing, they really very seldom discover things that are not already in the minds of the company present, yet there are cases in which this influence of the persons present must be absolutely rejected. The frequent apparitions that appear at the bedside of dying persons, no medium being present at all, is an argument that speaks against this theory of the invariable transmission of thought from bystanders. Then in the case of haunted houses, where suddenly chairs, tables, flasks, etc., begin to move around in whirling vortices, no one would speak of the power of mediums, the question being frequently one of uninhabited houses in which the mysterious phenomena sometimes perdure for several generations and even for centuries.

Lapponi, a Catholic and physician to the popes, — hence an unimpeachable witness, — records the case of the child Alfred Pansini, who at the age of seven during spiritistic trances would speak with a voice not his own, precisely in the manner of a true orator, frequently speaking languages of which he had no knowledge (French, Latin, Greek), even going so far as to recite in a marvellous way entire cantos of the Divine Comedy. At the age of ten, with his brother Paul, aged eight, without knowing how or why, he saw himself transported in half an hour from Ruvo to Molfetta. Another day the two children found themselves, in a scant half-hour from Ruvo, seated in a boat at sea near Barletta. Another time, in ten minutes they were at a distance from Ruvo and in front of the house door of an uncle of theirs, before whom Alfred made the prediction that they would not be able to depart next day, not until fifteen days had elapsed. In fact, the next day the uncle's horse was taken ill. Then the aunt hired a carriage to take back her nephews to Ruvo. But no sooner had they been reconsigned to their parents than they disappeared again, and again found themselves at Trani. Being sent back to Ruvo, they disappeared once more and found themselves at Bisceglie. Then, convinced that they were struggling in vain against superior powers, they betook themselves to Trani to await the expiration of the fifteen days (*Ipnotismo e Spiritismo*, Roma, 1906).

There are mental communications showing new mental faculties which cannot be explained by transmission of thought from the sitters. Such is the case of that English boy who had never left Great Britain and yet wrote rapidly in Chinese characters; and of that French lady described by Richet, who wrote whole pages in Greek, although she had never learned even the Greek alphabet.

Home one day told Soffietti that he saw near him the negro woman who had been his wet-nurse and who had saved his life when he was three and a half years old and was on the point of being drawn under a mill-wheel, — a circumstance that Soffietti had completely

12

forgotten and that was afterwards found to be true.

At another time the medium Home mentioned to Pisk a portrait of his mother with a Bible on her knees. Pisk began to rummage through the house and finally discovered a daguerreotype, taken twenty years before, in which the mother was depicted in precisely the attitude mentioned. Now it was impossible that Home could ever have seen it, even if he was not ignorant of its existence (Myers and Berret, *On Daniel Home*, 1900).

Still more important, both for their greater personal authority and in respect of the nature of the facts, are the observations of Stainton Moses (*Spirit Teachings*, etc.). Having entered into communication with a personality claiming to be one Horne, born in 1710, the son of a music-master, and who stated by whom he had been educated and with whom he had been intimate, Home undertook investigations, and found every specification to be most exact. Furthermore, when he requested him to write for him the last line of Virgil's Æneid, this was reproduced with accuracy. But, Moses being in doubt lest his (Moses') unconscious memory or his suggestion might have influenced him, he asked him to reproduce the last lines of page 94 of the last volume in the third row of his library, the very title of which he did not know. The lines specified were accurately written down. How is it possible to try to explain these performances by vestiges of unconscious cerebration if the vestiges themselves never existed? We may call them specimens of vision at a distance. But when the daughter of Mrs. Edmunds affirms that she has received a message from a certain woman named Debiel, who was then dead, — and it was true, though no one knew her, she having been five years in an insane asylum (Aksakoff), — there can be no question in this case of vision at a distance in any degree whatever. "A child entered into communication with us," writes Stainton Moses, "who gave the names of two of his brothers and the date of their death in India. No one knew them, and yet their names were verified by Valtser."

Especially noteworthy is a narrative given by Aksakoff. He was experimenting with two mediums seated at a table. The mediums were communicating the thoughts of a spirit, touching with the finger a small table that spelled out the letters of the alphabet. The Russian alphabet was called for, but the spirit wrote instead *emek habaccha*. "But that is not Russian," said some one, "and it makes no sense." The table replied, "Vale of tears." "But what does that mean?" "It is a phrase," said the table, "from a learned Portuguese Hebrew named Sardovi." A Hebrew dictionary was consulted and it was found that *nemek habacha* means " vale of tears," — a phrase found only in Psalm lxxxiii, which none of those present, not even Aksakoff, had ever read. But no trace was found of " Sardovi." On request the table corrected this name to " Cardosio." On consulting a biographical dictionary, it was found that a certain physician named Cardoso had lived in the seventeenth century, and that he had really used as an inscription on one of his books the words *Nemek Habacha.* Now how was it possible for this epigraph to be known by any of the company present, buried as it was in a forgotten book written in a tongue so little known? [1]

Later, Moses wished to communicate in Greek. Among those present only the son-in-law of Aksakoff knew this language, and there were found written the words σώματα ἀνθρώπων δίκαια εἰσί, which means " The bodies of men are just." Hippocrates has this very sentence to signify that the bodies of men are symmetrical. Now not one of the experimenters present had so much as read, much less studied, Hippocrates.

In 1887, at Vilna, a lady preceptress, Madame Stram, a writing medium, wrote as follows: " Lidia is here [Lidia had frequently appeared on other occasions] and Louis [her deceased brother] is also here, and wants to tell you that

[1] It might be a case of cryptomnesia, from the early studies of Aksakoff.

your friend Duvanel has died of hemorrhage."
Three days afterwards notification was received
by letter at Vilna from Neuchâtel of the death
of Duvanel, who had been an aspirant for the
hand of the preceptress, but had been refused
(Aksakoff, p. 413). In this case there was
neither clairvoyance nor unconscious telepathy
to exert influence.

But especially inexplicable as a part of the
action of the medium are certain features or
functions that rarely manifest themselves during
trances, but yet do so occasionally, — such as
vision and audition at a distance, the presentiment of the future, the knowledge of diseases,
the chemical sense for medicinal substances and
the instinct for remedies of which I gave instances (Chapter I) and shall give several more.[1]

AUTOMATISM

The greater number of the actions of the psychic are automatic, as is proved by the stereotyped character of the gestures, the uniform reproduction of the same graceful movements, etc.
(Morselli). In the case of the writing medium
the automatism is very plain, because his hand
is writing while his mind is elsewhere occupied
with subjects quite different from those of which
he is writing.

It is quite probable that this automatism de-

[1] For the power of seeing through material substance, see Aksakoff,
p. 457; vision at a distance, p. 452.

pends upon something that has been hitherto little noticed; namely, that almost all of the spiritistic phenomena of the medium have their origin on the left side (D'Espérance, Eusapia, Politi), or are perceived on the left side even when they come from the right, and that sinistrality is temporarily transmitted also to the controllers of the medium, — a sinistrality demonstrable by dynamometric figures, which showed after a séance a diminution of 6 kilograms for the right and 14 for the left (Morselli). Hence it follows that in the trance the work of the right hemisphere of the brain prevails, the one least adapted to psychical work and which participates least in the activity of consciousness.

Now, I ask, who animates this automaton? How reconcile with the automatism of the medium his multiplex activity and his artistic productivity? Outside intervention is required; and is not that of the spirit precisely what would be demanded, — a spirit for the most part powerless by itself, but which becomes powerful by associating itself with the living body of the medium under the conditions of the trance? It is in vain to assert that the unconscious action of the medium explains all; for when it is a question of a language, an art, totally unknown to the psychic, or medium, pray, what has this got to do with it?

Because it is something analogous to automatism (and we are considering automatic acts), it will be well at this point to note the extraordinary precocity of some psychics.

The child Alward not only moved tables too heavy for his normal strength, but made typtological communications. The child Yencker gave replies with raps when two months old. At the age of five months and a half he advised the return to London from his villa, his residence there being injurious to him on account of the fatigue incurred in going and returning. The nephew of Seymour wrote automatically when nine days old; at the age of seven months he gave typtological communications (Aksakoff, *Animisme*, p. 351; *Psichische Studien*, 1877, p. 467).

These are facts that could hardly receive credence were they not confirmed by similar wonders found among the Camisards. Camisard babes of fourteen or fifteen months, and even while still sucklings, will preach with the purest diction (De Vesme, *Spiritisme*, ii.). Vernet heard one of them, fourteen months old, speaking in pure French, although it could not yet walk. Bonnemère (*Les Camisards*, 1860) and Figuier (*Histoire du Merveilleux*, ii. 404) think this precocity to be the effect of religious exaltation; but this could not create a faculty that did not previously exist.

Most potent, then, is the power of the medium in spiritistic matters, so much so that it explains the greater part of the phenomena, but not all; and the complete explanation can be found only by integrating the mediumistic force with another force, which, although it is more fragmentary and transitory, yet acquires, by identifying itself with the medium, a greater potency. And this force, authenticated by the tradition of all ages and all peoples and by experimental observation, is pointed out to us as found in the residual action of the dead.

CHAPTER VII

Phantasms and Apparitions of the Dead

WHEN we are treating of the phenomena of phantasms, or spectral apparitions, we are reminded of Dante's counsel, —

> " Sempre a quel ver ch' ha faccia di menzogna
> De' l'uom chiuder le labbra quant' ei pote,
> Però che senza colpa fa vergogna."
>
> *Inferno,* xvi. 124–126.

("Always to that truth which has an air of falsehood a man should close his lips, if possible; for, though blameless, he causes shame [to himself by telling what fails of securing credence].")

In good sooth it is the best of advice, this, for one who wants to lead a quiet life, especially in the academic world, which has a propensity to dissimulate and deny intractable facts which do not admit of common and universal explanation, such as these very facts, that people are so shy of accepting, of an operant force that survives death. And yet I repeat, although it is dangerous to do so, no other explanation applies to these facts (since the action of the medium is in many cases insufficient to account for them) except this, that the dead are still endowed with power (or, rather, assume it under the stimulus of the medium) sufficient to impart those ideas and perform those feats which the powers of the medium and of the experimenters in the séance do not suffice to explain.

And just here I will recall the fact that primitive peoples, who believe in magicians and even manufacture them artificially, admit, to be sure, as I have already proved, a mighty power in these special mediums of theirs, but a power which is in great part based on the counsel and assistance of the spirits of the dead. In the potency of these ghostly beings all ancient peoples placed full credence (and this was perhaps the base and start of all the religions). Furthermore, as we shall see later, almost all barbarous peoples, even to-day, hold to their belief in it with a tenacity and a uniformity which ought to be considered, if not a proof, yet an important indication of the truth (see Chapter VIII).

Then, again, the replies, not rarely prophetic, though quite frequently vain and false, and most often in flat contradiction to the culture of the medium and the sitters, and the appearance in their presence of phantoms with such evident appearance of momentary life, can be explained (although the explanation naturally excites a shudder in the learned scientist) only by admitting that the presence of the medium in trance often induces the appearance and the activity more or less vigorous of beings, or personalities,

that do not belong to the living, but which for
the nonce take on their semblance and assume
many of their functions

RADIO-ACTIVITY

Yet, for all this, I would not undertake to
overthrow the positivist theory. I do not pro-
pose (need I say it?) to break a lance in defence
of pure disembodied spirits, — which are, besides,
beings of which we can form no conception, —
but of bodies the substance of which is so subtile
and refined as to be both imponderable and invisible except in special circumstances; such as the
radio-active bodies, which have the power of
emitting light and heat, and even other bodies
(helium), without apparently losing any weight
whatever. Now Lodge, in his address before the
Society for Psychical Research in London, com-
pares the materializations of spirits to " the mol-
lusk, that can extract from water the material
for its shell; or to the animal, that can assimilate
material for its nutriment and convert it into
muscle, skin, bone, or feather. And so in the case
of these living entities that ordinarily do not
manifest themselves to our senses, although they
are in constant rapport with our psychic world,
possessing, as they must, a kind of etheric body
(or, as we should rather say, radiant body), they
are able temporarily to utilize the terrestrial mole-

cules that surround them for the purpose of building up a kind of material body capable of manifesting itself to our senses."

Let me recall here the many indications of this radio-active state of the medium in the presence of the entities that I may assume to be the dead, — such as the operating of the electroscope by Eusapia while holding her hands suspended at a distance from it of four inches (a radio-active phenomenon); the impression of four fingers made by her on a prepared photographic plate covered with three sheets of very dark paper; the phosphorescent clouds floating over the head of the same psychic, and issuing from the abdomen of D'Espérance; the luminous bands and striations (taking shape in the form of spectral figures) that appear in the séances of Politi, Eusapia, and Randone (*Luce ed Ombra*, 1902); [1] the lights in the form of stars, and of globes from 60 to 70 centimetres in diameter, which do not burn and do not illuminate, which rise slowly, descend rapidly, frequently traverse space with rapidity, and are sometimes azure, sometimes green, or else yellowish (see Fig. 48), and respond at times to raps and frequently govern their movements as if intentionally, seeming as though they were projected and directed by a conducting wire, appearing at given hours for many years in succession without any influence

[1] See Fig. 48.

FIG. 48. LUMINOUS BANDS AS SEEN IN SÉANCES WITH THE RANDONES.

exerted on them by the medium (Aberden), and always moving from one point to another in equal times and in a true intentional direction, as at Berbenno and at Quargenta (*Arch. di Psich.*, xviii. 266–422).

To these phenomena must be added the fact of the reproduction in the dark of phantasmal markings and figures, such as the Count de Boullet obtained with the medium Firman, and Reiners also with Firman. This has been confirmed anew by recent experiments at Turin in the presence of Eusapia. A photographic plate covered with three sheets of dark paper was held by Drs. Herlitzka and Foà above the head of the medium in front of the curtain of the cabinet in order to photograph a phantasm that had appeared there. But the operation was obstructed by a formidable hand that did not belong to any one present, including the medium, and which tried hard to snatch the plate from the hands of Foà for the purpose of breaking it, as it had already done in the case of other plates (and this also proves the presence at the séances of energetic wills opposed to those of the medium and the experimenters). Foà stoutly resisted three assaults, and, after the third one, withdrew the plate, which did not show a reproduction of the face of the phantasm, but four huge fingers unlike those of Eusapia and of Foà.

This experiment, which should perhaps be connected with that mentioned above, of the impression left by the hand of Eusapia on a photographic plate, is indeed one of extraordinary value, because, leaving out of the account the radio-activity of Dr. Foà,[1] and that of the medium, because she was at a distance and her hand is entirely different, there remains the sole hypothesis that the radiations came directly from the incarnated body the image of which had been presented before, in the same way that imprints were previously obtained from similar phantasmal beings in paraffine and gypsum, — imprints that bore no resemblance to the limbs or features of the medium.

This is an experiment which brings us into very intimate relations, experimentally, with the phenomena, or, as I should rather say, with the so-called spiritistic organism, with those transitory and evanescent representatives of the life beyond of whose existence people wish, and do not wish, to admit the existence. It turns out, as I had already publicly stated some years ago, that those phantasmal bodies belong to some other state of matter, the radiant state, — a statement which

---

[1] The radio-activity of Foà is excluded because he, being an amateur photographer, has never noted the results of any action whatever of his fingers on hundreds of plates handled by him. It is a possible thing that during the séance with Madame Paladino his hand might have become radio-active. But then during the entire séance he had (and held long) in his hand three other plates upon none of which was to be seen the image of fingers. This excludes also the assumption that his fingers might have been fraudulently covered with radio-active substances.

has now at length got solid footing in science
and which is not only the sole hypothesis that can
reconcile the ancient universal belief in the per-
sistence of certain phenomena of life after death
with the postulates of science (which holds this
truth to be self-evident, that without an organ
there can be no function, and that there can be
no functioning of an organ without loss of
weight), but is also the only hypothesis that harmonizes with the phenomena we have under our
eyes in spiritistic experiments.

As a matter of fact, — except in rare cases,
such as those of Katie King in London and Eleanora at Barcelona, where these spirit forms
remain among us for days and years, — we rarely
see the face and body complete of these phantasms; most often we see only certain of the
limbs (hands, arms, etc.), which detach themselves from some part of the body of the medium,
or from the curtain of the psychic cabinet, exhibiting always an instinctive tendency to wrap
themselves in the curtain as well as in their astral
veil. When we touch them, we very rarely and
only for a brief moment perceive any solid form.
Usually we see emerging from the curtain or
from the skirt of the medium a true fluidic body
which is deflated and weakly dissolved when we
apply pressure to it, but which not for that reason
can we declare to be non-existent, but which
rather, and precisely on that account, we should

regard as incarnated in some material substance,[1] and a substance which eludes our touch because it is more fluid, more subtile, than a common gas (the existence of which last substance was denied, by the way, not long ago; and perhaps we would deny it still did not chemistry come to our aid). Evidently, however, these beings, or remnants of beings, would not possess the means whereby they could materialize themselves completely (incarnate themselves) if they did not get the temporary loan for their fluidic body from a part of the substance of the medium, who, while this is being done, is lying in a stupor, almost in the death-agony, through the loss of a part of the bodily substance. But borrowing from the power and the body of the psychic does not mean that the phantasm becomes identical with that personality.

That which we think we comprehend when we speak of anything as incorporeal is only the product of a fictitious conception. We mean at the utmost a kind of attenuated stuff, or consistency, incapable of longer affecting our senses. Virgil, in order to reconcile in the mind of Dante the idea of his (Virgil's) own proper materiality,

---

[1] Barzini, in his *Nel Mondo dei Misteri*, expresses himself thus: "The curtain is inflated and empty. That which on one side seems a human body in relief, and (covered by the curtain) exhibits movements, on the other side is a hollow in the curtain. I touch the inflations of the curtain on the outside: under the stuff I recognize the cheeks, the nose, the forehead; when I touch the lips, I feel my thumb pressed by the teeth — and then, suddenly, the curtain is deflated."

which renders him visible to his companion, with
the idea of his absolute transparency, says to
him, —

> " Ora, se innanzi a me nulla s' adombra,
>   Non ti maravigliar più che de' cieli,
>   Che l' uno all' altro 'l raggio non ingombra."
>   *Purgatorio,* iii. 28–30.

("If now in front of me nothing casts a shadow, marvel
not more than that which you marvel at in the heavens,
one of which does not put any impediment in the way of
another's darting through it a luminous ray."[1])

Precisely so. The ether that fills all space is a
substance, and yet is not directly perceptible. The
very air, the elements of which are known, — its
weight, density, elasticity, — is not habitually
perceived by us as a corporeal entity.

On the other hand, our senses possess a very
limited extension of perceptivity when compared
with the action of possible external forces.
Sound waves, for example, are perceived by us
in the interval between a minimum number of
vibrations and a maximum number; outside of
this sounds for us do not exist, nor, as a consequence of this, sonorous bodies. The same is true
of light, in the vast realm of which all beyond the
red and the violet rays escapes our perception.

Hence the fact of the appearance of entire
phantasms that took living form for a brief

---

[1] The allusion, as Fraticelli remarks, is to the revolving crystalline
heavens, or planetary spheres (of the Ptolemaic hypothesis), supposed to
be transparent. — *Translator.*

period, and occasionally for a long time, under
our very eyes, no longer remains completely in-
comprehensible and unreducible to the grand laws
of monism.   At any rate, the thing has been
proved over and over again.   The case of Katie
King, which was for three years under the observation of the most eminent English experimenters,
seems to me free from all suspicion, even as to
that most mysterious and most controverted phenomenon, reincarnation.   Florence Cook, without
the existence of any predisposition on her part,
felt impelled to take up the life of a psychic when
still under fifteen, after having been present at a
Spiritualistic séance at the house of a lady friend.
On this occasion the table in her presence rose
clear up to the ceiling of the room, and knocks
and direct writing revealed her extraordinary
power as a psychic.   After a few séances the
phantom form of a woman began to appear before
her, palpably visible to all present.   A trick being suspected, the medium was bound and the
bands sealed and she herself held immovable in
a niche in a wall, like a mummy, and placed under
the control of the well-known scientists Crookes,
Wallace, and Varley.   But for three years the
phantasm continued to appear.   She called herself
Katie King (presumably the daughter of Eusapia's John King). She would write and speak,
and was as tall as the psychic; but whereas Florence had long dark hair, Katie's was somewhat

FIG. 49. PHANTASMAL PORTRAIT OF KATIE KING.

blond and was cut short.   Her heart, auscultated by Crookes, showed 75 pulsations against the medium's 80.

The apparition of Yolanda, under the mediumistic influence of D'Espérance, also continued for three years, and it was found possible to photograph her (see Figs. 49, 50).

Marata, at Barcelona, in the fourth séance with the psychic Carmen Domingues, obtained the apparition of Eleanora, a phantasm completely materialized, who saluted the experimenters in a voice slightly veiled.   She disappeared; then, after a few minutes, returned again, went in and out of the cabinet several times, and once remained among the experimenters for nearly an hour, showing herself possessed of an uncommon intelligence and disposition.   During her appearances she sat down three or four times in a chair drawn out of the psychic's cabinet by herself, gave her hand to the spectators, allowed her chevelure of black hair to be touched, as also her white robe, which seemed to all as if made of the finest tulle and to gleam with luminous reflections (Aksakoff, *Animisme*, p. 620).

In 1860 Estella Marta appeared to her husband Livermore and continued so to appear for five years in succession, during 388 séances, held at night and in the dark, with the medium Katie Fox.   Her materialization was gradual, being complete in the forty-third sitting.   She was ac-

companied by a " guide " calling himself Frank-
lin, who, according to Spiritualistic tradition, was
a great organizer of spiritistic reunions. This
revenante could even endure the light, spoke a
little, but oftener wrote, — directly, with her own
hand, and in her own chirography; the writing
was often in French, *a language which the
medium did not know.* In 1866 she ceased to appear in a materialized form, but yet continued to
communicate messages and to allow spiritistic
photographs to be taken. In one of these appeared a relative of hers.

The phantasmal presentments of their own little
children appeared to Vassallo and to Porro.

I have myself been a witness of the complete
materialization of my own mother, as I have
related at length in Chapter II, where it was stated
that Morselli's mother also appeared to him (in a
séance with Eusapia), and more than once, but
was of a fuller bust and with less correct manners, exhibiting a deportment not her own. She
playfully bit him instead of kissing him, and held
a regular conversation with him by gestures,[1]
pointing sorrowfully to his spectacles and his
semi-baldness, as if she would make him understand how long a time had elapsed since she had
left him a bold and beautiful youth.

In a séance with Delanne in Algiers, Richet

---

[1] I get this from confessions made by him to the Countess Celesia and
to lawyer Bocca a few days after the event. He afterwards denied it.

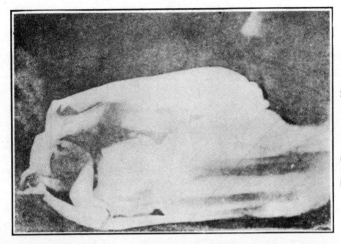

The Phantom of Yolanda.

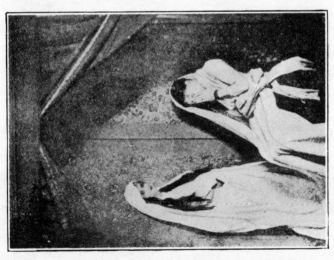

Fig. 50. Phantasmal Photograph of Yolanda with her Medium, Madame D'Espérance.

was favored with several apparitions of an Arab
phantasm called Benny Boa, who disappeared by
sinking through the solid earth, then reappeared,
pressed the hands of the spectators, and in response to a test with a solution of baryta showed
that he breathed out carbonic acid gas, a thing
that would assuredly have been impossible in the
case of a mere semblance of a living being (as
certain critics would suspect), nor could it have
been arranged beforehand by a trickster.

But we are able to draw a proof from our adversaries themselves. Morselli, in the rashness
of his anti-spiritism, when confronted by the
phantasm of the son of Vassallo and of the daughter of Porro, puts forward the hypothesis that
Eusapia had acquired previous information from
the families as to their physical characteristics,
or else had secured it from the subconscious states
of the sitters and obeyed their wish (p. 408).
But, if the latter form the rationale of the matter,
how does it happen that Edmond and Eusapia
could both cause phantasms of the acquaintances
of certain people to appear before them on the
very evening they had disembarked from ships
that had borne them from distant lands? and why
did not Eusapia perceive all the characteristics
of Morselli's mother in the depths of his subconsciousness, and why could she not there obtain
also correct ideas of the name? Why did she not
obey Morselli, who felt a positive repugnance to

having his mother's spirit evoked by her necromantic wand? And, on the other hand, why in
the world did she call up before Bozzano the
image of his hated wife with whom he had been
in litigation all his life? for most assuredly he did
not wish to see her after death; and, further, she
spoke to him in pure Genoese, a dialect that
Eusapia does not know. Why, if we are to stand
by his hypothesis, did she not reconstruct, clear
and complete, the figure of Giacosa, which she
could not only have read with great precision in
the thought of the company present, especially
in that of her illustrious son-in-law and friend
Albertini, and whose portrait she must have seen
on every street corner and in all the journals for
months after her death? The hypothesis which
has to serve for one has to serve for the others
also; and, if it will not fit all, then we must lean
to the other supposition, that the phantasms were
produced by something more than the externalization of the thought of the medium or of that
of the experimenters in the séance.

But Morselli finds proof that that apparition
was not his mother in its hesitation, and in the
error made in pointing out his facial defect, —
on the right instead of on the left, — and in only
giving the initials of his name. He does not perceive, learned as he is in the world of matter, that
the spirits, as Hodgson says, speak vilely (*negro*);
that the errors he alludes to were those observed

in all the spirits evoked, and that, employing, as they do, the vocal mechanism of the medium in a rough way and with the uncertainty of those who are employing it for the first time, they always make these mistakes. He lays stress also upon the fact that the phantasm had a fuller bust than his mother, not remembering that the phantasms assume the words, gestures, and body of the medium. This should also have explained for him the vulgar habit of playfully biting the beloved one which is common to all the other phantasms evoked by Eusapia and from whom they borrow it.

The fact remains that some at least of these ghostly visitors appeared — and not for a few brief moments merely — with the entire body, which presented the features of weight, temperature (see below), pulse-beats, and respiration. Of many of them the moral character could be fixed, — gentle, beneficent, apostolic, in the case of Katie King; vain and babbling for Walter and Phinuit; grave, austere, and haughty for Imperator; genial and ambitious for Pelham. Of two of them we possess portraits, taken together with those of their mediums and at the same time.

The spirit personality called Yolanda was a semi-barbaric girl, without native genius, but very curious. When she first appeared out of the shadow world, she did not know what a chair was, but tried to sit on its back, and fell. She did not exhibit any affection, and played with the children of Fidler because she was used to it. At the age of ten she barely knew a few letters of the alphabet, but had a great desire to be praised and approved. She knew at once the use of jewels. Her body was so real, so carnally feminine, that a person who took her for a real woman attempted to offer her an indignity, resulting in profound injury to the medium, to whom it caused an illness almost mortal (see D'Espérance).

But the complete phantasm is rather rare, and the phenomenon is rounded out and completed by those fragments of phantasms — arms, hands, etc. — which appear in almost every psychic séance. And even if these apparitions, complete and incomplete, had not appeared, should we not have the proof of their presence and action in those intelligent phenomena and acts, sometimes æsthetic and artistic, which take place at a distance from the medium, beyond her sphere of externalization, and which she has not the skill or competency to perform?

It is in vain for Flammarion to say that nothing unusual or rare has been revealed by the spirits and mediums which did not already exist in the capacities of mediumistic experimenters. In opposition to this I present the following questions: In a sitting where no sculptor was present, with a medium who would not have known how to sculpture an egg, how could those marvellous

sculptures be formed which even artists do not
feel they are capable of executing by long work?
And how could those paintings, some of them
truly marvellous, be formed?   And how could
Phinuit and Pelham produce predictions of
events absolutely unforeseeable and which yet
came true?

On a smaller scale the same may be said of that
series of intellectual acts, of little account to be
sure, but which suppose the aid of the hand of
another and of a skilled person, — such as the
playing of a mandolin, of a violin, of a closed
piano, — in all of which the difficulty is redoubled,
because we cannot comprehend how the externalization of the motive force of Eusapia could accomplish results in which she herself could not
succeed by employing her own normal woman's
hand, however skilful she may be; nor how she
plays a closed piano or a mandolin suspended in
the air; nor how she can put in motion a closed
metronome; nor how knots can be made in a cord
the ends of which are sealed together: whereas,
on the other hand, we understand how those
fluidic forms animated by the living body of the
medium can perform these feats, and we can comprehend how a spirit (more or less illuminated by
intelligence) building itself up out of the body of
Eusapia, or fusing itself with her body, can produce intellectual results which Eusapia herself is
not capable of accomplishing.

Worth noting is the reply given me once by the just mentioned psychic when, seeing a paralytic before me who spoke inarticulately, I asked, " Do you think the dead still have the diseases they had when living?"   "No," she replied, through the mind of John; "but how could men understand them if they did not appear in the state in which they saw them at the moment of death?"

On account of their great number and the profound earnestness with which they were gathered and examined, it behooves us at this point to mention the condensed records of phantasmal appearances studied in the magnificent work, *Phantasms of the Living,* by Gurney, Myers, and Podmore.

Out of the 5705 persons subjected to examination 96 had hallucinations.   Of these, 44 concerned persons dead many years before; 13, persons dead within a short time previous; 23 (or 1 in 248) had visual hallucinations of persons living, either sleeping or ill, and 1 in 40 of persons dead within the twelve hours.

Inasmuch as these figures exceed a thousand times those of the laws of probability, and since the greater number of these apparitions were unforeseen, and a certain number (93) seen by several persons at the same time and in various places, and many of them perceived by the sense of sight, of hearing, and of touch, we therefore have the practical certainty of the influence of the dying or of the just dead upon the ephemeral phantasm which in the greater number of cases presents itself before us only once.

And here note the curious circumstance that not rarely phantasms have been perceived also by domestic animals, which proves that they did not merely exist in the excited fancy of the human percipient. Samuel Johnson cites the case of horses that reared up when the horseman saw a spectral form. A " ghost " was seen in the air by two girls of thirteen and by a horse which shivered with fear and refused to go forward (Wallace, *Miracles*, p. 328).

Zecchini had a little dog that would come forth from his sleeping-place and leap about and bark with joy every time that the spirit of the young child Emilio was evoked. Emilio had been his playfellow. In the year 1893 a certain Danish dog who had a great affection for Madame F. was seen all of a sudden, at 9.15 by the clock, to jump up from his sleeping-mat as if he saw some one he knew and liked, then hide himself terrified under the bed. It was the very hour in which the mistress of the house received notice that Madame F. was dead.

We must therefore, I repeat, reinforce the psychic power of the medium by another power, however transitory; namely, that of the dead, pointed out to us by the traditions of all times and of all peoples and by experimental observation.

CHAPTER VIII

Belief in the Spirits of the Dead among Savages and among Ancient Peoples

PERHAPS the proof that appeals to me with most insistent force is the universality of the belief among all peoples (at least in the humble classes, who are frequently nearer to the fountain of truth than they seem) in the existence not only of mediums or magicians (see Chapter V), but of spirits, and especially the souls of the dead, active, operant, — sometimes beneficently and sometimes malevolently, — fluttering around us in the atmosphere, in houses, in the rocks, and who communicate with men especially through the agency of magicians or mediums.

To prove the universality of this belief, one needs only to weigh and ponder some of the data of that most excellent and erudite work, *Le Spiritisme*, by De Vesme.

The Veddahs have not the faintest shadow of a religion; yet they believe in the survival of souls and offer food to the shades of the dead to ward off their wrath. The Hottentots have no idea of a future life or of gods. Their souls seem blank pages (said a missionary) in the matter of religion; but then many of them, according to Lichtenstein (Ratzel, *Die menschlichen Rassen*), believe that the dead leave behind them ghosts, frequently malevolent. The Tasmanians, according to Bouvich (*Origin of the Tasmanians*), do not admit the existence of divinities, but people with spirits the rocks of the mountains, — malevolent spirits.

According to Letourneau, when the negroes of Africa affirm that all is finished after death, they find it necessary to add, " except the terrible spectre of the phantasm."

Worship among primitive peoples, writes Alfred Molury, being reduced to the exorcism of spirits and to the adoration of the amulet, the priests teach neither morals nor pious works, but are simple sorcerers whose business it is to get into relation with the spirits so much dreaded (*La Magie*, cap. ii.). " Among the Fuegians, the Tasmanians, the Australians, the Hottentots, no temples or religious rites are to be seen," says Letourneau (*Évolution Réligieuse*, lib. iii.). " Religion consists in the belief in the existence of anthropomorphic or zoömorphic spirits that people the grottoes and the trees, and no one among primitive folk has any idea of communicating with them. Later man comes to fancy that gifts and genuflections may change the decisions of the gods, made in his image; and, since the divinities are wanderers through the air, they

offer them a house of rest, which will later become the temple; and with the temple comes the
priest, who either in good or in bad faith claims
to possess the privilege of communicating with
the spirits and of serving as a mediator between
them and men."

Dr. Shepley Part, who was on the Gold Coast
and was there the witness of many spiritistic and
telepathic phenomena, observed, in respect to the
transmission of thought by unknown means, that
there are individuals in that country who succeed
in it at whatever distance, just as in transferring
themselves from point to point. In a night march
in a forest the caravan was preceded by a luminous globe that fluttered along in the air up to
the very gates of the city to which they were
going. The negroes said it was the double of a
spirit sent to them as a guide.

One day the doctor was informed by the natives
that, an hour and a half before, the governor had
entered Kumassi, a town five days' march away.
He asked a chief how he knew it, and the man
said he had means of communication more rapid
than ours, — methods that were the monopoly of
a kind of secret society. But the doctor very soon
understood that their clairvoyance was attained
by very simple methods and by means of continual practice. Yet there were very different degrees of it: first, simple clairvoyance; second,
a projection of the consciousness to a distance;

third, the same, with the power of materializing the entity projected and transporting objects, including the body itself, — the last a gift bestowed, however, on very few. The doctor saw in certain cemeteries nebulous masses which the natives claimed were the phantasms of the dead. He visited an ancient fortification built by the Portuguese in the seventeenth century, the temporary residence of the functionaries who make journeys to that region. One day, when one of these gentlemen was getting ready to go to dinner, he learned from his " boy " that a white man had come to take dinner, too. " Where in the devil is he? " said he. " He is sitting there at the table." And he pointed him out and described him and his Portuguese costume of the seventeenth century. The gentleman saw nothing; but the other negroes all affirmed that they saw it, and would not remain in the fort at night.

Du Chaillu, in his *Explorations and Adventures in Equatorial Africa*, says that the inhabitants of Gaboon have no clear idea of future existence, but believe that when a man dies he leaves behind him a ghostly form that survives for some time and haunts the place where the corpse was interred.

Winwood Reade (*Savage Africa*) notes that in the Congo the sons often kill the mother, in order that, having become a potent spirit, she may lend them assistance.

According to the Kaffirs, when a man dies he leaves behind him a sort of vaporous form resembling the shadow cast by his body when he lived (Bourchell, *Travels*, p. 550). In order to obtain a kind of guardian angel they select the spirit of a chief or of a friend, and invoke him when in great straits.

In Madagascar, according to a native doctor named Ramisiras (*Croyances Médicales du Madagascar*, 1904), " the superstition of the natives leads them to believe that the spirits of their ancestors always remain in the midst of the living, whether to lend them succor or to do them harm; hence their elaborate worship of the dead."

Indeed, Dr. Dancet knew a magician of the Bora race who invoked the souls of a captain and a lieutenant who had died in battle four years previous. Neither he nor the other natives saw anything; but they heard in the empty hut the words of command, which the natives could not imitate, and the gun-shots and cries and blows. It all lasted about twenty-five minutes.

When the Tuaregs of the Sahara, according to Duversiè, set out on long expeditions, their women, in order to get news from them, go and sleep on the tombs of their dead, evoking them and obtaining from them information the truth of which is afterwards authenticated. The geographer Pomponius Mela long before had observed the same thing. The Angelis, he says, know no other god than the spirits of the dead, and consult them as oracles. In order to have responses from them they sleep upon their tombs.

Mary Kingsley, in a lecture upon " The Forms of Apparitions in Western Africa," testifies that there are few persons in that region who have not seen apparitions either of a god or of the spirits of the dead. As to the priests, they claim to be in continual relation with the spirits. Often a god will take possession of a priest and speak through his mouth, but with another voice. Probably their more sensitive nervous system permits them to see things that we more obtuse races do not see. Their mind would in that case be a more sensitive photographic plate on which the world of spirits would be more readily impressed.

The Bayaka in the vicinity of the Congo believe that after death the souls of warriors dwell in the air and appear to the living in dreams to complain of the mal-treatment or neglect of their tombs, and to ask for revenge on their slayer (*Journal Anthrop. Inst.*, xxxvi. 1906).

The Awemba of Central Africa hold that the shades of the departed (*mipashi*) wander about in the groves where they were buried. Sometimes they incarnate themselves in the body of a serpent, or appear to the faithful in sleep, but more frequently are related to the living through the intermediary of a female psychic or magician. These women mediums take their names, imitate

14

their acts, give themselves up to sacred dances, fall into ecstasies (uttering words which the physician-priest alone interprets), and give useful information to the warriors and the hunters.

The physician-priests are the mediums of dead criminals; they eat the bodies of enemies, and spread abroad homicide and madness (*Journal Anthrop. Inst.*, xxxvi. 150. 1906).

The Australians refrain from pronouncing the name of one who has died, for fear of raising his ghost. According to Dumont D'Urville (*Voyage autour du Monde*, ii.), they go to the graveyards at night to communicate with the dead. See also Perron D'Arc (*Aventures en Australie*, p. 173). At Tahiti, in the Marianne Islands, exorcism is practised, and the natives think the shades of the dead watch continually over them. The aborigines of New Zealand believe in an intelligent and immaterial something belonging to a man slain in battle, and practise certain rites to shelter themselves from the revenge his shade would take (Spencer). Judge Manning, of Kehapaheha, tells us about a real Spiritualistic séance among the Maoris. One of their chiefs having died in battle, by request of many friends the *tounga*, or priest, invoked his spirit in the central public building, where all the people were gathered together in the dark. The first thing they knew they heard the words: " I salute all, I salute my family, I salute my friends.

Speak to me, you of my family." A brother of his said to him, " How do you feel? " " I am well," was the reply; and, when requested to give news of the other dead, the spirit promised to impart their messages. He asked that a pig and his gun be given to the priest, to the great grief of the brother. It being known that he had written and afterwards hidden a diary of his tribe, he was asked where it was to be found. He indicated the hiding-place, and it was at once discovered there.[1]

Dumont D'Urville says that the priests of the Tonga Islands seem to repeat all the phenomena which the ancients observed in their pythonesses and sibyls and which magnetism reproduces. Marner saw in Tonga individuals under the inspiration of the divinity who could truly divine the future to the sound of the drum, as among the shamans of Siberia.

Lafitte found that the American Indians believed in spirits, or genii of the dead, with whom certain privileged persons could communicate. According to Schoolcraft (*Indian Tribes*), the Sioux feared so much the vengeance of the spirits that homicide was unknown among them. Missionaries, in the volume entitled *Lettres Édifiantes*, tell of cradles transported through the air to distant points by the order of a priest. The medicine-man, or magician, during consultations

---

[1] *The Old New Zealand for a Pakeka*, 1878.

shakes the wigwam in which he sits, which by jerks and blows replies to questions, just as do the white man's séance tables. The divinations take place in a cylindrical cell made of oak bark, within the dark interior of which a man may stand upright. It corresponds to the mediumistic cabinet. Scarcely has the diviner entered when a great noise begins and voices are heard, one weak, the other very loud (that of the priest). The first, or weak, voice imparts the revelation.

Judge Larrabé saw an Indian medicine-man construct three little wigwams of hides, each hardly large enough to hold a man. He placed them about two feet apart. In one he put his moccasins, in another his leggins, in the third himself. Every Indian who wished to speak with a deceased person applied to the medicine-man, and soon the tents began to be shaken and voices issued from all three even at the same time, but they could be interpreted only by the medicine-man.

According to Fitzgibbons, the last governor of Bay Islands (Gibier, *Spiritisme*), there are many mediums among the American Indians, and they obtain better results than do our psychics. The spirits that choose them as the channel of their communications bear Spanish-American names, or affirm that they belong to the prehistoric races the remains of whose architecture are found imbedded in the tropical forests of Central America, and whose cliff dwellings are seen on the mesas and in the canyons of the Colorado and the Rio Grande.

But more curious still is the narrative of a certain " Henry," prisoner of the Hurons during the war of 1750. In the councils of this warlike tribe the question came up, Ought they to accept a proposal made by Sir William Johnson to send their chiefs to Fort Niagara to conclude a peace? The question at stake being one of the very highest importance, they wished to consult the spirit of one of their celebrated chiefs deceased, whose name was Great Turtle. This ghostly warrior manifested himself in the magic wigwam, first by shaking it, and then by his voice. On being asked if there were many soldiers at the fort, he disappeared and then returned, saying there were very few, but that there were many of them along the river in small boats, and further said that if the chiefs went there they would be loaded down with presents. And all happened as the voice said.[1]

Judge Larrabé tells how once a merchant had been waiting many days for a clerk of his, when

[1] The *locus classicus* for the true incident in American pioneer life, here cited by Professor Lombroso, I had the hap to find after considerable search. It is Chapter XXI. of a valuable and not very common little monograph published in New York in 1809, and entitled *Travels and Adventures in Canada and the Indian Territories, between the Years 1760 and 1776*, by Alexander Henry. The incident is told very interestingly in detail: the building of the magic wigwam, the entrance of the priest, the terrible hullabaloo of noises, and finally "the still small voice" of the spirit of "the chief that never lied " (Great Turtle). — *Translator.*

a medicine-man said he would give him news of him. So he covered his head with his blanket and said, " At sunset your friend will be here." And it was so.

The Esquimaux believe in spirits, the most potent of whom is a certain Cordarsuc, who has under him an army of inferior ghosts, many of whom are in the habit of putting themselves at the service of the magicians.

Jacolliot relates of a certain fakir that, having performed various marvels, — such as flights through the air, departures from the body and returning, — he said, in reply to the question of Jacolliot as to how he could do such things: " I have nothing to do with it; it is the spirits of your ancestors who do it. So true is it that I am going to set out and go a long way off, and the spirits alone will make you feel their power." And, in fact, when he was locked up in a room far from the palace, there occurred in the night a series of shocks (movements of tables and raps) that lasted till morning.

Now this is the thing that convinces me, — the occurrence of the same affirmation in India and in America; that in the one place as in the other the medium (or magician) is considered as the passive agent of the phenomena, while the spirit of the dead is the active operator, in spite of the fact that the very opposite would seem more natural and more in accordance with verisimilitude.

What we have seen as true in space, among the various peoples scattered over the surface of the globe, we might view also as occurrences in time, inasmuch as belief in the spirits of the dead has never suffered an interruption, from the earliest ages down to our day.

" I say nothing of Egypt and of its Book of the Dead," writes Brofferio (*Per lo Spiritismo,* Bocca, 1903, pp. 112 *et seq.*); "nor of India, which believes more in the other world than in this; nor of Persia, whose custom of calling forth the dead must have been imported, according to Varro (in Augus., *Civitate D.,* vii. 35); nor of the necromancy of the Babylonians.

" But it is known that the evocation of the dead was practised by the ancient Hebrews, since Deuteronomy forbids it (xviii. 10), and Saul consulted the spirit of Samuel called up by the Witch of Endor (Josephus, *Jewish Antiq.,* vi. 14. 2). In Greece, not merely the vulgar believed in apparitions of the dead, but the philosophers, especially the Platonists, and, first of all, the Pythagoreans. The latter went so far as to express wonder if any one said he had never seen a *daimon* (Apul., *De Soc.,* c. 20, citing Aristotle). Even Democritus said that visible and audible phantasms appear to men (εἴδωλα θεωρούμενα καὶ φωνὰς ἀφιέντα: Sesto, *Contro Mat.,* ix. 19; Cic.,

De Nat. Deor., i. 120), making announcement of
future events. The evocation of the dead was
a most ancient custom in Greece. So early as
the time of the composition of the Iliad, Ulysses
is represented as calling up the spirits of the dead
(*Odyssey,* xi. 23–50), — about five centuries before Simmias of Thebes, one of the characters in
Plato's *Phædo*, evoked the shade of Lysis, the
teacher of Epaminondas (Plut., *De Gen. Soc.*).
The Eleusinian mysteries were probably, as Du
Prel well says, necromantic ceremonies. It is
certain that the ψυχαγωγοί (psychagogues, sum-
moners of souls) made a practice of calling up
the shades of the departed in certain temples.
As early as the time of Herodotus that writer
speaks (v. 92) of a νεκυομαντήιον, or oracle of
the dead, near the river Acheron, to which the
tyrant Periandros sent, in order to question the
spirit of his deceased wife Melissa, and she gave
him a rational proof of her identity which de-
cency hinders me from mentioning. It is certain,
also, that Plotinus, Porphyry, and Jamblichus assert that the Alexandrian priests and philosophers called up spirits of every kind (theurgy,
goezia, — witchcraft, — and necromancy). Wallace cites a passage from Jamblichus which seems
like the description of a séance of the medium
Home.

"As to the Romans, the *Mostellaria* of Plautus
proves that the vulgar believed in apparitions.

Among the writers, Pliny, Suetonius, and five or six others speak of this. Both in the time of the republic and under the empire mediums sprinkled with blood practised the evocation of speaking phantasms from the abyss of Acheron, or Hades. Writers who show a knowledge of this are Cicero (*Tusc.*, i. 37; *In Vatinium*, ii. 6); Horace (*Sat.*, i. 8, 24, ss.); and Pliny (*Hist. Nat.*, 30. 2). Lucan (*Pharsal.*, vi. 452, ss.) describes the thing, the *modus operandi*. Several of the emperors were accused of it, among others Nero (Suet., *Nero*, 34) and Caracalla (Herodian, iv. 12. 3). There were even temples in Italy consecrated to this cult, the most celebrated of which was that of Lake Avernus at Misenum, spoken of by Virgil (*Æneid*, vi. 237) and Lucretius (vi. 740), and described by Maximus Tyrius (*Diss.*, 14. 2)."

In the same way other spiritistic phenomena — such as prediction of the future, typtology, incombustibility, levitation, immediate healing, xenoglossia, or "the gift of tongues" — we find duplicated in ancient times; for instance, among the Etruscans, and at the time of the Emperor Valens (emperor of the East), who put to death a certain Asiatic medium of Antioch who had typtologically predicted who should be his successor.[1]

[1] And also took occasion to execute any other magicians and necromancers on whom he could lay his hands. — *Translator.*

If we come down now to the Middle Ages and to Christianity, "Who can tell me," continues Brofferio, "how many souls have come from Purgatory to torment mortal men?" And, on the other hand, referring to "blessed spirits," Benedict XIV says (*De Serv. Dei Beat.*, iv. 1. 32. 5), "Innumera sunt apparitionum exempla, quibus sancti se eternam consecutos fuisse felicitatem ostenderunt" ("Innumerable are the instances of apparitions by which the saints have shown that they have attained to eternal happiness"). Furthermore, it will be remembered that St. Francis, St. Theresa, and St. Agnes gave proof of possessing the power of levitation.

Needless to say, many in modern times also have believed in spiritism and the apparition of phantasms, even before Swedenborg, and in our time, also, before the famous occurrences that took place in the Fox family at Hydeville, New York, in 1848, and from which modern Spiritualism dates. Kiesewetter gives us an accurate list of those who have written about it (between six and seven hundred). Wallace, in Chambers's Cyclopedia (1892), refers to the following: "The long series of disorders and noises that took place in the old hall at Woodstock in 1649; those that happened to M. Mompesson at Redworth, in 1661; those of Epworth, in 1716, in the family of Wesley, father of the founder of Methodism; the ghost of Cock Lane (case examined by Dr. Samuel Johnson, Bishop Percy, and other gentlemen); the extraordinary facts in the case of M. Jobson, in Sunderland, in 1839, which were studied and published by Dr. Clanny, member of the Royal Society, and certified as authentic by sixteen witnesses, among whom five were doctors and surgeons; and many less important occurrences referred to in the works of William Howitt, Robert Dale Owen, Dr. Eugene Crowell, and others."

Wallace cites only English examples, and knows nothing of those narrated by Du Prel, Perty, Jung Stilling, and a whole phalanx of German writers of this day, whose names the reader will find in the catalogue of Siegismund.

Certain persons wished to present before Lodovico, the Moor, a youth through whose mediation the spirits became visible, looking at men face to face. John Bee, the famous mathematician and astronomer at the Court of Queen Elizabeth, held a long series of spiritistic séances with the medium Kelley, and preserved reports of them, published in that day by Casaubon (1659). Cardano and Benvenuto Cellini possessed the mediumistic faculty. The former affirmed that he had spoken with the elemental spirits; the latter admits in the second book of his autobiography that he called up malignant spirits.

Finally, in the phenomenon of the doubling of the personality; in the levitation of sorcerers and

their power to act at a distance; in the divining-
rod (noticed as early as the time of Paracelsus
and of Agricola by those scholars, practically
operated by the married couple Beausoleil in
1635, procuring the discovery of 150 mineral
veins, being employed by Breton in 1690, by Pa-
rauguet in 1760, by the abbot Daramel, — who
in twenty-five years revealed by its aid 10,275
springs of water, — and by Ajmar, to whom it
revealed both springs and robbers), — in these
things, I say, and in the epidemic convulsionaries
of Louviers and of Loudun, who speak in strange
tongues (Turkish, Arabic, Hebrew), predict the
future and practise clairvoyance; in the phenomenon of the Camisard infants' prophesyings, and
the existence of invulnerability and incombustibility among certain of the Camisard adults; in
the phenomenon of the Quakers' inner light, and
the convulsionary Jansenists of the cemetery of
Saint-Médard, — in all these things we have rep-
resentations in quasi-modern times, of the same
phenomena that the spirits produce in the séance
cabinets of our latest psychics.

CHAPTER IX

Identity

MORSELLI is in error when he affirms that all the spirits that have revealed themselves up to the present time are either of obscure identity or hiding under a pseudonym, just for the reason that they are the creation of the medium. But take the case of the most important of all: it is certain that "Pelham" was Robinson; and "Katie King" was Miss Annie Owen Morgan. It is a fact that many dislike to reveal their name, just as did Morselli's own mother, and disguise their identity under the cloak of a pseudonym; but in intimate conversation, after figuring in many séances as "Imperator" or "Rector," they end by revealing themselves in their proper identity.

It must be confessed that to fix the identity of phantasmal personalities amid the labyrinth of tricks, confusions, and errors of speech (errors, as we shall see, often involuntary) and to separate the part played by the subconsciousness of the séance psychic and of the experimenters, is often a difficult thing; but there are cases in which it can be done. For example, the communications of Pelham have all the air of certainty.

Pelham belonged to a prominent family in the

United States, had studied law, but had afterwards given his whole time to literature and philosophy, and had published two excellent philosophical works. He had taken a great interest in psychical research, and had had many lively controversies with Hodgson on the survival of the soul, in which he did not believe, and had promised Hodgson that after death, if he could, he would try to communicate with him.

He was acquainted with the power of the Boston psychic, Mrs. Piper, having been present at some of her séances. In February of 1892 he had a fall from his horse which caused his death, he being still quite young. On March 12 he revealed himself to Mrs. Piper by automatic writing, his " guide," or spirit-control, being " Phinuit," who at first tried to stand in his way, but afterwards agreed to submit himself to his rule.[1]

Out of one hundred and fifty-six persons who frequented Mrs. Piper's meetings Pelham recognized thirty as friends of his, and had talks with each, alluding to their past and to their relations together before his death, of which Mrs. Piper could certainly have had no knowledge, nor could she get it from the subconsciousness of those present. They therefore prove Pelham's personal identity.

Thus he asked Howard if he was not occupied

[1] J. H. Hyslop, *Science and a Future Life*. Boston: Small, Maynard & Company.

in writing on the immortality of the soul, and said to him, " I will solve the problems, Katherine." This sentence would not be understood by any one who did not know that years before a young girl named Katherine Howard had been discussing space and eternity with him, and he had remarked to her, " I will solve these problems, Katherine." To Miss Vance, member of a society for mutual improvement in writing, he asked, " Who corrects your productions now that I am no longer there? " and spoke to her of her brother, who had been his classmate at college, and of her summer residence that had a vine on one side and a swing on the other. He recognized John Hart's sleeve-buttons as his own, which he had given him before he died. " My mother took them from a small box," he added, and " gave them to my father, who sent them to you." Seeing a photograph, he remarked, " It is your summer residence, but there is an outbuilding lacking." In fact, a hen-house did not appear in the photograph. He asked Evelina, daughter of Howard, about a book he had given her, containing a dedication. Remembering that he had taken her to task for her mathematical incapacity, he said, " I will not plague you any more to-day; but would you be able to tell us how much $2 + 2$ is? "

They placed before him the first lines of the Lord's Prayer in Greek, and after long perturbation of mind he translated them (with the exception of one line), although he had to call Stainton Moses to his assistance.

Now Mrs. Piper does not know a word of Greek; and, if she had read it in the thought of any one present, she would have been able to translate the whole and not a part merely. I may add that an Hawaiian woman appeared to Mrs. Piper in her trance, and gave replies in three or four words in the Hawaiian language, a tongue which nobody present understood. This is sufficient answer to the objection urged by some that the psychic gets from the subconsciousness of her company the ideas and facts she lacks.

Nor are these the only proofs of the identity of the departed that have been obtained through the intervention of Mrs. Piper by Hyslop, Lodge, and others.

One day Mr. Lodge asked that his deceased uncle " Jerry " communicate with Mrs. Piper, and reveal some incident in his life; whereupon the uncle replied: " We were in a boat that upset, and we had to swim to shore. Ask your brother Robert about it." No one knew anything about the matter, — neither Mr. Lodge nor Mrs. Piper; hence telepathy and cryptomnesia must be excluded. But Robert, on being asked, remembered that they really had been in danger of drowning, not because the boat had been overturned (case of the usual errors of the spirits), but because after they had got out of the boat they began to box and fell into the water. Now all the sitters were ignorant of this thing. Jerry also remembered that his brother Frank when he was a lad had once climbed onto the roof of a shed or barn and hidden himself there; for he had been striking a boy named John, and had been threatened with punishment by his father, but had escaped him. All this turned out to be true, but no one present remembered it.

Another proof of psychic identity is furnished by the communication of Mr. Hyslop's father, Robert. This gentleman had died in 1896. He had led a very retired life, being a sufferer from apoplexy, locomotor-ataxy, and from a cancer in the throat from which he afterwards died, and for thirty-five years he had not removed from the remote farmhouse where he was born. Religious, parsimonious, narrow-minded, he was accustomed to use in his speech a good many old saws and adages, which, it seems, he still employed in the other world: "Don't worry, it does n't pay"; "When you have n't got what you want, learn to do without it, and don't worry."

Up to this point the psychic could have got her material from the minds of the company. But one day she uttered these words: "How is Tom?" The allusion was to a horse that had died many years ago, and about which the son, Dr. James Hyslop, knew no more than that, so that he was obliged to make an inquiry in order to be able to explain the question. Robert also asked where a black skull-cap was which he had used sometimes. The son knew nothing about it (he was the son of the first wife), but his step-mother authenticated the reference, and confirmed the existence of a round bottle and a square block which he had kept in a drawer in his table, and to which he was continually recurring in his talks. " Do you remember the little black pen-knife with which I used to cut my nails and then put into my vest-pocket? " The son knew nothing of this, either; but the stepmother, on being asked, remembered it perfectly; " only he used to put it into his trousers' pocket and not his vest-pocket." He spoke of one son who did not amount to much, but again said in way of recommendation, " Don't worry." He recalled a Calvinistic preacher with whom he used to hold discussions on the future life.

He said to the son, " You had ideas of your own, which belonged to you alone." This was a stereotyped remark of his when living. He died of cancer in the throat; but, with the usual error of the spirits, he said to the son that he suffered from disease of the stomach, liver, and head, but, above all, of the heart. " It seemed to me that the stricture was so painful that I should choke; but I dropped asleep." It was ascertained that dyspnœa supervened when the beating of the heart was almost imperceptible, — which shows that even in the last moments of the death-struggle there may be consciousness.

He went on to speak of a hedge that he wanted to repair, and of taxes he had not paid before he died. The same foolish trifles, little errors, instances of lack of precision, which are constantly observed in the speech of mediums and their guides, or controls, whether they appear in Stainton Moses, Madame D'Espérance, or Mrs. Piper, are really a proof of identity, since they are a peculiar characteristic of them all (see next chapter), being, in fact, just what we might expect, since we are concerned, not with complete organisms, but fragments, which at best think and feel as we think and feel in dreams, and which, if they were of weak mind when living, we should expect to be so much the more so after death.

More important, both for personal authority and for the nature of the facts, are the observations of Stainton Moses (*Spirit Teaching*) which we have already presented, in Chapter VI, and others of which we now proceed to take note.

" One day," he writes, " there appeared to me a spirit who said he was Dr. Dee, once chemist and alchemist, lecturer at the University of Paris at the time of Queen Elizabeth, who visited him at Mortlake, where he died." All of which was found to be true by Moses in unpublished manu-

scripts at the British Museum. Another of his
communicators, a certain Zachariah Gray, said
he had been an ecclesiastic, and that he had written at Cambridge, in 1728, *The Immoral Hudi-
bras*. He wrote in a curious chirography which
could be and was proved to be authentic by comparing it with manuscripts preserved in the British Museum.

The foregoing well-established cases help us to
believe in other cases less well authenticated. For
instance, we read that Halle received at the rooms
of the medium Home a message from the daughter of Robert Chambers. When asked to give a
proof of her identity, she said, " Papa, my love,"
which were, in fact, the last words she uttered
before dying.

Knox communicated to Owen. He had been
dead three years, and when alive had promised
Owen, who did not believe in the soul, that if he
continued to exist after the death of the body he
would send him a message. Of this the medium
knew nothing.

Mori communicated to X a series of accidents
that had happened to him in the Far West, and
which his brother alone, living four hundred
miles distant, could possibly know.

The spirit of F. asked Barrett to bring him a
certain thing from his house. Barrett went into
the trance state, and presently there appeared on
his table the photograph of a daughter of his.

The photograph was in an album in a locked box of a bolted room.

A gentleman named Dowe had a son who was a ship's doctor and had died at sea. The captain of the ship sent the father twenty-two pounds sterling, together with a watch, both the property of the son. Now the spirit of the son appeared in a séance and said that he had been poisoned with the essence of bitter almonds, mixed (instead of mint) in the castor oil that had been prescribed for him, and that he had left seventy pounds sterling, and not twenty-two. The truth of the statement was afterwards judicially verified.

In 1857, in New York, a spirit-personality, unknown to everybody, appeared to the medium "Prosper." The spirit said he was E. G. Chamberlain, that he was about one hundred years old, had been a soldier, had eleven children, and had died in 1847 at Point Pleasant, — all of which was found to be true, except only that he was one hundred and four instead of one hundred. (See Aksakoff, *op. cit.*, on similar errors.)

A Baron Koroff, who died in April, 1867, had made a will, but it could not be found. In July of 1867 the spirit of Prince Wittgenstein informed the family, through the mediation of a psychic, of the place where it could be found, and the psychic was ignorant of the fact that the place was not known (Aksakoff, p. 569).

Owen received this communication from " Viola" at Naples: "I promised to remember you after death." She had, in truth, promised it twenty-two years before her death; but she had been dead forty years and no one remembered it, least of all the medium.

At London, in 1874, says Aksakoff (p. 477), a medium had communications from Abram Florentin, who said he had been a New Yorker, had died at the age of eighty-three years, one month, and seventeen days, and was an old soldier of the War of Independence in America. He gave violent wrenches to the table. He said he was happy to be freed from the miseries of life. The truth of all this was verified at Washington, and his widow said he was a violent man and had suffered much before dying.

During a séance with Eusapia, writes Faifofer to me, their friend Mainella was missed. He had remained at Pellestrina. "So Dolci begged 'John' to carry him our greetings. Two days afterwards Mainella came to my house and asked me if two days previously, towards midnight, we had sent John to him; for he had scarcely got into bed when he felt his head being caressed, and, suspecting it might be his friend in the soul-realm, he received confirmation of the fact by three raps on the ceiling."

The death of Querini at Polo in the Orient was announced to Professor Faifofer two months before it was known in Italy.

The death of Carducci was announced to him on the same day. " On the 18th of February, in the evening, our spirit-friends did not at once give us notice of their presence at our sitting, and we waited for them about half an hour. ' Remigio,' on being asked the reason why they had delayed, replied: ' We are all in a state of agitation and confusion here. We have just come from a festival — of grief for you and joy for us. We have been present at the death-bed of Carducci.' " He had died that day and in that very hour, and the news had not yet arrived by the ordinary channels (Faifofer, *op. cit.*).

In Paris a séance table gave by the usual raps the Christian and family name of the spirit who was speaking, and then added that he had been a pharmacist in Quebec, a married man, and that one day he got to doubting whether he had not caused the death of a certain person by a mistake in putting up a prescription, and to brooding over the serious loss that might accrue to him if it was discovered. He confided his suspicion to a friend, who was unable to comfort him, and in the end he went and drowned himself in the St. Lorenzo. The truth of this communication was verified.

Professor Faifofer — who, it is needless to say, is a most sagacious and illustrious investigator of natural and spiritual phenomena — again wrote me as follows:

" Last September I was at Chiusaforte. The

pythoness of the tripod said to me one evening,
'A telegram has come from Turin for you —
from Clelia.' I was not expecting a telegram;
the hour was late, and, thinking if it were not
some practical joke I should receive it in the
morning, I gave no attention to the communication. When the sitting was over, I went down
to the kitchen and there found the postman waiting for me with a telegram.

"I was present," continues Faifofer, "at a few
séances in Chiusaforte, in order to please a certain Signora Elisa Bien—. The signora was not
able to be present at the second séance, in the
course of which the table said to me, 'I loved
Elisa.' When I asked the communicating spirit
to tell me who he was, he refused, and begged me
to say nothing about it to Signora Elisa. But
after much coaxing he said his name was Gucone.
When the signora learned this, she told me that
before she was married (some forty years ago)
this Gucone had been in love with her, but that
through timidity he had not declared himself,
except to a lady friend of hers, under promise of
secrecy. He died soon after."

Here is another case: A certain lady (M. R.)
was asked typtologically by Schin— (who had
seen her only once when she was a young girl) to
tell her cousin Nicola to have nothing more to do
with certain friends of his, for they would get him
into trouble. She hesitated for some time to obey

this injunction, but one day received this further communication from the same S., " It is too late now, and you will be sorry." As a matter of fact, the police arrested Nicola and condemned him as being affiliated with Nihilists.

At a certain séance of the medium Madame Powel certain individuals wrote, unknown to her, the names of deceased persons on small slips of cardboard. One of the company present had begged the spirit of a lady acquaintance of his to prepare one of these for him, and without looking at it he mixed it with the others. Madame Powel pressed it against her forehead, turned pale, and swooned away. Presently she came to, and, lifting herself up, said (it was the spirit of the lady who had written on the cardboard who was speaking through her voice), " Tell Mr. Slavick that it was not accident or suicide that led to her death, but assassination, and it was my husband who committed the deed. What I say can be verified, and the letters will be found that prove it. I am Mrs. Lanor." This was the name written on the cardboard, and mixed with others by a third person who was ignorant of the purport of the writing. It all turned out to be true, and her husband, Lanor, was arrested (Aksakoff, p. 577).

The medium Carven fell into a trance at a public meeting in New York, but, in place of speaking, she kept making signs with her hands.

The communicating spirit was a deaf-mute who was speaking in the language of the deaf-mutes, — something of which the psychic was quite ignorant (Aksakoff, p. 542).

A personality named " Jack " once communicated typtologically that he owed a debt of $35 and some cents and had a credit of $15 with a shoemaker named A. Fact verified.

There was a schoolmaster who used often to feel an impulse to write automatically in the Latin tongue, although he did not know Latin at all. One day while he was footing it away from his native town, he felt his stick tremble in his hand. He relaxed his grasp and gave it free scope, whereupon it traced on the snow the words: " Turn back, your father died this morning. You will meet with R., who will give you information about it." He set out on his return to the village, and met R. on the way, who told him that his father had died by a fall from a barn. Later the schoolmaster fell ill and wrote with a pencil, " Day after to-morrow at three o'clock I shall die." He did die at the hour named (Gibier, *op. cit.*).

Doubtless many of my readers will be astonished to see here cited and gathered together cases that seem almost to lack verisimilitude. But what renders them less doubtful is their mutual adaptation and interrelation, which are such as to make of them a complete and coherent whole.

The case of Miss Laura Edmonds, daughter of Judge Edmonds, is a famous one in the United States. One day when the artist Green introduced to her a Greek gentleman named Evangelis, she began to speak to the latter in Greek, and told him that one of his most intimate friends, brother of Bozzaris, the famous Greek patriot, had just presented himself to her and told her of the death of one of his sons whom he had left in Greece in perfect health. The Greek gentleman, ten days after, received confirmation of the sad news. The same medium announced that she had received messages from a certain Dabiel who had died. Verified. Dabiel had been for five years in an asylum for the insane and no one knew him.

One day, says Myers (*Personality*, p. 282), between eleven o'clock and midnight, Mrs. Dadeson, while still awake, heard herself called by name three times, and saw the form of her mother (who had died sixteen years before) with two babies on her arm. She said to the daughter, "Take care of them, for now they are going to lose their mother." The next day she received the news that her relative had died from the effects of childbirth three months after having given birth to a second son.

Again, a man was found dead far from home, with his clothes covered with mud, and wearing some other cleaner garments which had been substituted for these. As soon as the news reached his home, one of his young daughters fell into a swoon, and, when she came to, she said she had seen the phantasm of her father with clothes on that were not his, and revealed the fact that a sum of money had been sewed into his own clothes. This fact was found to be true. The phantasm, then, had communicated two facts, one of which was known to himself alone, the other to very few.

Twelve similar cases of the appearance of apparitions are collected in *Phantasms of the Living*. Of these, three appeared at the very moment the dying person was hovering between life and death. In the case of the others the probability is that they appeared after death. It seems as if a promise made during life, or some other strong case of emotion, may influence the revenant. At any rate, such cases furnish most accurate proof of identity.

In one instance a consumptive had promised the young lady, his betrothed, to appear to her without frightening her in case he should die. And so he did, indirectly, just after his death, though not to her, but to her sister while she was out driving, and it appeared that he was then on his death-bed, and died two days afterward (Myers, *Personality*, p. 286).

Edwin Russell was on his way to sing bass in the church of St. Luke in San Francisco one Friday, when he fell in the street in an apoplectic fit. Three hours after his death the chapel-master Reeves, who knew nothing of his death, was visited by the ghost of Russell, who held one hand pressed to his forehead and in the other he had a roll of music. It is evident that his last thought had been that he would not be able to get to the meeting, and that in this way he was notifying Reeves of the fact (*Proceedings Soc. Psy. R.*, viii. 214).

It is well to note here the following revelations of Swedenborg, collected by Kant:

Madame Marteville was asked to pay a debt of her deceased husband, whereas she remembered perfectly his having paid it. But, do what she could, she could not find the receipt for the amount paid, and this of course was the only thing that would free her from the annoyance. In the mean time, actuated by no other motive than the wish to see close at hand the Swedenborg who had become so famous for his relations with the invisible world, she betook herself to him. On being asked by Madame Marteville if he had known her husband, Swedenborg replied that he had never seen him, because he had lived in London the whole time the deceased was in Stockholm. Eight days afterwards the spirit of her dead husband (a Hollander) appeared to her in a dream, and showed her where she would find a casket of finest workmanship, in which she would not only discover the receipt for which she had made so many hunts in vain, but also a magnificent pin of great value, adorned with twenty brilliants, which she believed to be also lost. She immediately got out of bed, lit the lamp, and ran to the place indicated by her husband. There, to her immense surprise, she found the casket, opened it, and found in it the receipt and the pin. Jubilant at having found it, she went to bed again, and did not rise till nine in the morning. She was hardly awake when her maid entered in haste to announce a visit from Swedenborg. As soon as he came in, and without knowing anything of the dream the lady had had, he told her that during the night he had conversed with many spirits, and among others with that of her deceased husband, with whom he would have liked to converse longer, but the spirit said he must visit his wife in order to reveal to her the whereabouts of a paper that was of the highest importance to her, and of a diamond breastpin that she thought lost. Swedenborg had called on the lady for the sole purpose of learning whether the spirit of her husband had appeared to her and whether he had actually afforded her the information of which he had spoken.

For proofs of the identity of phantasmal apparitions take the case referred to by Robert Dale Owen (*Crit. Exam. Existence Supernat.*). It appears that on October 15, 1895, at nine o'clock A. M., while Captain Sherbrooke and Lieu-

tenant Wynyard, both of the Twenty-third Regi-
ment, at Sydney, were drinking their coffee in
their dining-room, they perceived the figure of
a young man that passed slowly into the bed-
chamber. Wynyard suddenly exclaimed, " Great
God! it's my brother John!" Sherbrooke, who
did not know him, scenting possible fraud, taking
a lieutenant with him, investigated every room,
but found nothing. Finally there came a message, announcing to Wynyard the death of his
brother, which took place on the day and in the
hour when they saw him. But there is more to
be said: Sherbrooke, who had never known John
Wynyard, recognized in England another brother
by his resemblance to the phantasm that appeared before him at Sydney. The evidence is
here derived from the circumstance that the same
apparition was perceived by two persons, one of
whom did not know the personality that appeared.

Perhaps the case of the widow Wheatcroft
speaks with still greater force. This lady, on
the night of the 14th of November, 1857, at Cambridge, England, saw in a dream her husband in
his uniform, but with his hair in disorder, face
pale, his hands pressed against his breast, and on
his countenance an expression of deep emotion.
He tried to speak, but was unable to do so, though
remaining visible about a minute. She related
the event next day to her mother, and after some
time received a telegram announcing the death

of her husband as having taken place at Lucknow, in India, on the 15th of November. She told her solicitor Wilkinson that the date of the death in the official communication was certainly an error, that it must have occurred on the 14th, when she had seen the apparition. Now it is a singular thing that, a few days afterwards, the solicitor met with a noted medium (a woman) who said to him that she had seen at nine o'clock on the evening of the 14th of November the spectral apparition of a captain, who said he had been killed in India on that day afternoon. After new official investigation it turned out that he had indeed been killed in the afternoon of the 14th by the explosion of a bomb. Here, then, we have the case of an apparition presenting itself to the consciousness of two women, distant the one from the other, and the dates of the day and the hour of the two appearances and of the death were verified by a third person, and all coincided perfectly.

The medium Mansfield said to one of those present at one of his séances, " Wolfe, did you know in Columbia a man named Jacobs? " Wolfe said he did, and the medium continued, " He is here and wishes to let you know that to-day his soul was separated from his body." Fact verified. Here something was told that no one knew, — and it was not learned telepathically, because the medium did not know the dead man.

Another case. A séance table around which were seated four or five persons gave token by its movements of the presence of a spirit. "Who are you?" The table replied, by alphabetical taps, "Ben Walker." One of the sitters — not the medium — knew this name and asked, "Ben Walker of St. Louis?" "Yes." "I did not know that you were dead. When did you die?" The table rapped three times. "Do you mean that you died three days ago?" "Yes." (Truth of the statements verified by the questioner.)

Sometimes the departed have revealed the whereabouts of objects laid away or hidden by them when living. Brofferio cites certain cases in which a dream revealed where would be found a receipt that had been anxiously sought for. A case of this kind is related by St. Augustine (*De Cura pro Mortuis Gerenda*, c. ii.); another by Ernesti (*Opuscula Orat.*, ix.); another by Dr. Kerner (*Blätter aus Prevorst*, v. 75); and others by Perty (*Die mystischen Erscheinungen*, ii. 392); as well as that classic story of Dante's son to whom the father revealed where he had laid away the thirteenth canto of the *Paradiso*.

The most curious is that reported by Macnish in his *Philosophy of Sleep*, p. 81. It appears that Mr. R., of Bowland, was called into court to compel him to pay a sum of money that his father had already paid and that he was asked to pay again. He sought for the receipt in vain among the papers relating to the succession of the estate. The evening before the day fixed for the payment of the money having come, it was decided to pay on the morrow. But that night Mr. R. had no sooner got asleep than his father appeared to him and said: "The papers relative to this matter are in the hands of M., who has now retired from business and lives in Inveresk, near Edinburgh. I have recourse to him in this matter, although he never had charge of my affairs. If he has no recollection of it, recall to his mind that there was a little difference of opinion between us relative to the exchange of a piece of Portuguese money, and that we agreed to drink the difference at the tavern." Mr. R. thereupon went to Inveresk before going to Edinburgh, found the attorney, who had grown very old, and had forgotten the whole thing. But the incident of the piece of gold recalled the past to his mind; he found the papers and thus gained the case.

Brofferio was privately informed of the phantasm of a deceased lady who, through the intervention of a medium *a trasfigurazione*,[1] appeared unexpectedly to a certain individual, revealing to him in what place she had hidden, several years previously, her letters and her portrait.

But there are also communications in the

---

[1] That is, as I understand it, a psychic who has the power of evoking a phantasm and materializing it out of his own corporeal substance. — *Translator*.

nature of verifiable matters relating to persons
dead centuries before, — matters which on account of their small importance could not have
been preserved either by history or by tradition.
I find an instance of this kind in a communication
made to a descendant of Sebastian Bach by an
Italian musician named Baldassarini, who lived
at the court of Henry III of France, — a communication too long to give here, but which the
reader will find in the book of Delanne (*Le Spiritisme devant la Science*, pp. 399 *et seq.*). It is
sufficient to say here that the particulars of this
communication, in which Bach had no interest,
were found to be true solely by means of a small
strip of paper, found inside a spinet of 1664, and
having inscribed on it four lines of verse in the
handwriting of Henry III. The authenticity of
the king's writing was proved by comparing the
strip of paper with manuscripts of his existing in
the Imperial Library. In this case there could
not be telepathy, not even of an accidental kind;
nor clairvoyance, not even that directed by unconscious interest, not even by curiosity, since it
was not a case of mediumistic experiment, but of
voluntary communication.

Many of these occurrences, when considered
alone, may give rise to doubt, but viewed in the
ensemble they become a solid reality and certainty, — a certainty which arises from seeing
life incidents revealed, small in themselves and

unknown to everybody, but of supreme interest
nevertheless, not to speak of the revelation of the
whereabouts of hidden objects and of the complete
identity of writings of the form of which the
psychic was absolutely ignorant, the case being
frequently one of writings of several centuries
previous, etc.

There are certain typtological communications
that also furnish proofs of identity, the form of
the dialogue often fragmentary and contradictory,
and revealing admirably the tangle and confusion
in the conversation of several persons at once,
and always showing, furthermore, the intellectual status of the individual personality communicating; as, for example, when Statford, asked
with reference to an anatomical question, seeks
aid from the spirit of the eminent English anatomist Willis, not being himself an anatomist, and
when the spirit of the little girl " Nelly " says of
an object in a sealed box that is presented to her:
" The person who put it into the box did not feel
well at that moment. Inanition. Delicate. She
must be nourished. I don't know." Concerning
this curious mélange Mrs. Cartwright says, " Evidently Nelly was repeating the words like a par-
rot; and yet what she said was true, for the subject of this dialogue was anæmic (*Proceed. Soc.
Psy. R.*, xviii. p. 130). And the same Mrs. Cartwright, in another communication to " Pidding-
ton," corrects a communication of the child Nelly

about Bishop Benson, saying: " You ought not to allow her to chatter so. When she does it, you should send her to us."

In these fragmentary dialogues between individuals who correct each other there is such artless testimony that it excludes the idea of fraud and completes the demonstration of identity.

CHAPTER X

Doubles

THE reality of the existence of phantasms, of beings summoned into existence before our eyes in spite of the *date mihi ubi consistam*,[1] seems less paradoxical if we admit, with the ancient Greeks and Romans, the existence of the so-called "double" of the body, — in Greek εἴδωλον, in English *wraith*, in German *Doppelgänger*, in French *double*, — a phenomenon of which the legends of the ancients are full. But they had only a few instances of apparitions[2] and of dreams upon which to form their vague idea of the thing. But we, on the contrary, have a long series of clinical observations and experimental investigations, which, although when looked at one at a time may leave us in doubt, yet by their union acquire, like the stones in a mosaic, a certain appearance of solidity and integration.

---

[1] "Give me a foothold or fulcrum," — allusion to the saying attributed to Archimedes, Δὸς ποῦ στῶ καὶ τὴν γῆν (or τὸν κόσμον) κινήσω, "Give me a fulcrum and I will move the world, or the universe." — *Translator*.

[2] The Church admits the fact in the case of St. Anthony, St. Peter, and many others, and gives it the special name of "bi-location." It is well known that when Rhoda reported the arrival of St. Peter, the friends said, "Are you mad? Don't you know that he is in prison? It must be his angel" [*i.e.* his double]. — *Acts of the Apostles*, xii. 13–15.

The first experimental demonstration of the " double " is recorded in the investigations of Rochas, which are well known, though much disputed. He observed in certain sensitive subjects that not only their motivity (that is, the power of projecting and inciting movement), but their sensitivity itself, — which disappears during the magnetic, hypnotic, and mediumistic sleep, — is prolonged somewhat beyond the limits of the body. A first stratum of sensitivity follows the contour of the body and has a thickness of about an inch and a quarter to an inch and three quarters (3 or 4 centimetres). Around this, separated by intervals of from 6 to 7 centimetres, are other strata which succeed each other up to a distance of from 2 to 3 metres (say from 7 to 10 feet). Continuing the hypnosis still further, these sensitive strata become condensed into two poles of sensitivity, the one on the right and the other on the left of the patient. Finally, these two poles unite, and the sensitivity of the patient is now transferred to a kind of phantasmal enlargement of the body, — what one might liken to the garment on a manikin, and which possesses the power of lengthening itself under the orders of the magnetizer and passing through material objects while still preserving its power of sensation. According to Rochas and Morselli, Eusapia was endowed with this remarkable power. The pricking of a pin was perceived by her at a distance of an

inch and a quarter from her forearm, and about
two and a half inches from the back of her left
hand (Morselli, p. 213).

The existence of these *doubles*, which would
lend themselves so plainly to the explanation of
many mediumistic performances, might be considered proved (if the latter were worthy of complete belief) from the recent experiments of Dar-
ville (*Journal du Magnetisme*, 1907–1908). By
means of " passes " and other magnetic practices
he created a kind of double around two subjects,
Ninette and Martha, whose motivity externalized
itself reciprocally at a distance of several rooms,
in such a way that one struck against the other at
various points of the body, according to the order
given. Furthermore, on continuing the experiments, he saw a true phantasm take shape around
one of his subjects, at a distance of from 20 to
24 inches, and which could be somewhat prolonged. The constituent parts of this double ex-
haled in the form of an effluvium from the forehead, the bregma (or sinciput), the throat, the
epigastrium, and even from the spleen of the
medium. When it was dense, it took on the aspect
of the patient and became more or less luminous.
This double seemed tied to the body by a little
cord which began at the navel or the bregma or
the epigastrium; it had the visual power of seeing
through opaque bodies, and discerned what was
going on at a distance; its apparent organs of

sense took cognizance of taste, sight, touch,
whereas with the true sensory organs the patient
perceived nothing. When the phantasm (or
double) approached, it excited a sensation such
as that produced by cold, by blowing air, or by
shivering. If the hand was placed in the phantasm, you felt a sensation of cold and humidity;
in the dark the fingers appeared luminous. Some
subjects, by means of this double, can produce
raps and blows at a distance, and, like the Spiritualist psychics, open doors and boxes at a distance, and the like.

If the foregoing presentment is admitted to be
fact, it would not be difficult to understand that,
while the psychic activities of the body are dormant during sleep, the body's double might function in its stead and dart swiftly away to far
distant points.

DOUBLES IN SLEEP

Proofs of this, even to the point of experimental verification, seem to have been given to
Dr. Hyslop in a case that happened in a hotel
in Buffalo. One Sunday in the year 1907
D. C. W. S. awoke out of a profound sleep with
the impression of perceiving some one in his bed-
chamber. In fact, being wide awake, he saw his
wife at the foot of the bed in deshabille. He said,
"What are you doing?" She replied, "I came

to see about you," then approached him, embraced him, and disappeared. D. C. W. S. leaped out of bed, found the chamber dark, and lit the gas. In the morning he telegraphed to his wife, who replied, "We are all well." Returning home to New York after a few days, he was struck by the fact that his wife showed great interest in learning whether he had slept well Sunday night. She finally confessed that (having read in Hadeson's *Laws of Physical Phenomena* that if a person, at the moment when he is just about to lose consciousness in sleep, fixes his thought upon another person and desires to present himself before that person under certain conditions, that person will have a vivid and exact impression of the visit) she thought she would make a practical trial of the experiment. So, after she had gone to bed Sunday night, she fixed her thought on appearing to him that night and embracing him. The lady, I may add, tried several times to renew the strange experience, but did not succeed. "I remember," she said, "that I thought very hard and long before I went to sleep, and as long as I was conscious." She noticed, however, that the only thing that did not tally in her first experiment was the hour. She had the idea that the apparition ought to have appeared at eleven o'clock, but instead of that it appeared at seven in the morning (*Jour. Amer. Soc. Phys.*, New York, 1907).

DOUBLES IN TRANCE

We pass now to consider the activity of the double in the trance, or mediumistic, state, whether by the medium's developing a double or by his transferring himself to a distance while in a sleeping or a hypnotic state. Crookes saw the double of Mrs. Fay hand him a book from a distance of eight feet, and that, too, while she was tied to her chair. The daughter of Judge Edmonds could send her double to persons who asked for her. Lewis, the magnetizer, was requested by R. to go to his house and touch the shoulders of two ladies. A messenger was sent to verify the thing. Everybody in the house was found to be in a state of great excitement owing to " a ghost " (the double of Lewis) having, in full light, touched the shoulders of a woman in the kitchen (see Wild, p. 515).

Another case: a man named Bening was to give a lecture at T—. Not being able to send word in time that he could not go, he sent his double. This entity arrived at the club, made the signals agreed upon, said in low tones that he was not coming any more, and, when they were going to stop him while going downstairs, he sent his persecutors about their business with a couple of boxes on the ear, and disappeared. The matter was taken into court, but afterwards dismissed (Aksakoff).

DOUBLES IN THE NORMAL STATE

In Livonia, in 1845, in a girls' *pension* of forty-five pupils, one of the teachers, Madame Sage, was seen at the same time in two places. The two Sages were seated, — one at the blackboard, making a mathematical demonstration with the chalk, while the other had none. On another occasion Madame Sage was in the refectory eating in the presence of all the scholars, while her double stood behind her chair without eating, but imitating all her gestures. One day she was ill in bed with a cold, and a friend of hers, Madame Wrangel, was keeping her company by reading to her from a book, when she was suddenly stupefied with fear to see Madame Sage's double walking about the room.

Another day all the girls were working at their embroidery when they saw Madame Sage in the garden near by gathering flowers, while her double was seated in the hall in a large armchair, silent and motionless. Two girls went up to her and perceived that her body had a gaseous consistency, and little by little it gradually disappeared. Madame Sage, who had at first been working in the garden, remained as if in a state of sleep, and, on being asked, said she had thought of the empty seat and had been in fear lest the children, missing her, would make too much noise. This continued eighteen months, and she was finally dismissed on account of it. When leaving, she said, " This is the nineteenth time I have had to leave for the same reason " (Aksakoff, p. 500).

In the year 1828 Captain R. Bruce, while in his ship, bound for Newfoundland, suddenly saw in the cabin adjoining his a person unknown to him. He rushed out to give notice of it, but when he returned he found no one, but on the blackboard was written, " Steer to the northwest." Since there was no harm in that, he did so, and, as they were going, they discovered a wrecked ship. Boarding her, Captain Bruce found within the person whom he had already seen in his cabin. He was a passenger who had waked up from a profound sleep saying, " We shall be saved," affirming that he saw a ship that would come to their relief. He said he did not remember anything that occurred during his sleep, but that he found nothing to him unfamiliar in the succoring vessel; that he had had, he did not know why, a presentiment of being saved (R. Dale Owen, *Footfalls on the Boundary of Another World*, 1860).

Here is an instance from the life of our friend Eusapia: A nun, a former sweetheart of Signor R., appeared to him some ten times under the influence of Eusapia, kissing him, speaking to him, but always absolutely refusing to have her photograph taken. She was living, and her normal body was asleep during these phantasmal visits. In *Phantasms of the Living* there is a collection of 629 cases of apparitions of the living.

DOUBLES AMONG NEUROTICS

The existence of the double was ascertained in the case of certain neurotics. Pailhas recently observed (*Encephale*, fasc. 2) doubling of the personality after sensorial and peripheral alterations, — for instance, phlegmon (or tumor) and erysipelas.

Following are two cases sequent upon severe hemorrhages which afterwards produced excitements and *cenestesi*, states which were more active owing to the lowered vitality of the patient:

A woman forty years old, after profound hematemesis [1] and insomnia, felt pains in her head and in the right side, in which latter injections of ergotine were made. She would see a part of her body lying on a second bed near hers, and would talk with this second *I*, and wanted the food given to it which was offered to her, saying, " Hand it to her: I am not suffering." Another woman after a severe intestinal hemorrhage had the impression of being double, — that is, of having two bodies. If her right leg was cold, it seemed to her that she had two cold right legs. If she felt a joint move, she believed that she put

---

[1] Vomiting of blood. — *Translator*.

in motion two on the same side. The author
observed two other similar cases in a neuropathic
male patient who was sixty years old and in a
galloping consumption. While this man was
sleeping, he felt the presence of another person
beside him. When he was awake, he believed
that it was his double.

THE WRAITH IN THE NORMAL STATE

Here may be mentioned the case of Goethe,
who, on coming away on horseback from a field
of battle, after experiencing deep emotion, perceived the apparition of his own double riding
along beside him.

George Sand wrote (see *La Revue,* 1908, p.
135) : " I was persuaded that some one was with
me. Not seeing any one, I studied this prodigy
with immense pleasure. I marvelled at hearing
my own name, coming from my own voice. The
strange explanation came to me that I was double,
— that there was another *I* about me that I could
not see, but which always saw me, because it
always replied to me. I told it to come, and it
replied, ' Do thou come.' And it seemed to me
to draw back and to approach when I changed my
position."

We may then say, after a survey of the foregoing strange phenomena, that the existence of
the wraith, or double, is an ascertained fact for
all the more or less anomalous states of the psyche,

and especially in magnetic and hypnotic states. It
further appears that the double has the power to
go to a distance from its partner, and act with
quasi-independence of the proper *I*. Is it not then
probable that this double, just as tradition and
the Greek philosophy assert, remains whole and
perfect, capable of acting after death, standing
for what the ancients called the *anima,* the phantasm of the dead?

The double may furnish an explanation of many
spiritistic phenomena without having recourse to
the spirits of the dead, substituting for these the
action of the medium, — the body of the double, or
a part of it, acting at a certain distance from the
medium's living body, just as this itself would act.
Perhaps to the double belong also those more or
less incomplete limbs which are seen to emerge
from the body (the shoulders or the skirts) of the
medium; so also, perchance, with some of those
floating hands or arms which exactly resemble
those of the medium, so much so that they have
given rise to suspicion of deceit.

The double would also account for the visual
power, and the perception the psychic has as to
whatever takes place in the room in complete
darkness; explains perhaps the strange phenomenon of the transposition of the senses, by virtue
of which a person. sees without the proper eye,
smells with the knee, feels with the nose (see
Chapter I), etc.; and, finally, throws light upon

one of the strangest phenomena of hysteria, which heretofore we have not been able to account for. It may also solve the problem of clairvoyance, and explain the power of seeing through opaque bodies, and the possibility of distinguishing by touch alone metals which externally present no differences whatever, and how the body of a sleeping person can project a counterpart of itself to a great distance.

Finally, as we hinted, the double puts us in the way of comprehending the nature of the spirit of the dead; that is to say, how fluidic bodies (although that expression is not exact) can exist, and show, at least for a time, all the living faculties of the material body. The double, then, may be considered as the binding link between the psychic and the spirit of the dead; but the action of the latter becomes more exclusive when it appears as a true phantasm apart from the psychic, and when those arms and hands appear which have form and volume different from hers, and when there also appear actions such as the perception of the future, pneumatography, and writing made with a pencil between two slates without the direct intervention of any hand and exhibiting the special handwriting of the deceased, — forms of energy which the medium cannot possess, and which are hence due either to the phantasm alone or to the union of that with the medium.

17

CHAPTER XI

Transcendental Photographs and Plastiques

THE reality of the existence of phantasms and proof that they are not a subjective hallucinatory phenomenon are also afforded us by the so-called spirit photographs.

In March, 1861, Mr. Mumler, head engraver in the firm of Bigelow, Kennard & Co. (jewellers in Boston, Massachusetts), employed his leisure hours in making photographs. One day he detected on one of his proofs a figure that did not belong to the group he was developing. He concluded from this that the plate must have received a previous impression, and that it must have been put by mistake among the new plates. But a second proof gave the same result, with an even more distinct appearance of a human form. It is probable that Mumler had obtained the first spirit photograph.

The report of the wonderful thing spread rapidly, and very soon the unfortunate amateur was besieged by questions coming from every quarter. In order to satisfy the curiosity of people he was obliged to give two hours every day to this new branch of experimentation. Finally, his clientèle became so large that he had to give up his business as an engraver. Eminent persons posed before his camera incognito, and it was only afterwards that Mumler came sometimes to know them. It appears that the photographer agreed to all the conditions that his visitors exacted in the way of control, or verification.

The forms that appeared in the picture were, if I am well informed, those of personalities the recollection of whom was occupying the mind of the person who was posing.

Presently the eminent Boston photographer Black, inventor of the nitrate of silver bath, began to investigate Mumler's methods. Through the mediation of a friend who had just obtained proof of a phantasm, Mr. Black offered $50 to Mumler if he would agree to do his work in his presence. The offer was accepted, and Mr. Black made it a duty to examine with the most scrupulous and critical accuracy the objective, the plates, receptacles, and baths. He never once took his eyes from the plate during its preliminary preparation, and carried it himself into the dark chamber. Proceeding to develop it there, to his astonishment he saw a spectral form on the plate in the form of a man leaning on the shoulder of his friend. He carried away the negative and was so overwhelmed with amazement that he forgot at the time to pay his colleague.

In consequence of this authentification of his work Mumler was encouraged to continue his demonstrations publicly, and for this purpose opened a gallery in New York, where he succeeded in convincing his fellow-photographers Silver, Gurney, etc. Furthermore, he never refused to take his pictures in their own studios with their apparatus and their plates. The results were always the same.

But one day Mumler was arrested in New York on accusation of sorcery and fraud. His prosecutors were clamorous, but his friends brought many testimonials and he was released.

Many at that time tried to imitate Mumler, with greater or less success. With us in Europe, John Beathie, of Clifton (Bristol), was eminent among them all for the constancy of his devotion. He was a man of proved honor and highly skilled in photographic matters. It was his desire to have the most complete verification, and by way of precaution he made his experiments in the laboratory of a fellow-photographer named Josty, and employed an approved medium, Yutland. Nothing was obtained from the first seventeen poses, but in the eighteenth appeared a cloudy shape in the human form, and Beathie was encouraged to continue his trials.

In subsequent sittings they got nebulous images, which by degrees grew more and more distinct as they proceeded in their experiments.

FIG. 51. SPIRIT PHOTOGRAPH OF A WOMAN BURIED IN THE WALLS
OF CIVITÀ VECCHIA (WHICH ALSO APPEAR IN THE PICTURE).

At first appeared stars, or a cone superimposed on another shorter cone; then a cone in the shape of a bottle; then a star; next a luminous streak and a kind of luminous flying bird; finally a human figure.

The medium would indicate what kind of an image was to be formed before it appeared, and then it would materialize, appearing always first upon his forehead or on his face. The images appeared on the plates with much greater rapidity than in the case of normal images, and also in a light which would not serve for ordinary plates (*Psychische Studien*, p. 389).

Here also, as in other tests, it is evident that we are dealing with a substance invisible to the eye, and one that is self-luminous, and which reflects upon photographic plates rays of light to the action of which our retina is insensible, and which is formed in the presence of certain mediums, or psychics, and has such photo-chemical energy as to enforce the development of its own image before other images, and also has a progressive development. Thus in the first pose there is a star; in a second pose the star is transformed into a sun; in a third the sun is enlarged; in the fourth the sun is still larger, and out of it a human head unlimns — which proves the operant force of an intelligence that shapes these nebulous forms at will, as the artist shapes the clay.

Guppy, Reeves, Russell, Slater, Wagner, had the same success. Slater, who was an optician and at the same time a skilled photographer, and possessed the mediumistic power, obtained the portrait of his sister, on one side of which appeared the head of Lord Brougham, and on the other that of his friend Owen, who had said while living that if the other world existed he would appear to him. In general these phantasmal portraits do not appear in full length, but only as half-lengths, or at the most as far as the knees.

The publisher Dowe had among his employees a young woman who died at the age of twenty-seven and to whom he was much attached. Seven days after her death a psychic told him that a beautiful girl wished to see him, and that she held a rose in her hand for him. A month afterwards, at Saratoga, he made the acquaintance of another psychic, who never had seen him before. As soon as she had touched him she wrote on the slate, " I am always with you," in the handwriting of the girl. " On my return to Boston," he writes, " I paid a visit to the medium Hardy, and by her aid obtained the apparition of my friend, who told me she had given me proofs of her identity at Saratoga, that she was always near me, and that she wanted to give me her portrait, asking me to go to Mumler, the spirit photographer. I did so, but announced myself under the name of Johnson. My friend appeared and said to me, ' How are

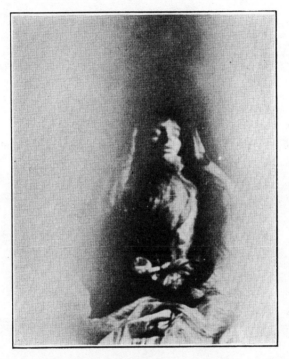

FIG. 52. SPIRIT PHOTOGRAPH OF BEBELLA.

you, Johnson? I never knew before that you were
ashamed of your name.'

" From the first two poses by Mumler nothing
was obtained. At the third, during which Mrs.
Mumler went into the trance state, my friend appeared and said to me, ' I shall be near you with
my hand on your shoulder, and upon my head a
crown of flowers.' I obtained the portrait precisely as she had described."

The foregoing is the case of one who was in
fact a sceptic as to spirits and distrusted the photograph. I selected this from among the photographs of Mumler, because, inasmuch as legal
proceedings were instituted against him, I wished
to exclude those that were not very thoroughly
substantiated by documentary evidence and that
were secured when doubts about him were most
rife.

The photographer Hartmann obtained similar
pictures, and, having been accused of trickery,
succeeded in getting a committee from among his
adversaries to be present at his experiments and
to take part therein.

What is most significant is the fact that these
photographs not only continued to be made in
spite of the noisy suits brought against the photographers, but that they still continue to be produced and are more and more diffused, even at
this day.

Take, for instance, the case of the girl Randone, a medium. On the 10th of September, 1901, Carreras found the girl Randone, fourteen years old, in a state of trance. Her brother observed the phantasm of a woman whose form partly hid that of his sister. Photographic apparatus being at hand, a picture was taken, and the developed plate showed not only the psychic, Randone, but the form of a girl wrapped in a veil, with abundant hair falling to her knees, and on the face the pallor and expression of death. Through the medium she said her name was Bebella, and that she was there to have her photograph taken. In November, 1901, the photographer Benedetto took the pictures of the Randones and of Signor Bettini by magnesium light. When the plates were developed, besides the figures of these persons there was seen a series of luminous and transparent bands (see Fig. 5, p. 16, *Luce ed Ombra*, Jan. 1, 1902).

A few years ago Carreras, in *Luce ed Ombra* (1904, fasc. 1), gave some account of the two Randones (brother and sister), who are unprofessional mediums, unpaid, and of spotless honesty. Through them he obtained some very curious spirit photographs. Carreras had gone to the rooms of Signora Mazza, a neighbor of theirs, and had found there Signorina Randone not feeling very well. For this reason she begged him not to go to his office, but to stay and take part in a séance. Her brother Filippo, also feeling

indisposed, did not go to his office, and indeed exhibited that abnormal condition which is the fore-
runner of trance.   They retired to their flat, and
Signora Mazza, who had concealed a photographic camera in a wardrobe, went to fetch it.
Not finding it, she went down to ask the two Randones about it.   She knocked and knocked, but
could get no answer; nothing but this communication by raps on the wall: " Photograph and
silence."   Half an hour later they went down to
their room and found the two mediums asleep and
amnestic,[1] Signorina Urania pale, livid, and
groaning.   Being with difficulty awakened, she
could render account of nothing.   Her brother,
still in the trance, spoke in the name of a spirit
named Cesare (who was often in the habit of
visiting him), and who now said he had brought
on the indisposition of the mediums to make them
stay at home for the photographic séance, and
that he had got one picture that was certainly
good, that of Bebella, and another that had not
turned out well.

The camera was placed on a table and pointed
toward Signorina Randone.   The phantasm obtained had facial features completely different
from those of the medium and showing that look
of the last death-agony that characterizes the bas-
reliefs of Eusapia Paladino's face.   The plates

---

[1] Dissociated from their own personalities and their own past. —
Translator.

in the camera had been placed there some days before by Signora Mazza, who had bought them of a photographer. There had been no camera in the rooms of the two mediums and there had been no one there during the time that the camera had been there. In the lower left-hand corner of one of the accompanying photographs (Fig. 53) the reader will observe a folded arm with sleeve showing straight lines. It is the arm of the medium while she was in trance close to the phantasm.

On another day the young man Randone obtained two photographs of the two ladies at a distance respectively of three and four feet (Fig. 3, *Luce ed Ombra*).

On the basis of the latest studies of Taylor and of Rochas (*Photog. Registra. of Spirit. Beings, " Luce ed Ombra,"* 1908, fasc. 9), spirit photographs are classified in the following categories:

1. Portraits of spirits of the departed, and various limnings of flowers, lights, and crowns, foreign to the thought of the medium and of the operators of the camera.

2. Objects which seem like statues, either sketches or pictures, reproducing mental images, conscious or unconscious, of the medium or of the operators.

3. Spontaneous tokens of intelligence on the part of the spirits of the dead.

Fig. 53. Another Spirit Photograph of Bebella, Trance
Companion of the Girl Psychic Randone.

4. Images of materialized forms that were visible to the persons employed in taking the photographs.

5. Reproductions of the double of living persons, — another proof of the existence of the double.

6. Tests in which only the mediums see certain constant images that are always the same and that no one else sees.

The accompanying photograph, obtained by the aid of the medium Miller, probably comprises three or four of these classes, as well as the luminous radiations that appeared in the Eusapia experiments of which we have spoken when discussing radio-activity.

Another demonstration of transcendental artistic power is furnished by the wonderfully executed sculptures by mediums totally ignorant of the art, and who therefore cannot be their real authors. See, for example, the sculptures obtained by the medium Eusapia in the figures herewith reproduced.

In 1879 the experimenter Denton succeeded in securing imprints in paraffine of a fluidic hand, while the medium (Hardy) was two feet distant from the paraffine. Afterwards he obtained the same when the paraffine was in a box, enclosed in a network covering of iron. The lid of the box was composed of two parts, one of which was closed by a spring-catch and the other by a bolt.

The box was also wrapped in a covering. Madame Hardy faced the box on its narrowest side. After forty minutes animated raps were heard, announcing success. The seals being removed and bolts drawn, a big hand was seen floating upon the cold water.

The sculptor O'Brien declared that scarcely one in twenty of the famous masters of the art could undertake to finish so admirably a hand like that, and perhaps might not succeed at all, " because," said he, " in our art, for the purpose of reproducing objects, we make use of the matrix in different pieces, which afterwards compels us to go to the trouble of chiselling away the roughnesses of the object in order to remove the disconnections made by the seams of juncture."

In 1877 we had the experiments of Reimer with this mysterious plastic art. The medium in this case was covered by a large cloth bag that concealed her head and hands. She was seated in a corner of the room. Her fingers are one centimetre longer and two centimetres larger in circumference than those of the hand produced, although some of the features of her hands — such as the wrinkles of age — appear among those characterizing the sculptured phantasmal hand, which was that of a young woman.

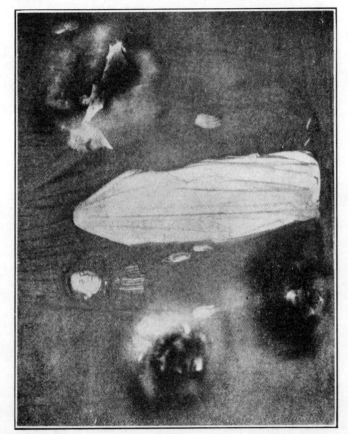

Fig. 54. Spirit Photograph taken by Rochas with the Medium M. A.

CHAPTER XII

Haunted Houses

HAUNTED houses furnish an important factor in the solution of the problem as to the post-mortem activity of the spirits of the departed.

The tradition of the existence of such houses is so ancient and so easily transmissible and infectious that we find words descriptive of the phenomenon in all languages: in German *Spuken*, in English *haunted*, in French *maisons hantées*, in Italian *case spiritate*, or *infestate*, as well as expressions in local dialects.

The proof of the existence of such houses is attested by many court decisions.

During the last days of December, 1867, at No. 14 Ghibellina Street, in Florence, subterranean noises began to be heard, and sudden and startling blows in the table around which the family was seated. Dishes were broken in the cupboards, there were showers of stones, and an invisible hand would press the arms of the inmates of the household, some of whom saw phantasms wearing broad-brimmed hats like those of the Brothers of Misericordia. The tenant haled the proprietor of the house into court to compel the payment of damages, and the court granted the petition on proof of the facts.

In the house in Naples owned by the Baroness Laura Englen, situated in the Largo San Carlo, No. 7, and rented by the Duchess of Castelpoto and her family, very remarkable manifestations took place at stated intervals, increasing to a maximum and then gradually declining. At the beginning there were raps and strange noises which generally grew more intense at the close of the day and at night. A little later the furniture began to be moved about, sometimes so noisily as to attract the attention of the tenants of the floors beneath. Once steps were heard, and a phantasmal form appeared on the threshold of the room and threw down a key. When the tenants left the house at night, on returning they would find the doors obstructed by furniture on the inside. As a consequence they demanded and obtained the refunding of the rent (F. Zingaropoli, *A House haunted by Spirits*, Naples, 1907).

Indeed, even the laws of the ancients made special dispositions for analogous cases (*Digest,* Tit. II. Law 27), just as Spain does now (Porzia and Covarruvio, *Variorum Resol.*, c. 6). And this particular kind of jurisprudence was in force as late as 1889 and after (Troplong, *Delle Perm. e Locaz.*, Cod. di Nap., 1802).

The jurist Dalloz has this to say on the subject:

FIG. 55 a. AUTO-SCULPTURES BY EUSAPIA.

" The question was discussed in the abstract, whether the apparition of spectral forms in an inhabited house constitutes a defect for which the lessor may be held by the lessee. The majority of writers on the subject gave an affirmative answer, and, as a consequence, taught that the lessee had the right to demand a dissolution of the contract."

CASES DUE TO MEDIUMISTIC INFLUENCE

It seems to me that haunted houses may well be divided into two great groups: namely, first, those revealing themselves to be such for a rather limited time (usually a short one), and in which may almost always be detected the operant influence of a medium (these should rather be called " medianic cases ") ; and, second, those in which the phenomenon is permanent and seems to exclude all mediumistic participation. Out of ten haunted houses that I have had the opportunity of examining I found four of this latter description. In one there were mysterious sprinklings of water; the continuous tinkling of little bells, even after the wires had been cut; the levitation of a lady from the floor, drawn up by the hair by an invisible power; the displacement of kitchen utensils, of furniture, and the movement of hats from one point to another even after they had been fastened with nails. The power-centre for all these phenomena resided in an hysterical girl.

As soon as she had married and removed to another city, the phenomena, which had lasted for two years, entirely ceased (*Ann. des Sc. Psych.*, April, 1906).

In another workman's home strange things occurred after midnight, such as the reversing of sheets, blows like cannon-shots, the opening of window-shutters and windows, — all as the immediate result of hospitality offered by the family to a girl affected with hysterical convulsions. By my advice she was sent away, and the phenomena ceased. They had lasted a trifle more than fifteen days.

In a little room on the fourth floor of a certain house inhabited by poor printers with a large family, frightful blows, or " raps," were heard in the wall contiguous to the children's bed. They sounded like a cannonade, beginning about midnight and not ceasing till the dawn of day, and terrifying all the families in the tenement. The investigations and researches of the police made it necessary to exclude altogether the hypothesis of any living thing being the cause of the occurrences. When the spirit that was believed to be at the bottom of the affair was put on the witness stand in a typtological séance, it replied several times, giving name, cognomen, and profession, — all turning out to be false. It affirmed that its object was to be revenged on the master of the house, whereas the house, at the time when the spirit pretended it had died, did not yet exist. There did exist, however, an unconscious medium in the person of a boy of eight years. When he was removed from the house, the uproar ceased; when he returned and went to bed, the phenomena recommenced; they grew weaker when he was ill (*Ann. des Sc. Psych.*, April, 1906).

In a *crèmerie*, or milk-shop, in Turin, similar noises, automatic movements, etc., were caused by a very young medium, six or seven years old, who was the son and grandson of psychics. But these phenomena lasted only eighteen days.

PSEUDO-MEDIUMISTIC CASES

In other cases the influence of the medium is less certain. The following are instances:

On the 16th of November, in Turin, Via Bava, No. 6, in a little inn kept by a man named Fumero, there began to be heard in the daytime, but to a greater extent at night, a series of strange noises. In seeking out the cause, it was found that full or empty wine-bottles had been broken in the wine-cellar. More frequently they would descend from their places and roll along the floor, heaping themselves against the closed door in such a way as to obstruct the entrance when it was opened. In the sleeping-chamber on the upper floor (which communicated by a staircase with the servants' room near the small public room of the inn) gar-

ments were twisted up and some of them transferred themselves downstairs into the room beneath. Two chairs in coming down were broken.
Copper utensils which had been hung upon the
walls of the servants' dining-room fell to the floor
and slid over long reaches of the room, sometimes
getting broken. A spectator put his hat on the
bed of the upper chamber; it disappeared and
was later found in the filth-heap of the courtyard
below.

Careful examination failed to disclose any normal cause for these performances. No help could
be got either from the police or the priest. Nay,
when the latter was performing his office, a huge
bottle full of wine was broken at his very feet.
A vase of flowers that had been brought into the
inn descended safely onto a table from the moulding above the door, where it had been placed.
Two large bottles of rosolio, which they were dis-
tilling, were broken in broad daylight. Five or
six times, even in the presence of the police, a
little staircase-ladder, which leaned against the
wall at one side of the main room of the inn, was
slowly lowered to the floor, yet without hurting
any one. A gun went across the room and was
found on the floor in the opposite corner. Two
bottles came down from a high shelf with some
force. They were not broken, but they bruised
the elbow of a porter, giving him a slight " black-
and-blue spot."

The people kept crowding in to see, and the police during their investigations gave the Fumero family to understand that they suspected them of simulating, so that the poor creatures decided to suffer the annoyance in silence. They even gave out that it had ceased (after an imaginary visit from me), so as to escape at least the guying, if not the damage. I began attentively to study the case.

I made a minute examination of the premises. The rooms were small. Two of them served the purpose of a wine-shop; one was used for a servants' eating-room, and was connected by a small stairway with a bed-chamber above. Lastly, there was a deep wine-cellar, access to which was obtained by means of a long stairway and a passage-way. The people informed me that they noticed that whenever any one entered the cellar the bottles began to be broken. I entered at first in the dark, and, sure enough, I heard the breaking of glasses and the rolling of bottles under my feet. I thereupon lit up the place. The bottles were massed together upon five shelves, one over the other. In the middle of the room was a rude table. I had six lighted candles placed upon this, on the supposition that the spiritistic phenomena would cease in bright light. On the contrary, I saw three empty bottles, which stood upright on the floor, spin along as if twirled by a finger and break to pieces near my table. To avoid a pos-

sible trick I carefully examined, by the light of
a large candle, and touched with my hand all the
full bottles standing on the shelves and ascertained that there were no wires or strings that
might explain the movements. After a few minutes two bottles, then four, and later others on
the second and third shelves separated themselves
from the rest and fell to the floor without any
violent motion, but rather as if they had been
lifted down by some one; and after this descent
rather than fall, six burst upon the wet floor (already drenched with wine), and two remained
intact. A quarter of an hour afterwards three
others from the last compartment fell and were
broken upon the floor. Then I turned to leave
the cellar. As I was on the point of going out,
I heard the breaking of another bottle on the
floor. When the door was shut, all again became
quiet.

I came back on another day. They told me
that the same phenomena occurred with decreas-
ing frequency, adding that a little brass color-
grinder had sprung from one place to another
in the servants' room, and, striking against the
opposite wall, jammed itself out of shape — as
indeed I observed. Two or three chairs had
bounced around with such violence that they were
broken, without, however, hurting any one standing by. A table was also broken.

I asked to see and examine all the people of the

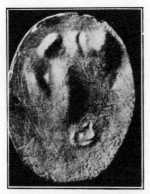
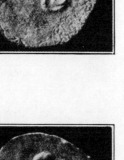
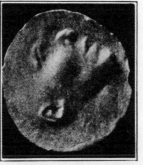

Fig. 55 b.   Auto-sculptures by Eusapia.

house. There was a tall waiter lad of thirteen, apparently normal; another, a head-waiter, also normal. The master of the house was a brave old soldier who from time to time threatened the spirits with his gun. Judging from his flushed face and forced hilarity, I judged him to be somewhat under the influence of alcohol. The mistress of the inn was a little woman of some fifty years, lean and very slender. From infancy up she had been subject to tremors, neuralgia, and nocturnal hallucinations, and had had an operation for hystero-ovariotomy. For all these reasons I counselled the husband to have her leave the premises for three days. She went to Nole, her native town, on the 25th of November, and there suffered from hallucinations, — voices heard at night, movements, persons that no one else saw or heard. But she did not cause any annoying movements of objects. During these three days nothing happened at the inn. But as soon as she got back the performances began again, at first furiously, but afterwards more mildly. The occurrences were always the same, — utensils, chairs, bottles, broken or displaced. Seeing this, I again counselled that the wife absent herself anew, and she did so on November 26.

On the day the woman left (she was in a state of great excitement and had cursed the alleged spirits), all the dishes and bottles that had been placed on the table were broken and fell to the floor. If the family was going to dine, the table had to be prepared in another place and by another woman, because no dish touched by the mistress remained intact. Hence one naturally suspected that she had mediumistic powers, or would have done so had it not been that during her absence *the phenomena were repeated in just the same way*. That is to say (to be specific), a pair of shoes of hers that were in the bed-chamber, on the dressing-cloth, came downstairs in broad daylight (half-past eight in the morning), traversed the servants' room through the air, passed into the common room of the inn, and there fell down at the feet of two customers who were seated at a table. (This was on November 27.) The shoes were replaced on the dressing-cloth and continually watched, but did not move until noon of the next day; and at that hour, when all were at dinner, they disappeared entirely! A week afterwards they were found, with heels to the floor, under the bed of the same chamber.

Another pair of ladies' shoes, placed in the same chamber, on the dressing-cloth, and carefully watched, disappeared, and were found only after the lapse of twenty days (folded up as if they were to be packed in a trunk), between the mattresses of a bed in the same chamber that had been turned upside down in vain *two days after the disappearance*.

When it was seen that the phenomena continued just the same, the woman was recalled from Nole, and they were repeated with the same continuity as before. A bottle of effervescent liquor, for example, in the inn, in full daylight, in the sight of everybody, slowly, as if accompanied by a human hand, passed over a distance of twelve or fifteen feet, as far as the servants' room, the door of which was open, and then fell to the floor and was broken.

After all this it occurred to the host to dismiss the younger of his two waiters. When he left (December 7), all the phenomena ceased. This of course makes one surmise that the motive force emanated from him. Yet he was not an hysteric, and was the cause of no spiritistic occurrences in his new home.

An instance of the exercise of mediumistic power which is somewhat uncertain, owing to the great distance between the medium and the house in which the power was brought to bear, is narrated by Augustus Hare in volume six of his *Story of my Life* (London, G. Allen, 1900, p. 365).[1] It seems that in 1891 a certain Mrs. Butler, who lived in Ireland with her husband, dreamed of finding herself in a very beautiful house, furnished with all imaginable comforts. The dream made a deep impression on her mind,

[1] I am indebted for this case to the courteous and learned Countess of Chanaz, who made an abstract of it for me.

and the following night she again dreamed of the same house and of going over it. And so for many nights in succession, until in the family circle she and her house of dreams became the subject of gentle raillery.

In 1892 the Butlers decided to leave Ireland and take up their residence in England. They went to London and procured from various agencies lists of country houses. Having heard of a house in Hampshire, they went out to see it. At the gate-keeper's lodge Mrs. Butler exclaimed, *"This is the gate-house of my dream!"* And when they reached the house she affirmed the house to be that of her dreams. The woman in charge proceeded to show the premises, and Mrs. Butler said she recognized all the details, except a certain door, which it turned out had been added to the place within six months. The estate being for sale at a very low price, the Butlers suddenly decided to buy it. When the bargain had been made and the money paid over, the price seemed to them so excessively low that they began to suspect there must be some grave defect, and communicated their suspicion to the agent who had sold it to them. He then admitted that the property had the reputation of being haunted, but that Mrs. Butler had no need to pay any attention to that, seeing that she herself was the phantasm that had appeared there!

This would seem to be not so much a case of

the action of a medium as of her double, which, as often happens to a person sleeping, darted over a vast distance from the place where she lay in the deep lethargy of sleep to that on which her thought was intensely concentrated in dream. The case is, however, almost unique.

TRAGIC CASES

On the other hand, in haunted houses which I may call tragic no medium is discoverable, or, at any rate, if found, his or her influence would have to be considered as a permanent thing, lasting often for generations or centuries. Popular legend, and frequently history also, attributes the noises heard and the appearance of spectral forms, often blood-stained and fierce, to scenes of violence that happened on the spot many years or many centuries previous. And in those cases of persons who suffered a violent death in the flower of their age there is noted a greater energy of action and a tendency to continue their former habits and to haunt the place of their burial. The most ancient example is that of the temple of Athena in Sparta, in which the traitorous general Pausanias was immured to die of starvation, and which was afterwards made uninhabitable on account of the terrifying noises produced by his ghost, until it was finally placated by a necromancer, or psychagogue.

It has been calculated that in England there are at least a hundred and fifty haunted halls, abbeys, schools, and hospitals, almost all of which have been in consequence abandoned by their tenants (Ingram, *Haunted Homes, etc., of Great Britain,* 1907).

Edmund L. Swift, Keeper of the Crown Jewels in the Tower of London, one day in the year 1860 saw a phantom bear come out of the room in which the jewels are kept; it is the same in which Anne Boleyn was imprisoned. The sentinel was unable to strike the bear with his halberd, but it dissolved away into the air like melted wax. The sentinel died the next day of the fright he had received (Ingram, *op. cit.*; see the same account in *Notes and Queries,* 1860).

Here belongs also the case of the lady in Scotland who in 1880 had rented an ancient castle, and one night woke up to see at the foot of her bed the image of a man without a head, and dressed in the fashion of two centuries previous. She awoke her husband, who, however, saw nothing. A few days afterward one of the inhabitants of the castle died. It was a tradition in the country roundabout that every time the headless ghost appeared some one in the castle disappeared from this life. The explanation was that at the time of the Civil War of 1660 a proscribed fugitive of the party of the Cavaliers, or Royalists, had asked hospitality of the keeper of the castle, and had been by him betrayed, being delivered by night into the hands of the king's enemies, who soon after beheaded him in the neighboring courtyard.

There can be no question at all in this case of supernormal power exercised by a medium, for it would have had to be perpetuated for three centuries.

" Miss Feilden writes me," says Hare (*op. cit.,* vol. iii. p. 78), " that during her youth her family removed to the Isle of Wight and rented St. Boniface House, between Bonchurch and Ventnor. She was accustomed to sleep in a chamber on the first floor, while the French governess and the other sister, Charlotte, slept in the adjoining room. The English governess had a room on the floor above. One night, while Miss Feilden and her sister were in bed, suddenly the door opened with a great noise and some one came into the chamber, producing a current of air. Then the bed-curtains were whisked up over their heads, and the bed-clothes dragged away. The two sisters leaped out of bed, and at that moment the mattress also was pulled forcibly away. They ran out of the room, crying for help. The English governess came down in haste, and the servants, being called, found things all right in the chamber, — the bed covers folded up and laid in three corners of the room, the mattress leaning against the wall, and the blanket by the fireplace. They found out afterwards that similar things had happened to others there, and that the house had the reputation of being " spooky." A lady had killed her babe in that room. Sometimes her ghost was visible, but usually she manifested her presence only by noise and movement of the furniture.

Glenlee, in Scotland, is a very lonely country house. Some years ago it was occupied by a lady who poisoned her husband to marry a young officer with whom she was in love and with whom she went away to live. He treated her so badly that she finally left him and returned to Glenlee, where she passed her time in sadly wandering through the halls of the house, until, grown old, she died. It is her ghost that was seen there, but which, it is said, ceased to appear after a Catholic tenant of the property had had Mass said in the house.[1]

At another time Mrs. Robert Gladstone was making a visit at the Maxwells', then owners of Glenlee. In the afternoon she went into the room assigned to her to rest, and presently it seemed to her that the space opposite to her was filling with mist. She thought it came from the chimney, but there was neither fire nor smoke there. She looked to see if it could come from the win-

[1] Several of these anecdotes were collected for me by the Countess of Chanaz, who crowned her kindness by interesting for my benefit Prof. Scott Elliott, who obtained direct information about Glenlee from the daughter of Mrs. Maxwell, mistress of the house.

dow, but outside the sun was shining bright. Little by little the mist seemed to take shape, until it became the gray figure of a woman looking at the clock.

Mrs. Gladstone fainted away through terror. When she came to, the figure had disappeared. As soon as she learned that that was a haunted chamber she left the house.

Mrs. Stamford Raffles also went to visit at Glenlee. It was winter. She woke up in the night, and by the light of the fire that was burning in the fireplace she saw the same appearance of mist, which little by little condensed until it formed a human figure that stood looking at the clock. She felt at the same time an intense cold; then fainted from fright after having tried to waken her husband, who was sleeping by her side, — but tried in vain, since her limbs and tongue seemed paralyzed. A little while after the Maxwell family left Glenlee for good.

In this case the phantasm is certainly to be accounted for by the house and the sad events that had occurred there, and not to the presence of mediums. The visitors provoked the appearance of the apparition by entering the room and especially by sleeping there, and not by any mediumistic gifts they might have. And yet the cessation of the phenomenon after the saying of Mass might lead one to regard the whole as the result of suggestion on the part of the living.

PREMONITORY APPARITIONS IN HAUNTED HOUSES

There is another kind of haunted houses which I will classify by the term *premonitory*, — houses in which the apparition appears at long intervals only and always serving as a premonition of the death of some one of the members of the household. Such are the famous White Lady of the Royal Palace in Berlin,[1] the White Lady of Avenel (in Sir Walter Scott's *Monastery*), the Dark Lady of Norfolkshire, and the Gray Lady of Windsor. Perhaps apparitions like these might be explained by that mediumistic power which many persons about to die possess, and which enables them to announce, even to those far off, their approaching end, by means of voices, raps, or the appearance of their double. The dying person would be, in this case, of the nature of a space-traversing medium to awaken the energies of the spirits of the dead attached to certain houses which may be considered as their appurtenance, and to which they are tied by the bonds of long habit.

In his *Story of my Life* (vol. iii. p. 40) Augus-

[1] She appeared in 1589, eight days before the death of the Prince Elector John George, and again in 1619, twenty-three days before the death of Sigismund, and also in 1688. In 1850 she foretold the attempt on the life of Count Frederick William the Fourth, of Prussia (De Vesme, *History of Spiritualism*, vol. ii., Turin). [This White Lady is popularly said to be the ghost of the Countess Agnes of Orlamünde, who murdered her two children.] — *Translator.*

tus Hare tells us that the celebrated Sir David
Brewster once went with his daughter to pay a
visit to the Stirling family at Kippenross in Scotland. In the night he took refuge in his daughter's chamber and asked her permission to remain
there lying on a sofa till morning, so terrified had
he been by the strange lamentations he had heard.
Miss Brewster's maid had also heard strange
noises that night and wanted to leave the house
immediately. In the afternoon Miss Brewster,
while on the way to her room, saw at the head of
the stairs a tall woman leaning against the ban-
isters. She asked this woman to send to her her
maid; but she only nodded her head thrice and
pointed to a door in the hall, then descended the
stairs. Miss Brewster spoke of the matter to
Mrs. Stirling, who was deeply agitated by what
the apparition presaged; for in the chamber to
which it pointed were sleeping Major Wedder-
burn and his wife. Before the year ended both
of them had been killed in the Sepoy Rebellion in
India. The tradition in the house was that who-
ever was pointed out by the ghost died within the
year.

One more instance under this head: In the
castle of Berry-Pomeroy the wife of the major-
domo of the House of Pomeroy had been taken
ill. Dr. Farquhar is called in, finds the disease
of a very light character, and asks the husband
as to the identity of the lady very richly dressed

whom he had met in the ante-chamber. The husband is struck dumb with amazement and fear,
knowing as he does that such a vision has for a
century and more always preceded the death of a
member of the family. His wife died in the night.

CASES IN WHICH NO MEDIUMS APPEAR

In other cases — the majority, in fact — there
is found not even this appearance of mediumistic
influence.

Solovovo (*Ann. des Sc. Psych.*, 1899, p. 173)
tells of a house in Russia occupied by two small
families of the patriarchal order, Kupréyanoff
and Nazaroff. The latter were in the habit of
buying in January and February for the whole
year's use quite stout sticks or chunks of wood,
weighing at least seven pounds each, which were
piled up in a row against the wall of the granary
to the height of twenty-one English feet. At ten
o'clock of a certain evening the family heard a
prodigious thumping and clattering in this wood-
pile. By the light of a lantern and three candles
they saw a stick leap out, not from the top, but
from the middle of the pile and fall on the ground
at a distance of several metres. The same thing
continued for forty minutes, during which
twenty-seven sticks were thrown out, to all appearance self-moved.

A curious feature was that the big hole left by
the departure of these sticks was not filled up

by the remaining sticks until the next day, when the whole mass was found to be compact, without a gap of any kind. The sticks did not fly out from one point, but from many, and always from the centre of the pile, never from the top or the sides. We must exclude the influence of animals and of men, and as a consequence that of mediums.

In a little house near Tedworth Judge Mompreson and his family were annoyed every night as soon as they had gone to bed by the beating of an invisible drum, which sounded ominously in the interior of the house, accompanied by a reeling dance of all the pieces of furniture, which were whirled about by invisible hands. The dogs hid themselves, and the judge himself was compelled to flee the house. It is a curious fact that this drum replied to questions by taps corresponding to the succession of the letters of the alphabet, just as in séance experiments of the present day. And yet it was as far back as 1662.

Dr. Morice (*Ann. des Sc. Psych.*, 1892, vol. iv.) made a careful study of a case occurring in the castle of T., in Normandy. This castle had been in existence since 1835, and was restored and used again as a residence by M. de X. In the month of October, 1867, extraordinary raps, or blows, began to be heard, with movement of tables, etc. They were renewed in 1875, and again more annoyingly in 1892. The castle was already notorious for having been in former days infested by maleficent hobgoblins.

In October, 1875, noises were heard as of steps upon the ground (at that time covered with snow), but no traces of footsteps could be seen. Armchairs and statues changed positions, large articles of furniture were dragged about, rapid steps were heard, and then came five loud raps on the staircase landing. On another day shrill cries, the sound of the galloping of horses in the hall. All this lasted from midnight up to three o'clock. Later the phenomena began to be noticed in the daytime as well. One day the wife of X, wishing to enter a room where the noises were heard, reached out her right hand, and the key leaped out of the lock and struck her on the left hand. Under the influence of exorcisms the nuisance diminished a little, then ceased, but again appeared in 1891. Here again we must exclude the hypothesis of a medium, even that reaching forward through a long extent of time.

Joseph Proctor (*Journ. Soc. Psych. R.*, Dec., 1892) communicated to the society a diary in which he had noted day by day the pranks and prodigies that took place in his father's house. During the indwelling of the first tenant — a certain X — nothing singular was observed. But the house was abandoned by X's successor on account of the strange things that took place in it. No sooner had a certain nurse entered the house than she began to complain of roarings, stampings, clamorous cries, which were heard in the adjoining room. These noises were heard by all the other inmates of the house.

Two months afterward one of the members of the household saw one evening a white form at the window. On another evening the custodian, his wife, and his daughter saw in the same place a priest in white stole. This apparition lasted ten minutes. At intervals during six months the nursery-maids were repeatedly thrown out of bed. Later the servant-maid saw at the foot of her bed the ghost of an old man with his fingers interlocked.

In the month of June a friend who was staying over night as a guest fled from his bed terrified by the sight of phantasms and by frightful noises. Two years passed, and then the inhabitants of the house heard their name pronounced here and there by invisible persons. Many and many a time there appeared before the children, while they were playing, the ghostly form of a nun, or the image of a pale head which vanished with a noise.[1]

After two years the tenants decided to abandon the house. The last night of their stay the noises and apparitions took place with redoubled

[1] One is reminded of the familiar apparition in Scott's *Antiquary* that vanished "with a curious perfume and a melodious twang." — *Translator*.

frequency. In their new home they heard no more noises and saw no more apparitions, as they had done in the ill-omened one they had left behind. On the other hand, those who succeeded them there were so rabidly persecuted by the poltergeists that they also had to give up the house. It was never rented again.

There is in the foregoing cases clearly no trace of mediums, except the influence of the Mass in two instances. To explain the phenomena (which were repeated for many years with different families, who, when they had changed houses, had no more trouble of the kind) we can have recourse only to the direct influence of phantasmal apparitions, which were, indeed, many a time recognized by those of the tenants who had mediumistic powers.

ACTS OF REVENANTS (NECROPHANIC HOUSES)

In other dwellings (which I will call necrophanic) the exclusive sway of the departed is evidenced not only by the appearance of their phantasmal fac-similes, but by their express declarations made in mediumistic séances that they were putting forth their powers (sometimes terrific powers) for such and such ends; for example, in order to inflict punishment for the reoccupation of the house or to revenge the honor of the family, or for moral and religious warning, etc.

Mrs. R., who in October, 1857, and for many many months succeeding that, lived in the manor house of Ramhurst in Kent, was disturbed from the very first day of her occupancy by blows on the walls and by voices that could not be explained and which terrified every one. A certain Miss S., who had been used, from infancy up, to the sight of apparitions (for she was at that time a medium), came to see Mrs. R., and scarcely had she entered the house when she saw at the entrance the forms of a couple of old people dressed in antique fashion, and they reappeared to her every day, surrounded by a kind of aura, or mist. The third time they spoke to her [in the mediumistic language] and said they had once been the proprietors of the house, that their name was " Children " (the old man said his name was Richard and that he had died in 1753), and that they were aggrieved that the castle, so dear to them, was now in the hands of strangers. Mrs. R., to whom Miss S. repeated the communication, continued to perceive voices and noises, but not apparitions, except that a month after, when she was one day about to go down to dinner, she saw in her room (in bright light) the two figures, as her friend S. had described them, and glowing on the wall above the head of the old lady, in phosphoric light, the words *Dame Children*, and some other words indicating that she was " earth-bound."

After a good deal of research Mrs. R. learned from an old lady that many years before she had known an old man who had been assistant keeper of the hounds for certain " Children " who lived then in the manor house. Among them was a Richard who had died in 1753, that is, a century previous. Robert Dale Owen discovered, moreover, in the Hasted Papers in the British Museum and in the History of Kent that a Richard Children had settled at Ramhurst and died there in 1753 at the age of eighty-three; that the family had in the sequel emigrated elsewhere; and that after 1816 the house had become a kind of farmhouse.

In such an instance as this we do not discover mediums as the cause of the phenomena, whereas traces of the activity of the departed, reaching back for a century, are testified to by two persons; and, when by chance a medium comes to the house, the name of the deceased is revealed both in writing and in mediumistic language, and the accuracy of the whole is confirmed by history, or rather by family chronicle (Owen, *Footfalls*, etc., p. 304; quoted in Alfred Russel Wallace's *Miracles*, p. 106).

Count Galateri relates that in 1852 his father, on retiring from the army in Annecy, acquired a villa, in which some years after certain strange events occurred: doors opened of themselves at night, pieces of furniture and boots struck one

against another, etc., so that it was decided to sell
the villa. During the last days of the stay there
the countess, noticing that the noises increased
in frequency and intensity in a small wine-cellar,
and in fact always issued thence, tried the expe-
dient of having excavations made there with a
mattock, and presently the uproar ceased.

In 1864, four years afterward, the two Galateri men saw a newspaper fold itself up automatically and reopen on the table. It was half-past
ten in the evening. At the very same hour, in
another house, the mother of the Galateri family
had been in a mediumistic séance at which her
deceased daughter said to her, "*I am going to
run and give a surprise to papa and brother.*"

In another séance the mother with another
medium affirmed that she saw at the door of the
haunted villa of Annecy, of which I have just
spoken, a soldier with a wooden leg, who confided to her how in a battle fought under Napo-
leon he was accustomed to despoil the dead, so
that he grew rich, and that with his ill-acquired
money he had bought that villa and in its wine-
cellar had hidden his little hoard. But now,
having repented of what he had done, he had
produced all those persistent noises to induce the
countess to search for the treasure in order that
she might distribute it to the poor.

Two years afterward, having returned to her
old home (the Annecy villa), she learned that

the then owners wanted to get rid of it at any cost, owing to the incessant clamor that occurred, notwithstanding the conjurations of the priest. She asked them to remain only two days more, dug in the cellar, and found a vessel containing several thousand francs in gold, which she distributed to the poor; and from that time forward the spiritistic phenomena ceased (*Luce ed Ombra*, Nov., 1905).

Here the action of the deceased seems perfectly evident and independent of any medium, and would find its explanation and proof in the cessation of the spiritistic antics after a wish expressed by the spirit of the dead man had been granted and embodied in a deed.

The same thing may be said of another case set forth by De Vesme in my *Archivio di Psichiatria,* vol. xvii. Crackings of whips, the overturning of articles of furniture, the turning inside out of women's garments, which were unexpectedly discovered to have been removed from boxes and wardrobes, then cut and placed on the window-sill, — such are some of the hobgoblin performances that took place in the house of a certain Fer— in Turin, Via Garibaldi, after the death of his sister, a lady of a very religious turn of mind. These pranks were repeated even out of the house, and wherever Signor Fer— went. They suddenly ceased after a typtological séance at which his sister confessed that she was the

author of all those occurrences, she being irritated at her brother's living illegally with a certain woman. She said that, if he would marry her, every annoyance would cease. And so it proved. Now neither the woman nor Fer— possessed mediumistic powers, and there was no one in the house who was gifted that way. Plainly the activity of the spirit of the departed is here shiningly conspicuous, nay, highly reasonable.

SUMMARY

If, then, there are cases, for the most part of a temporary nature, in which the phenomena of haunted houses can be explained by the active intervention of a medium, there are very many others in which the action of the medium is wanting, and the latter are the cases of longer duration, sometimes covering centuries, — cases in which the action of the deceased shines forth conspicuous and unique, verified by typtological communications or by apparitions, and by voices (perceived especially by persons of unusual sensitiveness), and observed and recorded by the most ancient peoples and preserved by all nations in their popular legends.

These haunted houses furnish the most ancient, the most widely diffused, and the least contestable records of the autonomous, volitional, and persistent activity of the departed, even at epochs extremely remote from the time of their death, their phantasms exhibiting certain special peculiarities: such as that of presenting themselves in garments of the fashion of their times, at fixed hours, days, and epochs, usually at night, preferably after midnight; or the habit of manifesting themselves (rarely) by the voice and in writing; of continually repeating the same movements, and especially those to which they were accustomed in life. Sometimes they make a show of violence, to revenge themselves, or to dissuade from evil actions, and occasionally for absurd and ridiculous reasons, — as in the case of the two Children, who believed themselves to be still the possessors of the castle abandoned a century previous; or as in the case of the White Ladies, etc., to announce the approaching death of some personage.

The phenomena are sometimes influenced, instigated, and multiplied by the presence of a medium. In that case they would not seem to be so mysterious. But in these instances the apparitions are more animated and vivacious and more continuous, although more transitory (appearing for periods varying from fifteen days to two years).

But the greater number of the apparitions take place, as we have seen, apart from any active intermediation of a psychic, — a very natural thing when we remember that they appear frequently in houses completely abandoned (sometimes centuries before), and continue there in spite of change of tenants, although not revealing themselves any further to these when they have removed to new habitations.

In that last fact lies the very nub of the proof of the independent action of the dead in haunted houses, — something not only confirmed by legend, but frequently by historical records. And while the majority of people are made aware of the presence of these spirits only through noises, blows, and disorderly movements, yet persons endowed even with slight mediumistic powers perceive them directly, in their proper dress and with their own facial traits (see the case of the Children).

There yet remains the mysterious problem how, without the aid which the body of a medium, of a living person, gives to the phantasm of the deceased, its activity can be displayed, and often with such energy. Certain individuals have given the strange and scarcely acceptable explanation that the spirits derive the material of their incarnation from the animals and plants of the deserted house. Twice I was given this answer by tranced mediums of whom I had asked the question.

It has also been affirmed that all haunted houses, even those that are free from mediumistic influence, have been under the sway of distant and invisible psychics. But phenomena are cited as apposite which would be better explained as a doubling of the personality, — such as that of Varley, who heard two blows in the wall of his room, distant more than five thousand English miles from the medium Home, who, in turn, knew of those blows because the same man, Ente, repeating the same thing in his house, had notified him of the concomitance and invited him to write to Varley about it, that out of the affair he might derive new proof of the reality of spiritism.

But this case, and that of Mrs. Butler, cited above, are rather cases of the doubling of the mediums, who transferred themselves to a distance for a brief moment and for a few nights, rather than cases of haunted houses. Even those of Lowestoft, spoken of by Aksakoff, are instances of apport to a great distance. In any case they are exceptional phenomena, and not frequent occurrences such as those in connection with haunted houses, and so cannot constitute a rule. Indeed, their extraordinary rarity and their distance from any possible medium operates as a bar to this explanation, whereas spiritistic phenomena are of frequent occurrence, and always take place in the immediate vicinity of the medium, rather more frequently on the left side than on the right, losing all active potency at a distance of eight or ten metres. A bar also to the theory of mediumistic action at a distance in the

case of haunted houses is, first, the frequent occurrence of these in lonely and abandoned sites,
where not only are there no mediums, but no
other inhabitants; and, second, the continued occurrence of the phenomenon through centuries,
whereas the medium cannot have a secular life;
and, thirdly, the fact that certain of these apparitions are repeated sometimes at intervals of many
years, and very often for a single time, coinci-
dently with some great and tragic event, whereas
the action of the medium must take place, not
once merely, but for months in succession.

The fact, by the way, that these phenomena of
revenants and poltergeists in haunted houses
occur in connection with cases of violent death
(suicide or homicide) is very striking. That
these mournful events took place so often in feu-
dal and barbarous times explains why the dwellings dating from those times are the most infested
by spirits. (In general, too, we may suppose that
the phantasmal bodies of persons who suffered
violent death, as in these old castles and halls,
would exhibit a greater activity and energy,
which they evidently do.)

Nor do these manifestations seem to be isolated. To haunted houses not subject to the will
of mediums must be added the malicious hurling
of stones by invisible beings, — cases very frequent, though not of long duration, — and these,
too, without any discoverable co-operation of a

medium. Here, too, belong the phenomena of luminosity, such as those of Quargnento, which began to be noticed by Signor Sirembo during the first months of 1895, and afterwards by Professor Garzino (instructor in chemistry) and by the civil engineer Capello and others.

These prodigies took place about half-past eight P. M. The dimensions of the luminous mass were about those made by a large lamp, though sometimes attaining a diameter of from 24 to 28 inches. The motion of translation was by leaps or bounds; the light moved from the little church of S. Bernardo to the cemetery, and about midnight returned to the church. The event took place at all seasons, but it was not every one who could see it. The light was known in the country roundabout under the name of " The Fire of S. Bernardo." In the church are buried the members of the Guasta family.

A similar phenomenon was observed at Berbenno di Valtellina. The movements there exhibited volition, always took place at a certain hour and between a field and a certain edifice. It is a flame that cannot be explained by any chemical law. For instance, among other things, it passes through trees without burning them. Everything shows that the phenomena are spiritistic manifestations, — especially if we recall how often in mediumistic séances luminous globes and ribbons appear in places where the manifestation of phantasmal entities occurs. But take notice that it was not possible to find in the vicinity of Quargnento and of Berbenno any trace of mediums.

It is very curious to note how in these latter days it is possible to examine and verify so many recorded facts of this kind, whereas for almost two centuries scarcely one was observed, except among the lowest strata of the population, who were not, we may say, in communication with the cultivated classes. The latter, at any rate, since they did not believe in the phenomena, even when they took place directly under their eyes, took no pains to examine them or make known their existence. Hence all memory of them was lost. To-day they take place, are perceived, and are studied, although, indeed, they are readily forgotten and encounter incredulity and derision.

Thus, in the Fumero case (described at the beginning of this chapter), if I had not persisted, and returned to the place, it would have been believed that, with the first appearance of the police or of myself, the phenomena had disappeared, and they could easily have been attributed to trickery, thereby completely diverting from them the attention of investigators.

CHAPTER XIII

Tricks, Telepathy, the Unconscious, etc.

HAVING reached this point, I fear lest my reader, in imitation of the famous Cardinal d'Este, may interrupt me with the exclamation, " Where have you found so many trashy stories? " or, worse still, " Have n't you allowed yourself to be deceived by the most vulgar class of swindlers? "

As a matter of fact, the first impression (and I have not been without it myself) is that it is a question of trickery, — all this medium business.[1] And this is the explanation that best suits the taste of the mass of people, since it saves thinking and studying, and makes the common man believe he is a more conscientious observer and more skilful than the man of science. Let us add that even the scientist must agree that no group of natural phenomena lends itself more readily to fraud and doubt than does that of Spiritualism. Because, in the first place, all the rarest and most important occurrences always take place in obscurity, and no experimenter can receive as proved truth events which take place in the dark

[1] See Abbott, *Behind the Scenes with the Mediums*, Chicago, 1907; Carrington, *The Physical Phenomena of Spiritualism*, Boston, Small, Maynard & Co., 1907 ; etc.

where they cannot be well controlled and observed. Then, again, the mediums themselves, whether involuntarily or not, often yield to deceit, and indeed are inclined that way; for, being for the most part hysterics, and false, as are all hysterics, when they feel their mediumistic power at the ebb, they want to supplement it by artifice. Some, being extremely suggestionable (as indeed they all are), engage in trickery in obedience to the secret urging of some hostile person present, as Eusapia once told me, who at Genoa had felt some one secretly ordering her to cheat and felt impelled to obey.

Let us not speak, then, of false mediums, hireling impostors, and jugglers by profession, who swarm in localities and countries where the belief in Spiritualism is most widely diffused. There is a regular literature of this subject, especially an American literature, that makes us acquainted with a whole arsenal of special weapons and apparatus used, it is said, by mediums in their cunning juggleries; such as false beards, masks, garments of finest muslin, phosphorescent substances, chairs containing hollow places from which the medium slyly draws forth his masks, or else with springs which, unbending, allow him to simulate true levitation.

Even Eusapia is not an exception to the general rule. We have seen that she has many artful wiles, both in the trance state and out of it. For example, she was once seen freeing one of the hands held by her controllers, in order to move a certain object near her or to give the raps; slowly lifting with one knee or with one of her feet the legs of the table; or feigning to adjust her hair, and slyly pulling out a hair in order to lower the balance-tray on a letter-weigher. She was also seen by Faifofer furtively gathering flowers before the sittings that she might claim them in the evening to be apports,[1] taking advantage of the darkness of the room. It seems, also, that she had learned from some mountebank or other certain special tricks, such, for instance, as simulating human faces by movements of her two hands wrapped around with a handkerchief folded in the shape of a turban. And yet her chief grievance, even during the séance, is to hear herself accused of fraud, — sometimes, it must be confessed, unjustly so, for it is now certain that supernumerary spectral limbs are superimposed on her true limbs and act as their substitutes. These phantom doubles used to be often taken for her normal arms.

Add to this the fact that no movement at séances takes place except in the immediate vicinity of the psychic, and especially in contact with her skirts, which makes some suspect artifice. Then it looks suspicious that the fluidic element

---

[1] Objects brought in through walls and closed doors and windows at séances by mysterious agency. — *Translator.*

gathers strength in the darkness and behind the material stuff of draperies, such as the portières of the medium's cabinet, from which so frequently come the materializations.

Again, when we seek to give precision to mediumistic manifestations by special mechanisms, the mediums often purposely cause them to deceive us, — not to speak of the fact that often, in experimental work, under identical conditions we do not get identical phenomena. (Thus some few mediums can operate in the light, while the greater number cannot.) Add that most of them show a vulgarity in strange contrast with the manifestations, apparently supernatural, of which it is supposed they are trying to give a demonstration, although even these manifestations often exhibit a vulgarity not seldom mingled with obscenity, in too sharp contrast with their pseudo-divine character.

To these objections, which are not without weight, we may reply, first of all, that no one denies the genuineness of the work of the photographer, in spite of the fact that he cannot develop his plates without darkness; and this truth, as Richet observes, by analogy may help us to understand how light may impede the development of mediumistic phenomena. On the other hand, thanks to the well-known contradictions that prevail in this field, we know of mediums — Slade and Home, for example — who could operate in full light; and in full light are revealed the strange wonders, or rather miracles, of the Hindu fakirs, so strange that the mere description of them makes us doubt. And Eusapia, also, although in general in her trances she is refractory and full of suffering, exhibits in full light an extraordinary series of phenomena, — such as modifications of the dynamometer and of the balance, or scales, and the moving of an enormous wardrobe. Modifications such as these that take place in the balance and the dynamometer prove that not rarely the precise methods of science can be applied with advantage to these phenomena so refractory to scientific treatment.

It is true that there are mediums, as I have just said, so cantankerous that at first they deliberately make the instruments speak false. But it will be readily understood that even they hate innovation, and are therefore averse to new mechanisms; and so, for that matter, is the whole human race. Indeed, Richet observed that the substituting of one table for another, as also the introduction of a new individual into the chain of experimenters, frequently interrupted the series of spiritistic phenomena. " The introduction of a new element," he adds, " into the conditions of an experiment does not always conduce to its success, especially when the experiment is concerned with things unknown or partly so."

Then, again, means and measures were taken

in the case of Eusapia to guarantee against any
trickery whatever, — such as tying her hands
and feet, or netting them in a circuit of electric
wires discharging into an electric bell, which in
turn sounded on the slightest movement of the
medium's feet. The psychic Politi was brought
to the Psychical Society of Milan enclosed naked
in a woollen sack. Madame D'Espérance was enclosed in a net, like a fish, and yet in this condition she procured the appearance of the phantasm Yolanda. The same thing occurred with
Miss Cook, who was surrounded by electric wires
in such a way that she could not move her limbs
without interrupting the circuit, and yet her Katie
King appeared, moved about, and wrote, while
the medium was in the cataleptic state.

And there have been physical experiments that
have the gravity and importance of all experiments made, as they were, with exact instruments, especially since they were controlled, or
authenticated, by the photograph. However true
it may be that spirit photographs have been
abused and made the subject of fraud, — for example, through an imprint made on the surface
of the plate by a thin pellicle, either by utilizing
certain chemical rays or certain substances, such
as bisulphate of quinine, which, invisible to our
eyes, are gathered in by the object glass of the
camera, so that a skull painted on the forehead
with this substance appears afterwards when the

plate is developed, — still every suspicion becomes weaker when it is a question of photographs made before a special commission of experts and men of indisputable fame, such as Zöllner, Finzi, Aksakoff, Volpi, and Carreras.

"Even the simplest of spiritualistic phenomena," says Brofferio (*Per lo Spiritismo*, pp. 33 *et seq.*), "could not be imitated without some study, and, above all, without considerable practice, which would be a difficult thing to hide. Writing or speaking is a very easy thing; but writing by putting one hand on a small hamper, or on a violin, to which is attached a pencil; or to write with impetuous haste while talking with some one; nay, to vary the handwriting every time a new spirit speaks, and to write the replies without mixing them up, — to do such things as this one would think would absolutely require preparation. The matter will seem still stranger to us if we stop to think that writing-mediums are numbered by hundreds. Of course one can conceive of some eccentric individual who might find amusement in a continuous imposture, useless and difficult as it is. But to think that this kind of a vocation could become epidemic is preposterous.

"Add that frequently the capacity for evil doing is lacking, as when, for example, the medium is a child. Imposture in writing-mediums seems to me absolutely impossible when a medium

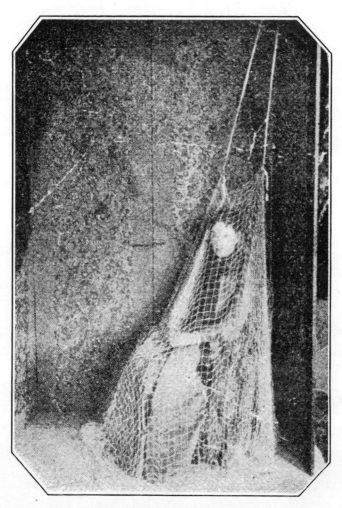

Fig. 56. Madame D'Espérance enveloped by the Net.

writes one communication with the right hand and another with the left, and gives a third *viva voce*, or when the letters of the alphabet are indicated to the medium by means of the planchette, but without his seeing them, and with the order of the letters changed. . . .

" The prestidigitators," continues Brofferio, " have not so far imitated spiritistic phenomena, except when they have been able to secure certain conditions. The first is that they should have with them all the requirements that the mediums have, and take all the precautions that the mediums take. The prestidigitator performs the trick which he has prepared beforehand, and it is useless to ask him to give another or to give it before or after something else. On the other hand, the phenomena obtained with the psychic are often such as are asked for, though not always, because the occult intelligence that produces them has also a will of its own.

" Indeed, the committee of the English Dialect Society has even gone the length of desiring that during mediumistic experiments the mediums should be watched by two of the best prestidigitators of London.

" The idea that the wonders of Spiritualism can be imitated is a widely diffused one among the public, but it is certainly not the opinion of the conjurors themselves. Jacob, prestidigitator of the Robert Houdin Theatre in Paris, and

Bellacchini, prestidigitator of the Court at Berlin, left declarations with the medium Slade to the effect that they could not do the things he did. Trollope (cited by Wallace) relates that Bosco, one of the most skilled conjurors that ever lived, used to laugh immoderately at the belief that the phenomena produced by Home could be thought imitable by the resources of his art.

"One cause of the so-called unmaskings of mediums is the current prepossession that the phenomena cannot be true. There are illusions of credulity, but there are also illusions produced by incredulity. Even the incredulous are in a state of expectant attention, which leads them to see what does not occur. If they do not see it, they divine it. They understand everything, they can explain everything. They have such fear of being made fun of that they do the mocking all by themselves, and to avoid the improbable they invent the impossible.

"And the same causes that produce the 'unmaskings' produce the legal prosecutions. The legal trial of Slade was set on foot in the interests of science, and the sentence was in part based on considerations drawn from the known course of nature. Hence the judgment of the court was derived from a prejudice, namely, that 'the known course of nature excludes the possibility of mediumistic phenomena. Now no one can accomplish the impossible, but only feign to do

so. Therefore all mediums are impostors.' The
logical outcome of this is that Spiritualists who
believe in the possibility of 'impossible' things
are imbeciles. So they are never called experts
(although they are the only experts there are,
and hence the only competent witnesses), and
when they are heard as witnesses they are not
believed.

" Finally, in regard to the spurious phenomena
produced by mediumistic impostors, by prestidigitators, and by sceptics, the Spiritualists reply
with Hellenbach that wigs do not prove that there
are no genuine heads of hair, sets of false teeth
that there are no natural sets; and so with
counterfeit money, dishonest packs of cards, etc.
When I have seen real facts, it is useless for Tyndall to come to me and say there are many pseudo-
facts. I know that coffee is also made with
chicory, with acorns, and with dried figs. I know
very well that it is not a sufficient guarantee to
buy it unground, for an importing grocer has
assured me that even the coffee beans are manu-
factured out of coffee grounds, and so skilfully
that I could not distinguish them from the real.
And yet, since I have sometimes drunk true
coffee, I am therefore (as respects coffee) in that
state of mind spoken of by Tyndall: I am afflicted
with an incurable credulity. Not even a Conti-
nental blockade that would deprive us of coffee
all the rest of our lives could cure me of the illu-

sion that such places as Mocha and Porto Rico exist. It is true that a phantasm differs a good deal from a cup of coffee; but the difference depends on this, that all who go to Naples go to the Caffè Nuovo, while nobody asks where Eusapia lives."

TELEPATHY

Those who shy at the hypothesis of the spirits of the dead as operant psychical agents have tried other explanations, — such as that the medium gets from the brain of the sitters the response to questions, and even images of phantasms, which she then projects in visible form. But leaving out of the account that this projection of phantasms does not occur in any other condition of life, — above all in such a way as to assume the pulse-beats, warmth, and weight of the living body, — I might perhaps admit that from some member of the company who knows a foreign language the medium acquires a temporary knowledge of the language itself, and also an extemporized acquaintance with physics and chemistry, just as he attains to faiths and philosophies, so that while he is an atheist in a group of atheists, he becomes pious in a pious company; but I do not understand how he can possibly obtain from those present what they themselves do not know, as when he speaks in the Hawaiian tongue, which no one present knows anything about.

I could understand how there might be telepathy in the case of Stainton Moses, who saw the apparition of one of his friends at the moment when, just before going to sleep, he fixed his thought upon him, or in the case of M. D., who appeared to two women after he had strongly desired to show himself to them. But, as James Hyslop says, the successive appearance before mediums of various communicators — five, six, ten times, with accurately individualized personalities — cannot be explained by telepathy. And we see in the séances of Mrs. Piper how what we must assume to be communicating spirits who did not know Mr. Hodgson knew how to indicate him. The very errors of the communications exclude the hypothesis of telepathy, while, on the other hand, they are well accounted for as the result of the difficulties that would beset beings who were endeavoring to develop their powers in the new sphere of life to which they had attained.

Telepathy cannot reveal events to come nor what happens to a dead person; as when Madame Meurier twice dreamed of seeing at the foot of her bed her decapitated brother, his head deposited on a coffin. In this case there can be no question of telepathy, since he was already dead when she saw him. In fact he had been decapitated by Chinese rebels. Hence the news was brought by some other intelligence than his living intelligence, for he could not transmit information of what was to happen to him after his death (Wallace, p. 344).

Again, we are told that the Rev. W., while writing his congratulations to a friend on his birthday, heard a voice saying repeatedly, "Why are you writing to a dead man?" His friend was really dead at that hour. The voice could not have been that of a living being, but served the purpose of advising him of his friend's death.

And so when there are announcements as to the future. Miss Curtis dreams of seeing a woman pass near her, then of finding her on the street, surrounded by a crowd, some of whom say she is alive, others that she is dead. The woman was a certain Miss C., her friend. Now the next morning Miss C. fell in the street, making herself ill. But how could telepathy enable her to see what had not yet occurred?

A certain New Zealand vicar was about to take a fishing trip to an island, in company with certain friends, who were to come to fetch him at dawn. As he was going upstairs, and afterwards in his room, he heard a voice say, "Don't go" And when he said, "But what shall I do when they come to call me?" "Lock yourself in," replied the voice. He comprehended that a danger was threatening him and decided not to accompany his friends. In the morning he learned that they had been drowned during the excursion. Here it could not have been the drowned persons who gave the warning, but other spirits to whom the future is not unknown.

"Telepathy," says Brofferio (*op. cit.*, pp. 237 *et seq.*), "is a double-edged weapon. If the phantasms of the living render useless those of the dead, they make them also a possibility. If a living being can appear and act at places distant from its body, that makes for the hypothesis that it can appear and act even when its body no longer exists. If the figure [or eidolon] of the body can separate itself from the body, it will perhaps be able to survive it. This is only an hypothesis. It is possible, on the other hand, that the apparition of a living being is the physiological action of one organism on another. But this also is at present only an hypothesis.

"But there is another positively decisive reason against the objection drawn from telepathy. When the phantasm seen and photographed does not resemble the medium, it cannot be an apparition of the medium. Then, again, when we get several phantasms different from the medium, the hypothesis of action by the double of the medium ought to be rigidly excluded. There is one other possibility to be considered, — the action of living personalities at a distance. But, when the departed are positively recognized, even this supposition is no longer admissible."

THE UNCONSCIOUS

Another solution might be found in the unconscious self. Indeed some psychic phenomena find their explanation in that singular state of the brain in which latent energies are set in motion, of which we have no consciousness and which develop a marvellous power.

Such, indeed, is the moment of the inspiration of genius (the poetic œstrus), which for so many reasons resembles the psychic state of the epileptic when in his fit. But putting forth bud and leaf, not in the brain of the vulgar convulsionary, but in that of the great genius, it gives us an inspired work instead of atrocious blasphemy or a black crime or a motor spasm.

" I often feel," writes Beaconsfield, " that there is only a step from intense mental concentration to madness. I should hardly be able to describe what I feel at the moment when my sensations are so strangely acute and intense. Every object seems to me animated. I feel that my senses are wild and extravagant. I am no longer sure of my own existence, and often look at a book to see my name written there and thus be assured of my existence."

Similar are the confessions of St. Paul, of Nietzsche, and of Dostoievsky.

" Suddenly " (writes the last named, in *Bezi*), " something opened before him, an extraordinary internal light illumined his soul. This lasted perhaps half a second.[1]

" There are moments (it is something that only lasts five or six seconds) in which you suddenly feel the presence of the eternal harmony.

" This phenomenon is neither terrestrial nor celestial; it is a clear and indisputable sentiment. All at once you seem to be in contact with all nature, and you say, ' Yes, this is true.' "

See also what Berlioz writes, in his *Mémoires* (p. 246):

" The empty void forms around my palpitating breast, and it seems to me that my heart, under the inspiration of an irresistible force, is evaporating and will dissolve by force of expansion. Then the skin of my entire body becomes burning hot and gives me the sensation of pain; my face and my whole body become red as fire. I should like to cry out, to call some one to my aid, that he might console me, guard me, keep me from rushing to destruction by holding in check the life which is fleeing from me.

" I have no idea of death during this crisis. The idea of suicide is not endurable by me. I do not wish to die; I wish rather to live, with a thousand-fold increase of energy. It is an attitude prodigiously prolific of happiness, and a frenzy of activity that cannot be subdued except

[1] See Dr. R. M. Bucke's *Cosmic Consciousness*. Philadelphia : Innes & Sons, 1901. — *Translator*.

by immense, all-devouring, furious enjoyments which shall tally the incalculable superabundance of sensitiveness."

Hear also the great Beethoven:

"Inspiration is for me that mysterious state in which the entire world seems to form a vast harmony, when every sentiment, every thought, re-echoes within me, when all the forces of nature become instruments for me, when my whole body shivers and my hair stands on end."

It is evident from these instances that where there is a maximum of productivity on the part of genius there is the minimum of consciousness. And so we understand how the creations of genius may be justified or confirmed by the dreams of the world's great men.

It is really extraordinary, the part that dreams play in the creations of genius.

It is well known that in his dreams Goethe solved many weighty scientific problems and put into words many most beautiful verses. So also La Fontaine (*The Fable of Pleasures*) and Coleridge and Voltaire. Bernard Palissy had in a dream the inspiration for one of his most beautiful ceramic pieces.

The same thing is revealed in the Confessions of Daudet and of Maury. "I have had while dreaming," says Maury, "thoughts and projects the execution and the direction of which denoted just as much intelligence as I possessed when awake; or, rather, I have had in dream ideas and inspirations that could never have entered my consciousness when awake. Thus in a dream in which I found myself face to face with a person who had been introduced to me two days before, there came to me a doubt as to his morality which I would not have had when awake."

Daudet created in a dream the following verses:

À JULIE.

Ainsi ne faut-il quand verrez l'heure suprême
Vous dépiter, ni pleurer, ni crier,
Mais, ramenant vos pensées en un même;
Ne faire un que de tout ce qui vous aime,
Regarder ce, joindre mains et prier.

Notes sur la Vie, 1890.

Holde composed while in a dream *La Phantasie*, which reflects in its harmony its origin; and Nodier created *Lydia*, and at the same time a whole theory on the future of dreaming. Condillac in dream finished a lecture interrupted the evening before. Kruger, Corda, and Maignan solved in dreams mathematical problems and theorems. Robert Louis Stevenson, in his *Chapter on Dreams*, confesses that portions of his most original novels were composed in the dreaming state. Tartini had while dreaming one of his most portentous musical inspirations. It was April (he says), and through the half-open window of his little room there was blowing a smart breeze, when all at once his eyelids drooped, then closed, and it seemed to him that he saw a spectral form approaching him. It is Beëlzebub in person. He holds a magic violin in his hands, and the sonata begins. It is a divine adagio, melancholy-sweet, a lament, a dizzy succession of rapid and intense notes. Tartini rouses himself, leaps out of bed, seizes his violin, and reproduces on the magical instrument all that he had heard played in his sleep. He names it the *Sonata del Diavolo*, one of the best of his works.

Giovanni Dupré got in a dream the conception of his very beautiful *Pietà*. One sultry summer day Dupré was lying on a divan thinking hard on what kind of pose he should choose for the Christ. He fell asleep, and in dream saw the entire group at last complete, with Christ in the very pose he had been aspiring to conceive, but which his mind had not succeeded in completely realizing.

The powerful influence the dream has on the genius is accounted for, as we have just seen, by the potent sway of the unconscious over his soul. Indeed it is the extreme ascendency of this that explains also how genius becomes subject to distractions of mind and temporary loss of memory, or amnesia. These symptoms recall very accurately the loss of memory in epileptics.

Illustrations of the absent-mindedness of genius are over-abundant.

"One day," writes Dr. Veretz, "Meissonier said to Dumas, 'If Giraud is not dead, I must have met him yesterday, and yet I did not recognize him and greeted him coldly. I afterwards remembered that it was the face of a friend, and now I realize that it must have been he,' and thereupon he ran to beg him to excuse him."

Grossi absent-mindedly destroyed in the toilet-room many pages of his *Marco Visconti*.

And here is Terti coming out of a conversazione salon with two hats in his hand, yet anxiously inquiring everywhere for his own (Stampa, *S. Manzoni*, vol. ii.).

Walter Scott, hearing some one sing at a social reception certain verses, said, "That is Byron's stuff"; but the verses were his own.

When Froude was talking with Carlyle about the posthumous publication of his Memoirs, Carlyle said he had forgotten everything he had written in them.

Manzoni's fits of distraction were very strange, although he was endowed with so marvellous a memory that he knew by heart the whole of Virgil and Horace. Once in a dispute about some historical topic it occurred to him to see what Gibbon said about it, and he found in the volume a marginal note by himself on the very point under discussion. "See what a memory I have!" he said, laughing. Another time he sent a book to a friend by mail, sealed so as to require full letter postage, thus causing a useless and relatively heavy expense to the donee, whose pardon he was obliged to ask afterwards. Once, when conversing with a friend, he cited a sentence that seemed to him admirable, but could not remember where he had found it. "I suspect," said the friend, " that it is yours " (*Dialogo dell' Invenzione*).

Several monographs have been written on the absent-minded doings of Ponchielli and Galuppi. Thus, according to Mandelli, Ponchielli used to go out sometimes in military uniform, with a stovepipe hat on his head and slippers on his feet. When it rained, he would often keep his umbrella shut and get a good wetting. He used to sip his coffee while playing billiards, and would often attempt to chalk the end of the cue with the sugar, and be in despair because he could not succeed. One day he was invited somewhere to dine, but went instead, at the appointed hour, to the inn, where he was disposing of the last mouthfuls when they came in search of him. On another occasion he was eating with an invited friend, and, sitting next a colonel, unknown to him, he took his wine and drank it all.

But *unconscious* is not equivalent to *nonexistent*. The subconscious powers may bring to the surface, and join in a prolific marriage, ideas and facts that had been forgotten, or nearly so, and which therefore had not existed at all in the active consciousness of the individual, but they cannot do the same for facts which he had never learned.

Hence, if we may concede to Flournoy (*From the Earth to the Planet Mars*) that the medium Smith, when she says she is speaking the Martian language, has received unconscious suggestions from old recollections of her own, or of persons present, about foreign tongues (and we can understand how, in the exaltation of the spiritistic trance, scattered and fragmentary notions might take shape, in the same way that, under the excitement of the œstrus of genius, latent and fragmentary ideas start into life all at once and are bodied forth in some discovery), — if we may concede, I say, to Flournoy that the medium has received such unconscious suggestions, we still are unable to go with him when he affirms that by the theory of the subconscious can also be explained the forty words of Sanskrit and the verses dictated by the same Flournoy, solely in virtue of the fact that she had seen the cover of a Sanskrit grammar.   Nor is it possible for her to have been able to reproduce the exact signatures of the mayor and the curate of a village in a remote district living at a remote epoch (1839), simply from her having once taken a pedestrian, but not a paleographic, trip through a neighboring valley.[1]

[1] Nor can we admit the unconscious when the medium is beaten or scorched by the spirit, — a thing that he must object to even in his unconscious states of thought.

If one end of a thread is tied to a woman's finger and the other end to a ring that dangles in the centre of an empty goblet, her age can be known, even though she is unwilling to tell it, because the ring will tinkle as many times as she has consciously lived years. This is very true; but the woman knows the number of years. Hence one part of the enigma is cleared up. But when the spirit speaks Chinese to a European who is ignorant of the language, but understands it while in trance, there is no use in talking of the unconscious, because in this case even the unconscious has to work upon acquired cognitions.

So Hyslop might get information about his father's black skullcap, his pocket-knife, and his habit of using in his talk old saws and proverbs, from the depths of his own unconscious memory of his early youth. But when Uncle Jerry spoke to Lodge about the danger he was in of drowning, with his brother Robert, and recalled how the other brother Frank climbed upon the roof of a shed to hide himself, these were things that happened in the youth of Professor Lodge's father, and of which he was entirely ignorant.

And so we may say of cryptomnesia [or unconscious memory]. Under certain circumstances, e.g., when I am at a great altitude, say six or seven thousand feet, I remember Italian, Latin, and even Greek verses which had been forgotten for years. But I know very well that

I read them in early youth. Similarly, during certain dreams in nights when I am afflicted with conditions showing intestinal poisonings, disagreeable moments of years previous (*e.g.*, the examinations made in 1896) are reproduced with precision, and with particulars so minute and exact that I could not possibly recall them when awake. Yet I observe that they are always fragmentary and incomplete recollections and depend more on the condition of the sentiments than on the intelligence.

During the night preceding his setting out to revisit his native village, which he had not seen for twenty years, Maury dreamed of meeting a certain man, who said to him, " Good-day, Signor Maury." Maury replied, in substance, " Excuse me, my dear sir, but I have not the pleasure of knowing you." The other, amazed and almost offended, declined to give his name, but said he was a friend of his father's, and tried to recall to his mind things that had happened in his boyhood in which they had mutually participated. All was in vain. Maury woke up smiling at the eccentric fellow who claimed to recognize him. But when he reached his native town one of the first persons he saw was the person who had recognized him in his dream, only he was older than in the dream, for he had dreamed of him as he was when he knew him many years previous. So his subconscious double during the dream had remembered and recognized that which his conscious ego no longer knew (Brofferio, *op. cit.*, p. 188).

We can understand as phenomena of cryptomnesia what Aksakoff recalls on the spur of the moment during the trance of Cardosio; and so of the inscription in a book of his, *Nemek habacha,* though he declared he had never seen those words; but this solution will not fit the case of a medium reading the last line of the last page of a book on a certain shelf of the library, the name of which he did not know. Nor will cryptomnesia explain the medium's revealing to him not merely the name of a certain person named Gray, who lived in 1628, but his being able to employ that person's own handwriting (see Chapter X).

CHAPTER XIV

Biology of the Spirits

THE facts relating to the activity of phantasms [1] are so numerous and so well proved that we can permit ourselves to construct their biology and their psychology. The phantasmal forms appear to us in the form of lights and ignes fatui, or else in the form of hands, or even the images of men, though rarely complete in shape. These images are frequently preceded by a luminous vapor in the room, and more often on the head and on the abdomen of the medium, — a vapor which always keeps getting more and more condensed until it assumes corporeal form. This shape passes from the immediate vicinity of the medium or the séance cabinet to some distance away and even moves around the room, making gestures and, more rarely, speaking, while the psychic in the mean time is in a state of supreme lethargy.

" As soon as I have entered the mediumistic cabinet," says D'Espérance, " my first impression

---

[1] According to Davin, sixty per cent of mediumistic phenomena should be attributed to spirits, sixteen per cent to auto-suggestion, and the rest to the action of the medium. But these calculations are mere inventions or guesses.

is of being covered with spider-webs.   Then I
feel that the air is filled with substance, and a kind
of white and vaporous mass, quasi-luminous, like
the steam from a locomotive, is formed in front
of the abdomen.   After this mass has been tossed
and agitated in every way for some minutes,
sometimes even for half an hour, it suddenly
stops, and then out of it is born a living being
close by me."

Phantasms are covered with a white woven
stuff, extremely fine, sometimes doubled, tripled,
and even quadrupled.   They seem to draw it out
from the clothes of the medium.   This mediumistic tissue is indispensable, as Katie King said to
Crookes, as the envelope of their fluidic organism and to keep it from dissolving in the light.
Many, however, keep to the old fashions of their
time and country, thus affording another proof
of their identity.   Frequently, when they find
a difficulty in forming themselves, or (so to
speak) solidifying themselves, completely, besides the assistance rendered by their mediumistic garments, they have recourse to that of the
portières of the cabinet, wrapping themselves in
these before they thrust out hands, arms, or head.
The head is thus divined (rather than observed directly) by means of the profile or by touching it.

In mediumistic sculptures or imprints, also,
they need to use this tissue, the impression of
which is distinctly seen on the gypsum or plaster

moulds. The phantasm materializes and grows out of the material substance of the medium, and certain ones have been observed to take on frequently a noteworthy increase in weight of body at the expense of that of the medium. Colonel Alcott, who in 1874 was experimenting with the psychic Compton, observed that, when the young girl-phantasm " K " appeared, the body of the psychic disappeared. Then he tied (and sealed with sealing wax) a string passing from the aperture of the medium's ear to the back of the chair in which she sat. Out of the invisible now stalks the spirit, which is at first found to weigh 77 pounds, later 58, and later still 52. In the mean time the medium had disappeared, but reappeared as soon as the phantasm had gone, yet without pulse or breath.[1]

So D'Espérance in 1893, while forming for herself Yolanda, saw that she herself had lost her knees and feet. But, if she touched the place where they normally should be, she felt pain. Hence an invisible part of them existed. This disappearance of the lower extremities was verified by many. Aksakoff himself made investigations among those who had seen her dematerialize herself. She herself directed the hands of the experimenters present in order that they might ascertain and thoroughly verify the disappearance of her legs. The witnesses authenticated

---

[1] Aksakoff, *Un Cas de Matérialisation Partiel.* Paris, 1896.

the fact that her dress during the dematerialization hung vertically close up to the chair, and that then it filled out again without the medium moving from her seat. While all this was going on, she was affected with severe prostration and experienced inordinate thirst, whereas under other circumstances she never drank. Gradually, as Yolanda disappeared, her sense of emptiness and of prostration diminished and she regained her strength. In one of Eusapia's levitation séances, also, Dr. Vezzano noticed that her lower limbs were lacking, and "John" explained that it was he who had caused them to dematerialize in order that her weight might be less for the levitation.

In the experiments in Paris it was found that during the levitation of a table the weight of the medium diminished just the amount that the table weighed, returning to the normal amount after the levitation had ceased.

Miss Fairland, sewed into a hammock which allowed the registration of the variations in her weight under the eyes of all the spectators, presented a gradual diminution to the extent of sixty pounds, — the half of her ordinary weight. As soon as a complete phantasm appeared, it began to walk about. When it disincarnated itself, the weight of the medium returned almost to its normal amount, so that at the end of the séance it had diminished by only three pounds (*Psychische Studien*, 1881).

Experiments with the medium Miss Wood revealed the fact (at the third séance) that the weight of the phantasm amounted to the half of that of the medium (*Light*, 1886). This same medium (Wood) was weighed by the balance of Blackbourne before and during the séance. Before she weighed 176 pounds. With the appearance of the phantasm this weight diminished to 83 and afterwards to 54 pounds. The weight of the phantasm was at first one-half and later seventy-five per cent of that of the medium.

The human forms assumed by the spirits are not such as properly belong to their existence, but form temporary incarnations by which they may make themselves known to us, and may therefore be extremely variable. They frequently take on the physiognomy, the voice, the gestures of the medium, but exhibit this peculiarity, that they change sometimes even in the same day, and assume an individual physiognomy and an individual moral character which may last for months (as in the case of Walter) and for years (as in the case of Katie King).

This metamorphic power the phantasms frequently transmit to their medium. Allan Kardec tells of a young girl of fifteen who would reproduce not merely the face, but the stature, mass, and weight of deceased persons, especially her brother. So Madame Krooke one evening saw her own face changed; she observed a thick black beard, and her son-in-law recognized by it his dead father. A little after her face changed into that of an old woman with white hair. But she preserved in the mean time her consciousness, yet felt through her entire body a pricking like that of a galvanic battery.

The phantasmal personalities develop, in the presence of the medium (especially under the influence of anger or offended vanity), a dynamometric force which once reached as high as 100 to 110 kilograms, and often attains to 80 and 90. With Bottazzi it went to 93.

Then there is the remarkable force exhibited (even at a distance from the medium) in haunted castles, — a force that opens very heavy doors and windows and flings showers of stones, not merely down, but up. It appears, however, from the confessions of the phantasms, that the forces acquired by them from the mediums rapidly diminish. The graphic registrations obtained with the drum of Marey, which was in communication with a rotating cylinder, traced very broad lines in two groups, the first with a duration of 23 seconds, and the other with a duration of 18 seconds. In each of the two groups it was clearly to be seen that the force diminished with considerable more rapidity than in the case of a medium or of a normal person.

Crookes and Richet both observed that phantasms have the normal temperature, and normal beating of the heart and arteries and respiratory movements, and proved further (Richet) the expiration of carbonic acid gas. A pain experienced by the phantasm is felt in the homologous part by the medium, — as if one had struck her instead of the phantasmal being. When Yolanda was amorously assaulted by an intruder in a séance, the psychic (who was at some distance away) fainted and became almost lifeless.

Often the spirits of the dead are held by an irresistible attraction inseparably united to the house where they long lived, or to the tomb in which their bodies were placed, and make themselves visible when the tomb is visited (Stainton Moses).

In cemeteries and places where sudden deaths occurred, Stainton Moses, the famous medium, noticed a great throng of phantasms that followed behind him as he walked. This explains (if we admit that chemistry has no solution for the phenomenon) the frequency of ignes fatui in cemeteries which (by returning at stated times and directing themselves from certain points to other well-determined points) seem to reveal thereby the expression of will.

The phantasm has the negative property, so to speak, of dissolving under the influence of strong light, — as wax is melted by heat. This was noticed in two experiments with Katie King.

We see by this how it is that phantasms do not manifest themselves in the daytime.

In the particular sites mentioned above they have the power of acting at night, even apart from the presence of the medium; but they are never visible as phantasms except in the medium's presence.

In Herlitzka's and Foà's experiments with Eusapia on a mercurial manometer, registrations were made that correspond to a pressure of 56 millimetres, which, given the proportions of the elastic membrane, indicated a pressure of 10 kilograms.

We are unable to measure the velocity with which spirits move through space. It is so extraordinary that it almost approximates the velocity of the wave-vibrations of the luminiferous ether. It seems to be 1000 kilometres [about 600 miles] in a half-hour (Sage, *Piper*).

In the instance of the flying brothers of Bari [in Italy; see previous chapter] it was proved that they had been able to transfer themselves (as if they were discarnate) over a distance of 45 kilometres [about 28 miles] in 15 minutes (facts authenticated and vouched for by the Bishop of Bari). See Lapponi, *Spedizione e Spiriti*.

The spirits often, as we have seen, produce an effect on photographic plates without being themselves seen, and a phantasm left the impression of four fingers on a photographic plate that was covered with three sheets of black paper. It is for this reason, as well as on account of other phenomena detailed on previous pages of this volume (such as the discharging of the electroscope and the phenomena of radiant bands and luminous globes that occur in séances and appear as imprints on photographic plates) and on account of the peculiarity these phantasmal beings have of comporting themselves under certain special tissues as gaseous bodies, that we have put forward the hypothesis that their molecular constitution resembles that of radio-active bodies.

The phantasms show very little inclination to express themselves in words; or, if they do, it is in a laconic form, as if it fatigued them to speak at length. Most frequently they use signs. Each one has a special kind of rap or a form of signal peculiar to him (or her).

Not rarely in their graphic sign-language they employ symbolic forms used by ancient peoples and by the prophets. Thus the woman psychic " Walt," an automatic painter, once felt impelled to paint three little angels in the midst of the plants and foliage of India. On that very day died three small children friends, almost at the same time as a friend of hers in India.

Here belong also instances of premonitions collected by Bozzano (*Archives des Sc. Psych.*,

22

1908). A mother saw flying in a deserted plain a little bird whose wings presently fell off. Soon after this vision her son died. Another saw a cataleptic in the house of a relative, whose death occurred soon afterwards. A lady acquaintance of mine one evening before going to sleep saw the image of a foot. She had been promised by another lady, her friend, that she would notify her in case of her being suddenly called away on a journey, and this was her unconscious method of notification. In general it appears that the spirits are ardently desirous of making themselves known to the living, and their failures only spur them on to new attempts. Their end once gained, they disappear. They employ for that purpose ways to which they are most inured.

Sometimes the spirits inflict themselves with impetuous violence upon a person to induce him to become their medium and thus enable them to communicate with the living, — as in the well-known case of Dr. Dexter. The Fox sisters were pestered by raps, denounced as impostors, and excommunicated from the church. They tried to get away from the spirits by changing their residence and town; but the blows and raps followed them and were constantly renewed. In like manner a certain spirit came many times to the séances of Stainton Moses to ask to be recognized. When he finally was so recognized by the brother of a certain S. P., he ceased to appear. He had died thirteen years previously (Moses, *op. cit.*).

According to Aksakoff, the spirit of a typographer once printed in the journal for which he had worked the notice, " To-day at three o'clock —— —— died." Inasmuch as no one knew of the death, and would not have the time or the inclination to write such a communication, it must have been his spirit that had evoked it.

In spite of their eager desire to enter into relation with us, — perhaps to reveal their personal power or to get news of friends and of events that have happened and of which in the beyond they are entirely ignorant, — the spirits show a strange aversion to revealing their names. In typtological communications they almost always give false names, or refuse to give their exact appellation. Some assume pseudonyms, others take very strange titles such as " Imperator " and " Rector " in the case of Stainton Moses, or " Phinuit " and " Pelham " with Mrs. Piper. But, if in time they become intimate, they sometimes reveal their personality, and Moses knew the true names of Imperator and Rector.

According to Moses, it seems as if, at the moment of his death, the spirit finds the manifestation of his personal existence more easy; and in support of this Moses adduced facts easily

verifiable. But according to Hyslop it is necessary for some time to have elapsed; for it seems
as if, immediately after death, they remain for
some days or months in a dumfounded or be-
wildered state. But the declarations of Pelham
to Mrs. Piper intimate a sudden astonishment, —
something one might expect under conditions
so new. Pelham thus describes the moment of
death: " All was dark to me. Then consciousness returned, but in a dim twilight way, as
when one wakens before dawn. When I comprehended that I was not dead at all, I was glad."
Altkin Morton, also, who killed himself in a
moment of despair, declared that after death he
did not at first recognize any one, but afterwards
remembered his own relatives and friends.

In general, it appears that those who meet with
unexpected death, especially in youth, renew the
achievements and perform the actions which
were habitual to them. Thus, after the sinking
of an English ship of war, the phantasm of a
sailor who belonged to the ship appeared at a
séance in London and said that the spirits of
sailors repeat in the other world the gait and
gestures habitual to them on the high seas in this
life. This assertion might seem fantastic, but it
is confirmed primarily by the legends of many
peoples, and also by what is observed in haunted
castles and halls, — the continual pounding of
hammers, the dragging of chains, the re-enacting

of crimes, and volleys of firearms kept up interminably, to the great despair of the proprietors.

I know of a servant, drowned near the villa of his master, who reappears by night and rinses the bottles and water-jugs of his employer as if he were still in his service.

Then, from the conversation of almost all the spirits, we learn that they have the whimsical hobby of not seeming dead at all and of continuing the habits of this life. If it is a physician, he continues to visit patients and give prescriptions; if it is a theologian, he preaches to us, etc. Dr. Hyslop's father continued to say, " Give me my hat," just as when he used to hobble painfully forth to meet some visitor. They seem to be automatic acts and expressions, as if performed in the unconsciousness of sleep or somnambulism.

In Mrs. Piper's forty-fifth séance with the two Lodges, the phantasmal personality calling himself " Phinuit " presented a spirit named Rich, who asked to send expressions of affection to his father. " My father," said Rich, in another séance, " is much afflicted by my death. Tell him that I still live " (the usual remark of spirits). And again, " Where are my eyeglasses? " and he touched his eyes with his hands; " father must have them, and my books too."

Nobody present could make anything of all this. But it turned out that he wore eyeglasses, and that he was in the habit of saying, when living, just as in the spiritistic dialogue, " Thanks, a thousand times."

According to Stainton Moses, the shades of the departed seem to retain beyond the veil all the desires and appetites, even evil ones, of this world, which they seek to satisfy by proxy, and ever keep urging incarnate men to involve themselves in vice in spite of the efforts of more highly developed souls who seek to hinder them in their nefarious task. In this way we might explain how it is that many men, and especially mediums, are the victims of spirits, who play them atrocious tricks, — throw water on their heads, pull the coverlets off their beds, and burn their clothes and the furniture of their houses, until they are obliged to pack up and decamp (Aksakoff, p. 297).

They are especially in the habit of breaking glass objects. In St. Petersburg a shower of stones fell upon the carriage of Mr. Phelps. He set down the facts in a note-book and the book was destroyed. He once had some spiritistic writings in a small box or drawer, and the papers took fire while inside and the smoke did not appear until they were burned up (Aksakoff, *Animisme*, p. 297).

When mediums or experimenters are dealing with insane spirits, Hodgson notes that the communications also are incoherent and insane.

A friend of Hodgson, Mr. A., once gave him

incoherent communications, and Pelham insisted that they should not go on because A. would be for some time yet confused in mind, having suffered from headache and neurasthenia. The spirit of the deceased Anna Wild once interrupted the interview with her sister and Mrs. Piper because it was time for Mass, and she did not want to be absent. Her sister said that, living, she had never missed attending Mass on feast days.

Yet it appears from the talk of certain of these phantasmal beings with D'Espérance that they are entirely ignorant of what is going on in the present life, and they accordingly desire and ask for news of this and that friend. Others are prophets, see into the future. This latter fact was known to the ancients, and Dante well expresses it (*Inferno*, x. 97–105), as I stated in Chapter I:

> " E' par che voi veggiate, se ben odo,
>   Dinanzi quel che 'l tempo seco adduce,
>   E nel presente tenete altro modo."
> " Noi veggiam, come c' ha mala luce,
>   Le cose," disse, " che ne son lontano;
>
> .   .   .   .
>
>   Quando s' appressano, o son tutto è vano
>   Nostro intelletto."

(" It seems that you see beforehand what time brings with it, if I rightly hear, and have a different manner with the present." " Like one who has imperfect vision, we see the things that are remote from us," he said. . . . " When they draw nigh, or are, our intellect is altogether void.")

The phantasmal control Phinuit, in America, made this prediction to Mrs. Pittman: " You will go to Paris, will suddenly be affected with disease of the stomach and head. A pale blond man will treat you for it." He refused to say whether or not her disease would end in death. She said there was nothing the matter with her stomach, and that she had no intention of going to Paris. But shortly after she was obliged to go, was taken ill with stomach and nerve ailments, was treated by Dr. Herbert, a blond, but died of her complaints.

Phinuit declared to Harsen that he (Harsen) was a very robust man, but had a disease in the membranes of the nose, — which was true. In answer to a request he said that Harsen had had a pain in his right shoulder and pointed out the spot. On another occasion Phinuit indicated the point in his chest where he felt pain, and said it was due to violent muscular exercise, — a true statement. Again, he told Mr. Lodge that his son had something the matter with the fleshy end of his finger, and that a few days after the malady, which had been in the heel, would be localized in said fleshy end of the finger. It happened as predicted.

It is certain that the spirits of the dead exhibit the personal peculiarities they had when living, only in a more conspicuous way. Thus the phantasm of a very violent-tempered captain, although he was communicating through a psychic of most gentle disposition, exhibited a strange violence, interrupting the sittings by an outrageous series of cuffings and blasphemies.

D'Espérance relates of a certain Sveen that he appeared to her begging her to send news of him to Stron in Sweden, saying that he had died, but had first made a great fortune in Canada and was there held in high esteem.

Faifofer told me of phantasmal beings who more than once obstructed his séances, offended because several séances previous a certain other spirit had been invited. If the spirits that are communicating with you are not taken seriously, they are indignant and cease to speak, or else reply in sharp and pithy retorts to your epigrammatic remarks (Hyslop).

When little children die, their phantasms, when they manifest themselves, reproduce the gestures and words of childhood, and ask for their toys; but, when they have been dead for a long time, they act and speak like men, whereas their relatives can only remember them as children. This is another proof that the consciousness and the unconsciousness of the medium have nothing to do with these communications, since evidently they would speak of them as still children if they had seen them as children.

For instance, Pelham being the intermediary for a child, the mother spoke to him of it as a

child.   Then Pelham said, " But he is no longer
a child, he is a man."

It seems that they completely lose all ideas of
time and space, or else err about them. We can
understand how they have no idea of space, because distances do not exist for them, and they
are seen to go and come in a few minutes from
one point to another point that is distant several
hundred miles.   Their obliviousness to time is
a stranger thing, since we see Pelham, on being
requested to go to see what a certain person is
doing at a given time, return, saying that he
has seen him doing not what he was actually
doing then, but what he did the day after and
what he thought the day before.   In contrast
with these peculiarities it appears that the spirits
never forget certain objects that belonged to
them when living.   These objects have an attraction for them when there is a special recollection
connected with them.   Certain objects serve as
landmarks for them in their confusion, refresh
their power of association of ideas on the matter
in hand.   In the technical mediumistic termi-
nology of Mrs. Piper these objects are called
" influence."   They recall the objects put into
the hands of hypnotized persons, — such as hats
and letters, — in order to put them in the way
of remembering or predicting events past or to
come that concern the person to whom the objects belonged.

When "an influence" is presented to the medium, — that is, an object that once belonged to the deceased, — it makes the old memories and ideas live again in said medium, and all the more in proportion as the objects have been in his (or her) hands. Phinuit seemed to find in these "influences" many a source of information. Also the spirit "Imperator," in his function as guide or controller of other communicating spirits, made use of "influences" with Mrs. Piper to retain the communicator and hinder him from slipping away from the subject and becoming incoherent. "Give me something," said he to the medium, "to hold him with, to clear up his ideas." In the midst of the confusion it formed a nucleus around which the thoughts of the disembodied being might crystallize.

The intelligence of these discarnate personalities, even in the case of those who were in life of strong intellect, being now deprived of their own organism and being obliged to make use of the brain of the living, is but fragmentary and incoherent. When a long time had elapsed since their death, disembodied persons seemed to Stainton Moses to be dazed and confused in revisiting the familiar scenes of earth. You would say they were embarrassed in reinvesting themselves with the old habits. Many are sincere, but the greater part are rude and unseemly jesters, allow themselves to be influenced by suggestion into accepting for true those facts that never occurred. Many spirits remember nothing of their past. Numbers of them cannot orient themselves except in the circle of their intimate friends and acquaintances.

When Stainton Moses passed from one séance circle to another, he received only vain and fragmentary disclosures, imparted typtologically in a meagre way. But in a circle composed of a few very intimate friends he at once got most important communications.

The discarnate personality styled " Pelham," in Mrs. Piper's séances (see Hyslop), says that in trance the ethereal body of the psychic parts from its comrade the physical body just as it does in dream, " and then," said Pelham, " we take possession of it for the purpose of communication. Your conversation reaches us as if by telephone from a distant station. Our forces fail us in the heavy atmosphere of the world, especially at the end of the séance."

The spirit of Robert Hyslop, in the Piper séances, said every little while to his son, " You interrupt me; I ought to go now, for my power is failing me and I don't know what I 'm doing." So Pelham kept insisting thus: [1] " When clear communications are wanted, you must n't stun them with questions. In order to reveal them-

[1] He is speaking as master of ceremonies, or psychopomp, for a throng of alleged invisible Dantesque shades at the séance. — *Translator.*

selves to you the spirits put themselves in an environment that discommodes them a good deal. They are like persons who have received a blow on the head and are in a state of semi-delirium. They must be calmed, encouraged, assured that their ideas will immediately be of great importance. To put ourselves into communication with you we must penetrate into your sphere, and we sometimes become careless and forgetful as you are. That is the reason why we make mistakes and are incoherent. I am as intelligent as I ever was, but the difficulties of communicating with you are great. In order to speak with you it is necessary for me to re-enter the body and there dream. Hence you must pardon my errors and the lacunæ in my speech and memory."

This spirit " control " Pelham, speaking again in a similar strain, says that the words of the wisest persons who have left the material body but a short time are incoherent and inexact, owing to the severe shock of being disincarnated and their arrival in a new environment where everything is unintelligible. Their inability at first to make use of the organism of the medium is great; but little by little they become clear in their expressions. Thus at first George Pelham could not be understood, but afterwards became extremely lucid in his speech.

" Friends," said Pelham, " do not regard us
with the eye of the critic. A spirit who communicates with you through a medium is like one
who is trying to climb up within the trunk of a
hollow tree."

It seems to the spirits that all the light comes
to them solely from the medium.

" When Mrs. Piper is in the trance state,"
said the discarnate Phinuit, " I take possession
of her. A medium is for us a lighthouse, while
you non-mediums are to us as though you did
not exist. But every little while we see you as
if you were in dark apartments lighted by a kind
of little windows, which are the mediums."

Aksakoff put this question to a spirit, or supposed spirit: " You say you have a visual organ;
how does it happen, then, that you cannot see
certain things except through the medium?"
The ghost gave him a very sensible reply, which
I give here in abstract:

" I see those things. But our sensations are
quantitatively and qualitatively different from
yours. So that it is one thing to see a thing for
myself, and quite another to see it so as to give
you an account of it. To do this it needs that
I see it as you would see it; hence I need the
medium."

If it is difficult to express one's self in words by
means of an interpreter, so much the more difficult must it be to get a blind man to understand

colors through an interpreter. The questioner and the spirit are like two prisoners who would like to communicate through a closed door, and one of them is deaf and the other blind. This illustration may perhaps account for the obscurity and incoherence of many messages.

"If I often blunder," said Pelham, "it is because I am making use of an organism which does not fit me well." Hyslop noted that many spirits made communications that were unworthy of them. It is very much the same thing as it is with us in dreams when we firmly believe we have composed something of memorable worth; but, when we are awake and write it down, it excites our pity.

Sometimes these discarnate individualities write with their own proper signature, though Pelham could never succeed in doing so. Often they write in a formal lithographic hand on account of the superior potency of the right hemisphere of the brain of the medium while in trance. Many times the words are written with the letters in reverse order, as *latipsoh* for *hospital*. Hence an enormous quantity of errors and also involuntary blunders in the communications of spirits. Hence also the very natural and proper uncertainty or doubt which some spiritistic messages awaken in cautious minds.

During the communications through Mrs. Piper to Dr. Hyslop and Mr. Hodgson, when the

spirit of Rector was present, mistakes were made
in many English names. For instance, the name
Carruthers appeared as Charles, Clarke, Clar-
ake. The name of Robert Hyslop's second wife
was Margaret, or familiarly "Maggie." But
this latter never appeared. Hodgson called
Rector's attention to it; but he, being unable to
remember it, gave up the task to Pelham, who
at first was vexed, but afterwards said, "Well,
I'll go and hunt. If she has a name, I'll find
it." After a quarter of an hour he returned with
the name "Margaret," but not "Maggie." Now,
if the communications were telepathic, or read-
ings of the thought of the medium, these names
ought to be found at once and accurately spelled;
for it is evident that a son ought to know the
name of his stepmother and uncle. And the fact
of failures like these proves that the spectators
cannot influence spiritistic communications in
the slightest degree. Take for an example the
following: At a séance with Mrs. Howard the
message came, "There is a person named Far-
nam who wants to speak with you. He wants
to ask about your aunt Ellen, whose servant he
was for many years." Aunt Ellen was thereupon visited, and it was found that she had really
had as gardener forty years previous a man
named Farnwood; but Mrs. Howard had never
heard his name mentioned.

Dr. Hyslop made a statistical calculation regarding the more important communications made in 15 sittings with Mrs. Piper. They were 205 in number; and of these 152 were found to be true, 16 false, and 37 indecisive. Then, in regard to 927 matters of detail alluded to in these communications, 717 were true, 43 false, and 167 undecided.

It will be said that the communications came telepathically. But, since many of the things revealed were unknown to those present, how are we to understand a telepathy that reaches sources of information in individuals remote and unknown, while even in wireless telegraphy distance is of great importance? If all the disclosures were telepathic, how is it that so many were confused and false? And how was it that the communicators kept losing the idea of time, whereas among the living this ever endures as a matter of supreme importance? Then, among the hundreds of speeches, each one was marked by an individual style. Imperator was always biblical, and haughty to the point of presumptuous vanity and fickleness. Pelham was impatient, genial, of noble ambition as to his personal reputation. Robert Hyslop always spoke (as in life) of not worrying.

But, if the communications with the beyond have been up to this time fragmentary and uncertain, it is because the means of communication have been crude and unsuitable. Still the

23

methods have been continually perfecting. It is
now over half a century since the Fox sisters in
America began to ask that responses should be
given, yes or no, by a certain number of raps,
and it is a long time since another American asked
that the raps should indicate the letters of the
alphabet. The first care of the spirits when they
discovered this method of communicating was to
say, "You ought to announce this truth to the
world." But the announcement was not well
received. The Fox family incurred grave dangers. Then, by counsel of spirits, a small table
was adopted, which was more convenient than
a wall. Next a pencil was fitted to the table;
then the pencil was attached to the planchette,
and finally taken in the hand. After this the
spirits wrote independently of the hand of the
medium. Then they materialized themselves. So
there has been great progress. And to-day the
latest step in advance is the attempt to use me-
chanically exact graphic methods, — such as
Marey's drum, for example, in measuring and
studying the psychology and biology of the inhabitants of this vast unseen realm.

We should expect the influence of the medium,
when compared with that of the spirit of the
dead, to be preponderant, because the one possesses a complete organism, and the other not.
The spirit, too, can do nothing without the aid
of the medium.

The special conditions of the trance (in which, as in certain hysterical attacks which we have studied in the first part of this volume, by the paralysis of certain centres certain others are intensified) give to the medium at a stated moment extraordinary faculties, which she certainly did not have before the trance and which ordinary persons do not have. Above all, the action of the unconscious is intensified. Those centres which seem dormant in the ordinary life come into activity and predominate. Matters forgotten years ago are recalled (cryptomnesia). The thought of persons present is divined and assimilated. This explains how mediums in trance know every person who is present at a séance, even if they see him then for the first time; how they read in his thought the story of his life; how they speak his language, difficult though it be (xenoglossy). But the psychic cannot apprehend, and so manifest, what is not in the thought of the members of the séance, nor what is not in the present. When that does take place, when without literary materials the medium writes a romance, makes a statue without the slightest assistance whatever from a sculptor; when he communicates matters unknown to anybody; when he writes with the peculiar handwriting and in the style of the deceased (a style wholly unknown to all present); when he pencils sentences with a closed double slate without the

action of the arm, — these things happen because with the power of the medium there is associated another power that has, even though tran-
siently, those gifts that are denied to the living;
namely, the ability to read the future, to extempo-
rize artistic powers, and the like.

INDEX

INDEX

Also in this series:

DEATH-BED VISIONS
The Psychical Experiences of the Dying
Sir William Barrett

Visions of living friends and relatives seen by people at the moment of death . . . Music heard by the dying, and by those attending them . . .

Visions of heaven and of deceased loved ones . . . The psychical experiences of the dying remain as puzzling — and as momentous in their implications — as ever.

Death-Bed Visions, first published in 1926, is a classic account of such experiences by one of the most distinguished early psychical researchers.

'Many people who have been through the 'near death experience' find that their view of their own lives has been completely transformed . . . If Death-Bed Visions *can produce even a diluted version of this insight, then it undoubtedly deserves its place as one of the great classics of psychical research.'*

COLIN WILSON

THE SOUL OF THINGS

Psychometric Experiments for Re-living History

William Denton

Psychometry, the power to 'see' the history of an object when it is placed in contact with us, was believed by William Denton to be possessed by everyone. His psychometric experiments produced amazing results which make compelling and enthralling reading.

First published in 1863, **The Soul of Things** remains the best available book on psychometry, a classic in literature of psychical research that raises questions about the human mind that have yet to be answered.

In my opinion, this is one of the most important books in the history of psychical research, and its neglect for more than a century is nothing less than a tragedy. It is also — as its new readers will discover — one of the most exciting books ever written.'

COLIN WILSON